YEATS

A Psychoanalytic Study

YEATS

A Psychoanalytic Study

BRENDA S. WEBSTER

Stanford University Press
Stanford, California
1973

Stanford University Press
Stanford, California
© 1973 by the Board of Trustees of the
Leland Stanford Junior University
Printed in the United States of America
ISBN 0-8047-0846-0
LC 73-80623

Published with the assistance of
the Andrew W. Mellon Foundation

In memory of my father
Wolfgang Simon Schwabacher

Acknowledgments

I wish first to thank Professor Thomas Parkinson of the University of California, Berkeley, for lending me his microfilms of the manuscripts of Yeats's plays held by the National Library, Dublin. I am deeply grateful to the many people who read the manuscript at various stages and, with their comments, helped to shape its development: to Professors Robert Alter, Thomas Flanagan, and Alexander Zwerdling, all of the University of California, Berkeley; to Professor Rudolph Binion of Brandeis, Professor John Unterecker of Columbia, and Professor Harold Bloom of Yale.

I am grateful also to members of the San Francisco Psychoanalytic Institute for an increased understanding of psychoanalytic theory, and especially to Dr. Norman Ryder for reading and criticizing the manuscript. My debt to Dr. Estelle Rogers is incalculable. She gave of her time and knowledge with the utmost generosity, and provided invaluable help in preparing the final draft of the manuscript.

I should like also to thank Professor Norman O. Brown of the University of California, Santa Cruz, for his encouragement, and since publication is a form of encouragement, Harry Slochower, editor of *American Imago*. (Parts of Chapter 2 of this book, dealing with *The Shadowy Waters*, were published in slightly different form in *American Imago*, 28 [Spring 1971]: 3–16.)

To Dr. Anna Menchen and Dr. Kurt Eissler, I owe an increased awareness of certain problems and their possible solutions.

Muriel Bell has been a steadfast friend during the years of work on the manuscript, and I am particularly grateful for her skilled editorial assistance.

Passages from the unpublished letters of W. B. Yeats to Mabel Dickinson are quoted with the permission of the Yeats estate and the director of the Bancroft Library, University of California, Berkeley. Material from the variorum editions of Yeats's works is quoted with the permission of the Yeats estate. Selections from the following published works are quoted with the permission of the Macmillan Publishing Company (New York): *Autobiography, A Vision, Collected Plays, Collected Poems, Letters of W. B. Yeats* (ed. Alan Wade), *Mythologies.*

B.S.W.

Contents

Introduction

MY MAJOR AIM in this book is to follow as closely as possible the track of the creative process in Yeats's work, beginning with the germs embedded in fantasy and daydreams. How does Yeats first embody fantasies and daydreams in his poems and plays? How do they change and develop? How, finally, is Yeats's view of himself and his body related to his progress from the dreamy, highly stylized, and emotionally monotonic early work to the hard, concise richness and complexity of his late poems? While concentrating on the inner dynamics of his works and showing how details, symbols, and character fit various emotional patterns, I shall try to correlate such patterns with suggestive facts from Yeats's life.

Yeats's earliest work, with its themes of death and escape and its main symbol the garden island, reflects his characteristic early response to psychic conflict—a tendency to flee into dreams or illness, an almost paralytic passivity, and a sense of identification with his mother's weakness. Other early preoccupations—feelings of anger and deprivation—emerge in a series of plays with hunger as a central theme.

The 1890's represent a period of transition. Yeats's symbol-laden disembodied style reaches its apex in the obscure and dreamy mysticism of *The Shadowy Waters* and the *Rosa Alchemica* stories. The *Rosa Alchemica* stories, however, contain signs that Yeats is dissatisfied both with his style and with his self-representations. They give him a bad feeling about himself and increase his sense of dissolution and despair. In August 1896 Yeats met Lady Augusta Gregory, and in the early 1900's under her beneficent influence he began to reverse some of his negative feelings about himself. With her support, he developed a new ideal of the poet-bard who created from joy and immersion in reality. He now saw the body as a source of sexual and creative energy, and his feelings about it stimulated a new aesthetic of organic form. At the same time, he began to clarify and harden his style.

In the first decade of the twentieth century Yeats ceased to obscure conflict with an embroidered style. As he wrote in his poem "A Coat," "There's more enterprise / In walking naked." He was able to admit more of reality into his work. This new self-confidence was made possible by his changing attitude toward himself and by his belief that he was protected by a benevolent force, conceptualized as *Anima Mundi*. Imagined contact with *Anima Mundi* made him feel loved, and also less responsible for the threatening material he now included in his work.

Equally significant was his recasting of impulsive material in a hard, beautiful, and acceptable form, as image or mask. One of the most striking of Yeats's new hard images was the virile unicorn. Identification with the unicorn permits Yeats to express violent aggression; at the same time, its qualities of coldness and hardness protect Yeats from feeling overwhelmed by his impulses. This unicorn, derived from unconscious fantasy, appears in several plays as an agent of destruction. In *Where There Is Nothing*, Yeats portrays a precursor of this beast engaged in Nietzschean violence. Destructive violence continues in *The Unicorn from the Stars*, and in *The Player Queen* destruction is joined to sexuality: the Unicorn is to mate with a Queen and initiate a New Dispensation. The theme of the mating of beast and queen undergoes many permutations, culminating in *Purgatory*, where a son watches the ghosts of his bestial father and aristocratic mother mate on their wedding night. Yeats's imagined participation in the unicorn's sexuality appears to be an attempt at active mastery of trauma. For reasons to be detailed later, both the content and the tone surrounding the unicorn and related figures—their bisexuality and awesomeness—suggest fantasies or impressions of parental intercourse derived from early childhood.

Yeats's middle years are characterized by an absorption in mask and persona. He had noted earlier that when he created he entered a state in which his eyes did not "flinch before the bayonet."[1] With his theory of the mask he made an aesthetic of his introspective musings about the psychic origins of creativity in the transcendence of weakness and passivity. Cuchulain and other Yeatsian heroes embody his ideal state of "creative joy without fear," and through them he is able to release new emotions—while defining his own brand of stoicism. Mask-wearing is expressed by active striving, and through his heroes and beasts Yeats steadily increased his capacity to replay emotional traumas with himself in control, to turn passive suffering into active mastery. Later, in *A Vision*, Yeats schematized his feelings about his evolution from limp and dreamy aesthete to mask-wearing, powerful poet.

In old age, I will argue, Yeats's earlier fears of castration and loss of integrity were reawakened by declining potency and approaching death. The heroic mask no longer sufficed, and Yeats increasingly turned to other means of dealing with his fears. The most important of these means, the use of a talismanic object, can be observed in his great poems "Sailing to Byzantium," "A Dialogue of Self and Soul," and "Byzantium." Talismanic objects had played a role in Yeats's work as early as *Oisin*; in these late poems he uses them in a more inclusive way to hold intact his body image. With the help of these objects he can entertain fantasies of fusion and loss of self and come to terms with concomitant feelings of anger and hostility. Throughout these poems, Yeats attempts to make death less fearful by regarding it and the afterlife it leads to as an extension of artistic creation. In the artifice of eternity, the dead self is recreated in a more beautiful and permanent form, as Yeats's golden bird.

[1] W. B. Yeats, *Mythologies* (New York: Macmillan, 1959), "Anima Hominis," p. 325. Hereafter cited as *Mythologies*.

ONE

Islands

FEW POETS have been so acutely aware of dreams and their importance to art as William Butler Yeats. Late in life, Yeats theorized about the nature of dreams and their importance to creativity as a gateway to images stored deep in the self. But it is in his earliest work that we see most clearly how images from his unconscious or buried self, after passing through the medium of daydream, are transformed into poetry and fiction. The early work has certain dreamlike qualities—as if the psychological substance of daydreams were translated with little change into poem or story. Much of this work can, in fact, be described as an extended daydream, which lessened the weight of "youth's dreamy load" that "none can have and thrive."

In this chapter we will examine a number of related images and emotions that appear both in Yeats's daydreams and in his earliest works (through 1891). The principal theme of the daydreams seems to be escape from reality at any cost, whether by retreat to an island or by death. The island retreat, however, proves to be a place not only of peace and joy but also of danger and temptation. Other images to be discussed here—the garden, the waterfall—similarly express conflict severe enough to paralyze a man, while at the same time representing elements of an imagined paradise that is a source of creative energy.

The characters associated with these ambivalent images, particularly the women, seem at first to be categorizable as either good or evil: the goddess Niamh and Dhoya's spirit mistress, or the paralyzing Enchantress and the bearded witch. But on closer inspection the personae moving through these ambiguous symbolic landscapes prove equally ambiguous: Niamh is in some respects a demon, and the bearded witch an aspect of the poet's image of perfect love.

Yeats represented himself in this symbolic world, with fair consistency, as a dreaming, passive hero who is either paralyzed or in some other way unable to function as a man. As we shall see, this passivity was a response to Oedipal conflict, which was a source, too, of the creative energy on which Yeats drew. This point will emerge most clearly in the discussion of *Oisin*, but all the works discussed in this chapter—and in particular their symbolic settings and the relationships between the characters in them—throw light on the forces driving the poet to seek refuge and on the significance of the refuges he created for himself.

In the section of the *Autobiography* titled "Reveries over Childhood and Youth," Yeats relates several daydreams of his childhood. The first, a very early one, seems to have been stimulated by a rumor of a Fenian rising:

> When I had begun to dream of my future life, I thought I would like to die fighting the Fenians. I was to build a very fast and beautiful ship and to have under my command a company of young men . . . brave and handsome . . . and there was to be a big battle on the sea-shore . . . and I was to be killed.[1]

What is striking about this daydream is its intense combination of grandeur and masochism, a combination that reflects Yeats's early attitudes toward death.

In his first reported memory Yeats recalls going to bed in terror when a servant tells him that someone "is going to blow the town up." His second memory is of Sligo days, when, he says, he was "very unhappy." After praying for death for several nights, "I began to be afraid that I was dying and prayed that I might live" (*Autobiography*, p. 3). Neither of these memories speaks of death as beautiful or glamorous, the qualities stressed in the daydream. On the contrary, they reveal great anxiety about being killed or blown up or about dying, a fear resulting from a feeling of guilt,

---

[1] *The Autobiography of William Butler Yeats* (New York: Macmillan, 1953), p. 9; hereafter cited in the text as *Autobiography*.

from the thought he had sinned and deserved punishment. In the reminiscence of Sligo days Yeats goes on to say that he was miserable, out of both loneliness and fear of his grandfather, a stern and famous sea captain. "I think I confused my grandfather with God, for I remember in one of my attacks of melancholy praying that he might punish me for my sins" (*Autobiography*, p. 5). This grandfather-God is replaced by a voice in his head that is "sudden and startling" (*Autobiography*, p. 7) and often reproves him. Yeats calls it his conscience; in his writings of this period it alternates with external images in chastising him for sin, the exact nature of which will become clear later in this chapter.

The dream of death on the seashore is a fantasy of atonement, in which the hero voluntarily accepts punishment for guilty wishes. By depicting himself as a hero dying for a noble cause, he made the underlying self-destructiveness more acceptable. Yeats seems to be combining here two of his most characteristic methods of dealing with anxiety. Throughout his life, whenever he greatly feared something, he either denied his fear by a show of gaiety or heroic nonchalance, or presented the feared event as something wished for. Thus his earliest remembered fantasy, "I thought I would like to die," shows the same method of dealing with fears of death and punishment as his great late poem "Sailing to Byzantium," where the hero prays for death with more eloquence but for similar reasons.

The unhappiness to which death seemed at times the only alternative is illustrated by a memory that contrasts strongly with the daydream of the fast and beautiful ship: "I am sitting on the ground looking at a mastless toy boat with the paint rubbed and scratched, and I say to myself in great melancholy, 'it is further away than it used to be,' and while I am saying it I am looking at the long scratch in the stern" (*Autobiography*, p. 3). The explicit sexual connotations of the image—with the female nature of the ship underscored by the scratched stern and missing mast—as well as the intense emotions associated with it, suggest that we are dealing here with a screen memory, in which the receding ship represents a longed-for woman. When Yeats was a child, he spent much time with his stern, eccentric relatives at Merville, in County Sligo, and even when he was with his parents, he felt that his mother was emotionally unavailable to him. Mrs. Yeats was continually in low spirits because of her husband's poverty and her own ill health.[2] She shared the "strain of depressive melancholia" so marked in the Pollexfen family, and, according to her husband, was "not at all good at housekeeping or child-minding."[3] It seems likely, then, that the longed-for person represented by the scratched and mastless boat was Yeats's despondent mother.

One obvious way in which Yeats could try to solve the problem of feeling abandoned by his mother was to identify with her (a solution that was to cause many problems in his later relationships with women), even at the cost of seeing himself as broken and worthless. This interpretation will be borne out by our analysis of the plays, when we see how closely at times Yeats identified with female weakness. If the toy ship represents his feelings about himself as broken or worthless, the fast and beautiful ship is his effort to construct a new self-image.

In its purest state, the daydream of death does not appear in the earliest work. By extending the fantasy to dreams of ships and faraway places, Yeats shifts the focus from death to escape, bravery, adventure. The thought of death has not left him ("I often said to myself how terrible it would be to go away and die where nobody would know my story" [*Autobiography*, p. 11]), but it is connected now with the desire to be remembered, the desire to achieve something memorable in real life, not just in fantasy.

Yeats began to develop alternatives to death-wish fantasies as means of dealing with his terrors of death and his loneliness: he dreamed of himself as a magician, capable of bringing the crea-

---

2 W. B. Yeats, *Memoirs*, ed. Denis Donoghue (London: Macmillan, 1972), p. 47; hereafter cited as *Memoirs*.

3 William M. Murphy, *The Yeats Family and the Pollexfens of Sligo* (Dublin: Dolmen Press, 1971), pp. 34–35, 53 (Yeats's sister Lily supported this charge of her father's). John Butler Yeats wrote his brother Isaac, "Susan could not have boiled an egg. I never left home without wondering what would happen in my absence" (p. 48). According to Murphy (p. 49), Susan's incompetence and her hostility toward her husband's career strained the marriage to the breaking point. This work is hereafter cited as Murphy, *Yeats Family*.

tures of his imagination to life, and he dreamed of escaping to an island paradise from which all fear and sorrow would be banished.

The magician dream, which was to compete for many years with the dream of death on the seashore, took shape in adolescence, when the physical signs of maturity began to correspond to long-established desires, and Yeats became, as Richard Ellmann has pointed out, more deeply involved in daydreams.[4] Scientific interests served as a pretext for evening trips to a cave above the sea, where he played "at being a sage, a magician or a poet." His earlier idol, Hamlet, is joined by Manfred on his glacier, Prince Athanase with his lamp, and particularly Shelley's melancholy Alastor, who disappears, drifting slowly away on a river between great trees. Yeats notes that his father's influence was at its height during this period, and he reacted in part by daydreaming of isolated and melancholy heroes (*Autobiography*, p. 39). In addition, the works he admires contain many hints of forbidden or incestuous passion and hostility toward a father or father-figure. Hamlet murders his uncle, Manfred has probably committed incest, and Alastor is suffering from extreme melancholia; the women chosen to accompany these heroes are "lawless women without homes and without children." (The fact that these women have no children means that they can devote their love completely to the young heroes, and suggests that in Yeats's fantasy they represent their opposites, i.e. ideal mothers.)

Yeats's uncle, unlike his father, was melancholy and devoted to magic, and under his approving eye Yeats "nursed" a new ambition: to live on a little island called Innisfree, opposite a wood. This ambition is not wholly new. Instead of death, it presents both an alternative form of escape and Yeats's first attempt to work his fears and guilt feelings into a traditional framework. The island, he explains, is a refuge from sexual temptation: "I thought that having conquered bodily desire and the inclination of my mind towards women and love, I should live, as Thoreau lived, seeking wisdom" (*Autobiography*, pp. 43–44). Innisfree was par-

---

[4] Richard Ellmann, *Yeats: The Man and the Masks* (New York: Dutton, 1958), p. 28; hereafter cited as Ellmann, *Man and Masks*.

ticularly appealing, he tells us, because of its connection with an Eden myth—"a story in the county history." On the island there had once been a tree, guarded by a monster, that bore the fruit of the gods. A young girl asked her lover to get some of the fruit for her. He complied with her wish, but tasted the fruit and died of its "powerful virtue" after reaching the shore, whereupon "from sorrow and from remorse she too ate of it and died" (*Autobiography*, p. 44). Thus the island provides an escape from "bodily desire" and guilt, but at the same time harbors something forbidden, the desirable but dangerous god food. Yeats says he was twenty-two or -three before he gave up this dream, which appears in a variety of forms in his early poetry and prose.

The daydream of escape to an island paradise first takes literary form in *The Island of Statues*, a verse play written in August 1884 and described by Yeats as "An Arcadian Faery Tale." The island here is paradoxically a place of intense joy and acute danger, and the play's "savage and decadent theme," as Harold Bloom points out in his recent work on Yeats and poetic influence, "is curiously Yeats's own."[5]

As the play opens, two shepherds are having a singing contest for the love of the shepherdess Naschina. Their rival and the play's hero is Almintor, a hunter whose outstanding characteristic is ineffectuality. His arrows, representing his desire, twice miss the mark. When we first see him he has just missed a heron (which symbolizes beauty), and at the end of Act I he misses the flower of wisdom. When Almintor speaks of his love, Yeats defines it as being like the love of Paris for Oenone "long ere an arrow whizzed or sword left sheath,"[6] i.e., long before the siege of Troy precipitated by Paris's abduction of Helen; the contrast is between innocent love (Arcady is the world before the Fall) and sexual passion.

Naschina is as bored with Almintor's innocent love as Paris was

---

[5] Bloom thus at one stroke dismisses, correctly I think, two outworn critical notions about *The Island of Statues*—that it is innocent (a "picture play with Spenserian shepherds," as Ellmann calls it in *Man and Masks* [p. 37]), and that it is derivative. *Yeats* (New York: Oxford University Press, 1970), p. 53.

[6] Russell K. Alspach, ed., *The Variorum Edition of the Plays of W. B. Yeats* (New York: Macmillan, 1966), p. 1229; hereafter cited as *Variorum Plays*. All citations of the plays, unless otherwise noted, are from this volume.

with Oenone's. She wants action even if the consequences are
tragic. Her desire for the combative masculinity of a dragon-killing knight, rather than the "song" and "toys" of innocent children,
shatters Arcady and sends Almintor on a quest not for a dragon
but for a forbidden "goblin flower." The flower grows on an island
isolated by the sea and guarded by an Enchantress. The Enchantress turns the unlucky seekers of the flower into "moon-white
stone." Almintor is called to the island by a maiden's voice; her
song links the flower to Eden's forbidden fruit:

> *Voice.* When the tree was o'er-appled
> For Mother Eve's winning,
> I was at her sinning.
>
> · · ·
>
> And I sang round the tree
> As I sing now to thee:
>
> · · ·
>
> From the green shaded hollow
> Arise, worm, and follow!
> (pp. 1233–34)

Yeats's hero Almintor is commiting the original sin, goaded on by
a woman. The epithet "worm" suggests both sexuality and weakness.[7] Yeats identifies Almintor with the childlike innocence of
unfallen nature, but also, I think, with a kind of passive femininity.
Yeats's discussion of Blake's worm symbolism is enlightening in
this respect. After listing the worm's symbolic possibilities, he concludes that "viewed as a worm, male is female."[8] Certainly Almintor as worm is far from the dragon-killing knight Naschina yearns
for. Even when he shoots his arrow at the goblin flower, he relies
for success not on his own powers but on the will of the gods. He
misses and is turned to stone.

   [7] In his old age, Yeats gave "worm" an explicitly sexual meaning in "The
Chambermaid's Second Song," where the phallus with its "butting head" is
"limp as a worm" after the sexual act. Peter Allt and Russell K. Alspach, eds.,
The Variorum Edition of the Poems of W. B. Yeats (New York: Macmillan,
1957), p. 575; hereafter cited as *Variorum Poems*. All citations of Yeats's poetry
refer to this edition unless otherwise noted.
   [8] Edwin J. Ellis and W. B. Yeats, eds., *The Works of William Blake* (London:
Quaritch, 1893), vol. 1, p. 4. Yeat's interpretation of Blake's worm symbolism
occupies pp. 413–20.

Almintor clearly is not what Yeats later thought of as a hero, either. Naschina, who resembles Shakespeare's Rosalind—there are many borrowings and similarities of tone in the dialogue—surpasses him in wit and strength. She in turn pales beside the Enchantress, not simply because an evil character is easier to portray than a good one, but because the Enchantress interested Yeats more than Naschina did. He says in a letter to a friend that the part of the Enchantress, as well as that of Vivien in *Time and the Witch Vivien*, also dating from 1884, was written for his cousin Laura Armstrong to act.[9] This cousin was engaged to a man with whom she often quarreled. Yeats, who had no hopes of marrying young because of his family's penury, could safely think himself in love with her, and he became her confidant (*Autobiography*, p. 46). It appears from the one surviving letter between Yeats and Laura that they addressed each other as shepherds (*Letters*, p. 117). Thus it was natural that he would write an Arcadian drama with a part in it for his cousin. *Island of Statues* is, then, the first of Yeats's plays written around and sometimes for a beloved woman. In a letter to his main early confidant, Katharine Tynan, Yeats says that Maud Gonne interested him because she reminded him of Laura, yet that even Laura interested him only as myth and symbol. A symbol, it would seem, of unattainable desire as a stimulus for art: Laura, he writes, "woke me from the metallic sleep of science and set me writing my first play" (*Letters*, p. 117). We shall return to this statement later, but now let us look more closely at the Enchantress.

Although she may be a prototype for the later queens, the Enchantress is not a queen but the female embodiment of the magician, the role Yeats was most interested in at the time. Like her counterpart in *Time and the Witch Vivien*, she desires unlimited power and is punished by death. Her death is the occasion for the most moving speech in *The Island of Statues*, a protest against death itself:

[9] Allen Wade, ed., *The Letters of W. B. Yeats* (New York: Macmillan, 1955), p. 118; hereafter cited (primarily in the text) as *Letters*.

Ah, woe is me! I go from sun and shade,
And the joy of the streams where long-limbed herons wade;

. . .

I shall not in the evenings hear
Again the woodland laughter, and the clear
Wild cries, grown sweet with lulls and lingerings long.
I fade, and shall not see the mornings wake,

. . .

I dream!—I cannot die!—No! no!
I hurl away these all unfaery fears.
Have I not seen a thousand seasons ebb and flow
The tide of stars? Have I not seen a thousand years
The summers fling their scents? Ah, subtile and slow,
The warmth of life is chilling, and the shadows grow
More dark. . . .

. . .

Oh, death is horrible!

(pp. 1253–54)

In later plays, it is generally the man who must die for his pre-
sumption.

This is one of the very few traditional "happy endings" in the
plays: the hero lives and is united with the heroine. Significantly,
however, he is united not with the Enchantress, to be played by the
girl Yeats loved, but with Naschina. Maud Gonne, who was to be
his next heroine, "altogether favored the Enchantress and hated
Naschina" (*Letters*, p. 106).

In some respects this play shows the Yeatsian hero before he
really starts his quest for the perfect woman. He is questing, to be
sure, but though the object is the flower of immortality and truth,
the impetus comes from Naschina, his rather ordinary though demanding love. The ordinary woman will gradually fade from
Yeats's work (she is present as the Friend in early drafts of *The
Player Queen*). From now on the hero will be inspired not by an
ordinary woman, but by a perfect one, immortal, fay, or queen.
Later Yeats wrote, "The clouds began about four years ago. I was
finishing the 'Island.' They came and robbed Naschina of her
shadow" (*Letters*, p. 88). In gaining the flower, that is, Naschina
lost her soul (became immortal and thus shadowless). The remark
suggests Yeats's growing obsession with immortal women who will
entice his heroes through cloudy dream landscapes. In *The Island*

of Statues the hero has no real contact with the Enchantress. From a distance she changes him into moon-white stone. The Enchantress's coldness is shared by many of Yeats's later heroines. The repellent aspect of this coldness appears when the Enchantress changes into a slimy green frog before she dies. Naschina is left to comment on her death:

> As figures moving mirrored in a glass,
> The singing shepherds, too, have passed away.
> O Arcady, O Arcady, this day
> A deal of evil and of change hath crossed
> Thy peace.
>
> (pp. 1255–56)

Yeats tended to write companion pieces exploring different aspects of a single theme. *The Seeker,* a dramatic poem in two scenes, was printed along with *The Island of Statues* and shares its epilogue. The hero of *The Seeker,* unlike Almintor, comes into direct relation with the spellbinder, who is seen to be the true object of the quest. The quest, however, fails in an ironic manner. When the Knight finally sees his beloved, he finds that she is a sexually ambiguous bearded witch. The poem's hero is a dream-led knight who has been searching all his life (through "spice-isles") for a visionary figure that promises more than human joy. The beginning of the poem presents a marked contrast to the apparent natural innocence of *The Island of Statues.* Dreams are described as ravenous animals, "red-eyed panthers" circling around their "dreadful brood" (p. 1259), and when the shepherds try their flutes, they emit shrieks, not music. When the Knight asks for directions, the shepherds in great agitation warn him against the woods:

> Seek not that wood, for there the goblin snakes
> Go up and down, and raise their heads and sing
> With little voices songs of fearful things.
>
> (p. 1260)

These snakes sound very much like the voices singing of temptation near the goblin flower in *Island of Statues.*[10] The Knight ig-

---

10 In a later poem of this early period, "The Man Who Dreamed of Faeryland," Yeats has fishes of silver raise their heads, sing, and drive the man from peace. *Variorum Poems,* p. 126.

nores the snakes' warning and advances to a ruined palace, where
he sees a motionless figure, his beloved, the object of his quest.
Bowing down before it, he asks it to speak, but not as if its words
would be unfamiliar:

> Even from boyhood, in my father's house,
> That was beside the waterfall, thy words
> Abode, as banded adders....
>
> (p. 1261)

"Banded adders" links the figure's words with the "fearful things"
told by the goblin snakes and with the serpent of Eden. Even in
boyhood, supposedly a time of Arcadian innocence, the tempting
serpent words were with the Knight. The object of his quest is the
(characteristically Yeatsian) supernatural figure, who supersedes
the biblical forbidden fruit or goblin flower of *Island of Statues*.
In addition, *The Seeker* reveals a closer connection between passivity and the quest; i.e., here it becomes clear that it is the incestuous dream itself that paralyzes and isolates the seeker and at
the same time leads to his quest. Whereas Almintor, naturally non-
aggressive or passive, was prompted by love for a woman to engage
in a masculine quest, the object of the Knight's quest and his love
are the same, and it is the poisonous or dangerous dream that leads
directly to his passivity and isolation.

The Knight's desire for the love of a visionary figure is associated with a waterfall. Although the waterfall image does not
become a favorite, Yeats uses it in the early autobiographical novel,
John Sherman, in connection with his desire to escape to Innisfree, and also in a later dream poem, "Towards Break of Day."[11]
In the poem, the waterfall of his childhood, which he longs to
touch, becomes a symbol of the poet's ideal woman, his mother or
sweetheart. This association seems to have been present, consciously or unconsciously, in *The Seeker* as well. The words that
abide by the waterfall cut the boy off from masculine pursuits and
make him a "coward in the field." The Knight is known as the
"Knight of the Waterfall," i.e., a man who is like a woman. If the
waterfall can be identified with the poet's image of the ideal woman

---

[11] *Ibid.*, pp. 398–99.

in boyhood, his mother, then the tempting words that disturbed his innocent relation to home and waterfall may represent an incestuous dream. This would make psychological sense of the ending, where the horrified Knight finds that his love is "Infamy."

The Wanderings of Oisin (1889), Yeats's first long narrative poem, brings together all the emotional material we have observed in the earlier work and in the daydreams—his fears of death, of his grandfather, and of sin, his longing for a comforting mother, his island fantasies—in a coherent pattern that will be repeated with variations throughout Yeats's work. *Oisin* is therefore extremely important to an understanding of Yeats's later work. According to Bloom, who sees the poem as a typically Yeatsian version of the Romantic quest, "*Oisin* is probably Yeats's most underrated major poem. . . . The whole of Yeats is already in it, as he himself always knew."[12]

Besides being the first complete representation of the Oedipal drama, *Oisin* provides abundant material for an investigation of the way Yeats symbolized the human body. His method, which is reasonably clear in *Oisin*, remains essentially the same throughout his work. To the earlier representations of the female body as a wooded island, a waterfall, and a broken boat, he adds a representation of the interior of the female body as slimy stairs and domed cavern. This symbolism was probably unconscious—Yeats says that the images in Book II of *Oisin* came to him in a waking dream (*Letters*, p. 87)—and is balanced by a conscious and more ordinary presentation of a Victorian lady compounded of misty vapors. The device of splitting aspects of reality into two components, in this case pure, helpless, and beautiful as opposed to disgusting but powerful, is characteristic of the later Yeats, as is the symbolic representation of parts of the body. It was in *Oisin* that Yeats first represented the male organ as a hard, precious object, as a scepter and "word sword." Indeed, sexual symbols of all kinds abound in *Oisin*. These symbols are important not in themselves but for what they tell us about Yeats's feelings toward the body and its functions—for instance, that a woman's genitals are dis-

12 Bloom, *Yeats*, p. 87.

gusting but that the womb is a place where one receives magical powers, both sexual and poetic. Symbols like the sword have a defensive function: they protect against fears of castration and death.

The use of such symbols is connected with Yeats's characteristic pattern of defense, which is observable in Oisin's reaction to St. Patrick: fear followed by laughing defiance. When this defense fails, we see an equally characteristic deflation associated with masochistic imagery: Oisin sees himself as old and broken on the anvil of the world. The pattern of fear, defiance, and deflation, with its corresponding imagery, recurs in the drafts of one of Yeats's most famous poems, "Sailing to Byzantium." When we have understood the pattern and the defensive function of symbols like the sword, we are in a better position to understand more complex symbols like Byzantium's golden bird. But that is in the future; let us turn now to *Oisin*.

Except for Bloom, *Oisin*'s many critics have tended to find the work escapist and inferior to its sources in Irish myth. Ellmann has rightly pointed out that the three allegorical islands to which Oisin travels—the Isle of Joy, the Isle of Many Fears, and the Isle of Forgetfulness—are not merely refuges from life but representations of it.[13] On one level, Ellmann suggests, each of Oisin's three island voyages represents a stage of life: childhood, adolescence, and senility. More personally, he suggests, the three islands represent Yeats's idyllic boyhood in Ireland, fighting in London with English boys over being Irish, and daydreaming at Howth. He also finds a political level, in which the chained lady represents Ireland.

Although Ellmann relates the poem to Yeats's life, he does so in a way that fails to suggest the seriousness of Yeats's myth and the importance of the poem for his development. Yeats is not just representing isolated elements from his childhood; he is representing a conflict central to both life and work, with a progressively unfolding psychological pattern. It was the necessity of fully ex-

[13] Richard Ellmann, *The Identity of Yeats* (New York: Oxford University Press, 1954), pp. 17–20; hereafter cited as Ellmann, *Identity*.

pressing this pattern that led Yeats to add two further islands to the single island of his source.

Just as in reality Yeats always connected the beloved Sligo with his mother and the hated London with his father (whose work forced the family to move there), the joyful landscape in Book I of *Oisin* symbolizes the mother in her ideal aspect, and the dark towers of Book II the father in his fearful aspect. Moreover, the islands represent states of mind as well as people and places. Oisin moves from joy (the Isle of Joy) to conflict or guilt (the Isle of Many Fears) to repression (the Isle of Forgetting), a psychologically necessary progress. An understanding of this basic psychological pattern illuminates many of Yeats's more conscious themes, such as the conflict between Christianity and paganism (which critics like A. G. Stock fail to see in relation to other elements),[14] by showing how they relate to his inner life and the structure of his defenses.

The writing of *Oisin* cost Yeats his "greatest effort" up to this time. The strain involved can be seen from his letters, which show the conflicts concealed by the poem's decorative surface.[15] The tension between a natural reluctance to put emotion-laden material into words and the drive to create art out of inner struggle may partially explain the vague style of *Oisin*—and of the early work in general. The dreamy cadences of this style lull the reader, so that he notices not what is happening in the poem, but the manner of expression, the music, the imagery, and the remote and exotic settings. The style disguises meaning while conveying emotion through a dreamlike mood that one feels but does not understand. At times the feeling produced is directly opposite to the meaning, as in the dream poem "Cap and Bells," where a fable of self-destruction is embodied in dance-like patterns and delicate imagery suggestive of life and beauty.

14 A. G. Stock, *W. B. Yeats: His Poetry and Thought* (Cambridge: Cambridge University Press, 1961), p. 20.
15 To my knowledge, the only other critic to have dealt similarly with this subject is Morton Irving Seiden, in "Patterns of Belief—Myth in the Poetry of William Butler Yeats," *American Imago*, 5 (Dec. 1948): 259–300. Seiden devotes most of his attention to *Oisin* and *A Vision*, but he also discusses the function of myth and its relation to poetry.

Yeats was aware of this highly charged but obscure quality of his early work and its connection with dreams. He compares *Oisin* to a dream that loses its value in being written down: "I am like people who dream some wonderful thing and get up in the middle of the night and write it and find next day only scribbling on the paper" (*Letters*, p. 87). *Oisin* also resembles a dream in having its real (emotional) content under symbolic disguise. Yeats admits that he alone has the key to the symbolism with which he has disguised his meaning in Book II (*Letters*, p. 88). Nevertheless, we can make at least a small rent in what Yeats referred to as the screen of "clouds" surrounding this Book, and begin to interpret the poem's riddling symbols.

Oisin contains many examples of the poet's ambivalence toward the longed-for woman. The title was originally "Oisin / and / How a Demon Trapped Him." In revision this title was dropped, but the concept of woman as dangerous and destructive was one Yeats intermittently shared with St. Patrick, who serves in the poem as Oisin's interlocutor. The poem does present two competing views of woman: St. Patrick's, in which Niamh is an "amorous demon," and Oisin's, in which she is the daughter of love and poetry. Yeats's clear preference for Oisin's heroic attitude toward love can be seen as an attempt to defend against his own feelings of sin and guilt, his fear of death, and his ambivalence toward women.

In Book I the goddess Niamh is introduced as a figure associated with both death and sexuality: she entices Oisin away from ordinary life to the Isle of Joy (referred to in Celtic myth as the "Isle of the [Ever] Living"), which is also traditionally the isle of the dead, where there is perfect satisfaction and love. This construct not only sets up an imaginary place where all frustrations are banished, but successfully denies the fear of death. The love-death motif becomes a constant feature of Yeats's work. Oisin describes Niamh as he first sees her in terms of a mixture of red and white, which represent purity and passion and are both dangerous; her moon-like pallor links her to ideal love and death, her red lips to the destructive Helen of Troy: "And like a sunset were her lips, / A stormy sunset on doomed ships" (I, 22–23). For the most part in Book I, however, Niamh's death aspect is relegated to the background and the sexual or life aspect emphasized: the demon is a demon not of Death but of "the little death."

Niamh's connection with love and nature is suggested by the dress in which she first appears, which is embroidered with birds and beasts and held by a shell, later to be used by itself as an emblem for woman. Yeats immediately identifies her as the child of love and poetry. She wants to take Oisin with her to the Isle of Joy, the land of perfection and satisfied love. "Music and love and sleep await, / Where I would be when the white moon climbs, / The red sun falls . . ." (I, 103–5). The poem presents a series of contrasts between the moon and the sun and the values, people, or states of mind associated with them. The Isle of Joy is under the auspices of the moon, and Niamh is an aspect of the queenly moon goddess, carrying off her man on a white steed with a golden crescent between its ears. Although Yeats had not begun to work out this contrast systematically, the falling sun stands for the land Oisin rides away from, his everyday reality, and, by extension, his father, the warrior king Finn, whom Oisin leaves behind weeping.

The fact that union with the ideal woman can only take place away from the solar influence of the father suggests the forbidden, i.e., incestuous, nature of the union. Oisin's father laments his son's capture as death, but from Oisin's point of view it is the father, or Sun, that dies: as Oisin and Niamh ride away they see the sun sink. Music rises from the sun's dying flames as though celebrating its sacrifice, and immediately afterward trees "like sooty fingers" rise trembling out of the warm sea (I, 171). The image, obviously phallic, is also a birth image. Out of the sun's fiery death there is born a combination of sexual and poetic power. The birth, moreover, is associated not only with the warm maternal sea out of which the trees rise, but specifically, in the sootiness of the trees, with the sun's ashes. Yeats's comparison of the movement of the trees to drumming fingers (a movement caused by hundreds of song-birds in the trees' branches) suggests a link between the rhythmic movements of the sexual act and poetry or poetic meter.

Rhythmic movement, along with images of flame and rose, creates a general feeling of beauty, free sexuality, and harmony on the Isle of Joy. And in his portrayal of the Isle's chief figure, Aengus, god of love and poetry, Yeats again links poetic and sexual powers. Aengus is seen as a young man dreaming in a clay house, an obvious reference to the house of "clay and wattles made" Yeats wanted to live in on Innisfree. In spite of his passivity, Aengus has an instrument of great power—a flaming scepter. Yeats associated flame not only with passion and madness, but with the isolation of the poetic talent—in the Knight and here again in Aengus. The dancers in *Oisin* worship the scepter, kissing it with red lips and touching it with their fingertips (I, 258–59). Aengus responds to the dancers' adoration with a poem of praise to generation, which in the first version of the poem begins, " 'Tis joy makes swim the sappy tide" (I, 261). The flames are then directly linked to the moon by the assertion that men's hearts are "drops of flame" wrung from the moon (I, 276), only to be imprisoned in the body. Yeats will eventually write of angels who make love in an incandescence of the whole being, but here unity is expressed only by the dance over which Aengus presides.

The imagery throughout this section reinforces the association between poetic and sexual powers. The scepter, like the twisted horn and the seashell, serves as a defense against fears of dissolution and castration: the scepter belongs to Aengus and is under his control, but is not part of his body and cannot be destroyed. The scepter also serves to externalize the active, masculine part of Aengus, who is himself "beardless" and dreamy.

Dancing is one of Yeats's favorite symbols of harmony between the opposites of spirit and flesh, the "pale blossoms of the moon" and the red roses of the earthly paradise. But in *Oisin* Yeats is thinking primarily of the flesh. His world of the everliving is a world of nature before the Fall, ruled only by love. There are continual echoes of Blake in Yeats's exaltation of individual energy into a commandment because "joy is God." Constraining the free expression of energy in joy or sex is external moral or religious law. The dance on the Isle of Joy concludes with a song to the stars, the "slaves of God" (I, 331). God, as Harold Bloom points out, is clearly related to Blake's Urizen,[16] who holds men in iron

---

[16] Bloom, *Yeats*, p. 101.

bonds and connects each man to his brother by law. He is also the threatening, anti-instinctual God of St. Patrick. "Fasting and prayers," says Oisin, are the two things he most hates (I, 360).

Although there is an explicit opposition between joy and generation on the one hand and repression of instinct on the other in *Oisin*, there is nothing similar to Yeats's later description of "nymphs and satyrs" who "copulate in the foam."[17] Niamh and Oisin merely embrace. The drumming fingers, the ride, and the dance upon the "woody central hill" (I, 323) may be rhythmic equivalents of intercourse, but though the sensual imagery and the panting and swooning of the characters carry sexual implications, nothing is made explicit. The result is an undefined merging of sex and spirit rather than an opposition between them.

The portrayal of Niamh and Oisin astride the galloping horse has similar erotic implications. The galloping rider, whether on horse or unicorn, is an image insistently recurring throughout Yeats's work. For reasons I will go into later, it seems to be a transformation of the primal scene, that is, of Yeats's parents having intercourse. Whether observed or imagined, such a scene would first have caused fright, which Yeats later attempted to master by changing it into something beautiful: a man and woman entwined on a swiftly galloping horse. (Unicorns ridden by angels in *Where There Is Nothing* and the mating of Unicorn and Queen in *The Player Queen* are later derivatives of this image that similarly suggest the "goodness" or beauty of intercourse.) In *Oisin*, as in later versions of the galloping rider image, Yeats is ambiguous about the respective roles of man and woman. Oisin is completely passive; the description of Niamh whispering to herself as she binds and winds him in her "triumphing arms" (I, 107) has a slightly sinister quality, as though Oisin were indeed, in Patrick's words, being "trapped of an amorous demon" (I, 4, variant).

The Isle of Joy episode begins with an emblem of Oisin potentiated as both man and poet—the trees that rise from the sea filled with birds. It ends with a sign of impotence—a broken warrior's lance.

17 "News for the Delphic Oracle," ll. 35–36, *Variorum Poems*, p. 612.

The island to which Oisin travels in Book II, the "Isle of Many Fears," represents Oisin's struggle against guilt. The fearful demon that inhabits it is the father who repeatedly arises to chastise Oisin. Oisin and Niamh, entering the battered door to the "dark towers," come upon a stairway; at the top they find a lady in chains, a figure surely derived from Blake's Oothon, who was bound by Reason for giving her love. She is Niamh's counterpart—like Niamh she is connected with the moon, being "wrought out of moonlit vapours" (II, 70)—and represents not only the guilt attached to incestuous desire but the mother enchained in possession of the father. By breaking her chains and freeing her, Oisin not only denies guilt but repeats the crime of Oedipus.

When Oisin leaves home in Book I, he leaves an essentially male world dominated by his father and rides with Niamh to an essentially feminine landscape. The Isle of Joy is bathed in moonlight, covered with roses, and dominated by the "woody central hill." In Book II, the father returns to punish: the dominant feature of the Isle of Many Fears is the threatening, dark towers. After his marriage Yeats was to make such a tower with its stair his home and his unique symbol. Now its ownership is still in question. In *Oisin* Yeats uses the bisexual nature of the tower to explore his feelings about both male and female bodies. The outside of the tower is masculine and threatening, the inside is feminine. More specifically it represents the female genitals and the womb. The genitals are seen as worn with use: the door through which water gushes is battered and repulsive; the stairs are covered with green slime. The lady at the top of the stairs represents woman without her sexuality. Her ideal beauty is insubstantial, dependent on her asexuality and lack of vital body functions. She is the culminating loveliness of the "foam-white seagull" (II, 105), detached from the loathsome nether regions. At this point Yeats was unable to face a fact he later accepted, that "Love has pitched his mansion in / The place of excrement."[18] This dichotomy between moon-woman and slimy stair may help explain the curious symbol at the end of *The Island of Statues*, in which the dying Enchantress becomes a slimy

---

[18] "Crazy Jane Talks with the Bishop," ll. 15–16, *Variorum Poems*, p. 513.

green frog. Death removes the enchanting or illusory qualities of
her beauty, and she is seen in her repellent genital aspect.

The end of Oisin's symbolic journey within the towered fortress
is a great cavern:

> A dome made out of endless carven jags,
> Where shadowy face flowed into shadowy face,
>
> . . .
>
> . . . and the high dome,
> Windowless, pillarless, multitudinous home
> Of faces, waited. . . .
>
> (II, 144–49)

The womb-like quality of the cavern is obvious. More interesting
is the cavern's connection, in a context where it is clearly seen as
a symbolic womb, with what Yeats calls *Anima Mundi*, a pool of
universal thought and feeling that borders on the unconscious of
every man, who draws on and then sends back to it whatever he
thinks or feels. Like *Anima Mundi* the cavern is a repository of
past memories: "loaded with the memory of days / Buried and
mighty" (II, 150–51). More strikingly it is the place where Oisin is
given the sword, identified in an early version of the poem as a
"Druid word sword" (II, 174, variant), with which he is to fight
the demon. The sword, which symbolizes both masculine potency
and the magic or potent word,[19] is the gift of the moon-woman who
finds it in the cavern, just as in later years words and images would
appear as gifts to the poet from *Anima Mundi*.

The sword is by no means a unique instance of Yeats's using
words as magical weapons. When he was bullied by an English boy
at school he reacted by giving the boy an order, "Rise upon Sugain
[hay foot] and sink upon Gad [straw foot]" in Irish, which he knew
the boy would not understand, and which when translated was
seen to imply that the boy was so stupid he could not tell his left
foot from his right. On another occasion Yeats suggested that his
uncle pronounce the name of the angel Gabriel to frighten away
his nightmare visions. Later, when Yeats was overcome by an inner

---

[19] In the first draft of his autobiography Yeats wrote, "A man must know
how to speak in Ireland just as a man in old times had to carry a sword."
Memoirs, p. 21.

force at a London seance he used the words of a powerful poet, Milton, to dispel evil. Significantly, the words he quoted were, "Of man's first disobedience and the fruit." He said later that he could not remember a prayer (*Autobiography*, pp. 20, 162, 64). It was as if an immediate confession of sin (linked to his own incestuous fantasies, the possession of forbidden fruit) through the medium of great poetry would save him.

The Druid word sword is linked to Mannanan, God of the Sea —his name is on it—and placed in the context of opposition between heroic (sexual) pagan activity free of guilt and Christian inhibition and masochism, symbolized by Christ's "milk-pale face / Under a crown of thorns" (II, 134). In the first edition of *Oisin* Yeats stressed both Christian guilt and masochism in a detailed description of the monks' abasement before God's thunder:

> Trembling, on the flags we fall,
> Fearful of the thunder-ball
> Yet do with us whate'er thou wilt,
> For great our error, great our guilt.
> (II, 208e–h)

Against Christianity's reinforcement of the superego and the demands of conscience, Yeats sets up the pagan Irish hero, who hears in the thunder not the sound of his guilt but the "laughing Fenian horn" (II, 213). Using the mythological history of Ireland to support his personal struggle against the demands of conscience and feelings of guilt, Yeats portrays the Christians as ineffectual opponents not only of heroic activity but of poetry: "the lying clerics murder song / With barren words" (II, 196–97). They are incapable of dealing with either "ravening Sorrow" or "the hand of Wrath" (II, 199). The demon is, of course, not a Christian demon but a pagan one; nonetheless Christianity and its emphasis on sin fit in imaginatively with Yeats's struggle against both his father and his sense of guilt. The image of the grandfather-god is brought in to enrich the image of the father-demon.

In the treatment of the demon, we see Yeats's ambivalent feelings toward his father: the desire to rebel and the desire to identify. The father is both a fearsome figure who stands in the way of the son's consummation of his love for his mother, and a weak figure threatened with exhaustion or corruption by the sexuality of the rapacious female. Yeats's fantasies of successful rebellion against his father can be seen in Oisin's confrontation of the demon. When the demon sees the word sword, he feels threatened and undergoes a series of transformations. These fantasies can in turn be linked to Yeats's statement that his magical studies helped him to achieve his first degree of independence from his father.[20] One of Yeats's problems in freeing himself from his father was the similarity of their ideas. His pursuit of mysticism was one of the few ways Yeats found to oppose or defend himself against his father; hence the Druid word sword.

The similarity of thought between father and son meant that Yeats had a problem not only of defense but of identity. This is reflected in the mingling of attributes and sharing of possessions between the demon and Oisin. The sword and the tower, symbols of masculine power, are linked to both of them. Yeats seems to be asking himself, who is more potent, my father or I? Oisin enters the demon's tower and unchains his woman—referred to in one version as his "prey"—and takes the magic sword. The demon as Oisin first sees him is anything but the fearful creature we have been led to expect. In fact, as he sits desolately by the runnel's "stony and bare edge" (II, 157), he resembles Yeats's later self-image, the old man of *At the Hawk's Well*, who sits by the empty well waiting for water. But there is a more important resemblance to Yeats's description of himself as a prematurely aged "white-haired youth" in "The Two Titans." Both descriptions include rhythmic movement with an autoerotic quality: the demon in *Oisin* rocks back and forth, "passing to and fro / His hand along the runnel's side, as though / The flowers still grew there" (II, 161–63); the youth in "The Two Titans" "nodding to and fro sang songs of love, / and flowers."[21]

20 Ellmann, *Man and Masks*, p. 41.

21 Lines 35–36, *Variorum Poems*, p. 688. In *The Myth Against Myth: A Study of Yeats's Imagination in Old Age* (London: Oxford University Press, 1972), published as this book went to press, Daniel Albright suggests that the demon is a projection of Oisin's sexual and aggressive impulses, and more particularly that the allegory reflects Yeats's struggle with autogratification (pp. 98–105).

Both demon and youth crave life-giving moisture: the demon
sits by the trickle of water, the youth kisses rain in crevices. Both
also crave the fertility that moisture brings: children and flowers.
In this mood the demon resembles the Fisher King, wounded and
impotent in a parched land, and Yeats obviously had no difficulty
in identifying with the demon in this role. But when threatened
the demon can make a great display of potency. (He has two sides
to his nature just as his eyes have two colors—snow-white, the
feminine narcissistic side, and angry red.) He arises in the huge
phallic shape of "a great eel." With his sword Oisin can kill him
or reduce him to impotence—a "dripping and sunken shape" (II,
179, variant)—but he is always reborn, and thus the ownership of
tower and lady remain in question.[22]

As in the later unicorn imagery, there is an apparent link between the phallus and the soul or essence of a man. The demon
says that his tower is dropping "stone by stone" and his soul de-
cays "like rotted flesh" (II, 236, variant). The rotten flesh recalls
the corpse, whose watery decay in turn relates to Yeats's slimy
images for the female organs. The male, impotent or worn out by
passion, is seen as female. Given Yeats's later theme of leprosy falling from the moon in a context that expresses fear of women, the
demon's description of his crumbling tower may disguise an unconscious fantasy of the penis being eaten away by a leprous disease
caught from a woman. The life-giving "warm sea" from which the
phallic trees were born in Book I becomes in Book II a tomb, a
slimy devourer of individual energy, which Yeats sees as being re-
absorbed: the moon goads "the waters night and day, / That all be
overthrown" (II, 238–39).

If Book I of *Oisin* represents flight to a dream world where in-

22 Michael Sidnell suggests in his forthcoming book on Yeats that the demon
is Edward Dowden, Professor of English Literature at Trinity College, Dublin.
Yeats's antagonism toward Dowden would fit, in Book II of *Oisin*, with a struggle
against repressive forces—paternal control and Christian repression. It seems
to me a mistake in emphasis, however, to see conflict with Dowden as central.
Yeats often combined the traits of several people in his characters. Moreover,
as Sidnell points out, Yeats criticized Dowden freely in his prose; it was because he was expressing his feelings toward his father that he resorted to disguise here. Yeats's quarrel with his father's friend simply reinforces his basic
quarrel with his father.

cestuous fantasies are satisfied, and Book II a struggle with Oedipal guilt, Book III shows the conflict repressed; in the Isle of Forgetfulness, Oisin sleeps.

The images of impotence with which Book II ends are picked up in the beginning of Book III, where the trees are "dripping and doubling . . . / Like an army of old men" (III, 15–16). The feeling has changed, however, from one of despair at impending dissolution to one of desire for sleep, death, as a release from sexuality: the old men are "longing for rest from the moan of the seas" (III, 16). The male element, moreover, is united in a comradely retreat (an army) from the female and demanding sea. The imagery has an onanistic quality. The sound of the bell-branch that puts Oisin to sleep is described in terms of a delicate touch—trickling water and the caress of a snowflake—that pierces "the marrow like flame" (III, 68). The rhythmic swaying of the branch in Oisin's fingers adds to the suggestion of sexual stimulation, and is paralleled by the lines about God, who "Could fondle the leaves with His fingers, nor go from His dew-cumbered skies" (III, 38). Yeats's description of the sleeping Oisin contains more than a hint of sensual abandon: "his knees in the soft star-flame, / Lay loose" (III, 43–44). The feminine receptivity of the loosened thighs is developed in Yeats's description of Oisin falling asleep: "a softness came from the starlight and filled me full to the bone" (III, 72). The starlight entering Oisin's body suggests divine impregnation. The whole opening sequence of Book III seems to represent a male retreat from the female and is followed by autoerotic fantasies in which Oisin takes a female role.

Yeats's letters reveal that it was while he was finishing *Oisin*— probably in the fall of 1887—that his mother had the first of the two paralytic strokes that affected her mind.[23] Since he apparently had

---

[23] Hone says the stroke occurred at the end of the summer of 1887 (Joseph Hone, *W. B. Yeats: 1865–1939*, 2d ed. [New York: St. Martin's Press, 1962], p. 56). Murphy places it early in the winter of 1887–88, saying that the family's return to London in 1887 "cracked Susan's spirit" (Murphy, *Yeats Family*, p. 51). Yeats wrote to Katharine Tynan in August 1887 from Sligo, where he had gone to work on *Oisin*, that " 'Oisin' goes ahead famously. The country helps one to think" (*Letters*, p. 51). This does not sound like the letter of a man whose mother had just had a stroke, though in the same letter he spoke of fighting daydreams—sexual fantasies or fears, perhaps—to get time for his work.

completed Book III by then and was working on the rewriting, the
stroke probably had no direct influence on the feminine attitudes
represented on the Isle of Forgetfulness. It undoubtedly frightened Yeats, however, and intensified both his fears of dissolution
and castration and his conflicts. The rewriting of Book III became
more difficult. Yeats reports that "between a severe cold and cough
and that savage graybeard, Oisin, I have had a bad time of it";
and then, still at Sligo, "This finishing off of 'Oisin' is a great relief. . . . It has kept me out of spirits and nervous" (*Letters*, p. 52).

Dhoya, a short story finished by the time the letter just quoted
was written, connects Yeats's depression and loneliness with a longing for a comforting mother. Dhoya, a giant isolated in a forest
cave, has a constant dream of a finger resting on his forehead, a
presence that sighs softly; "gradually . . . he began to long for this
mysterious touch."[24] This was written at the same time as a letter
from Sligo in which Yeats writes, "My mother is somewhat better,
is to come down here, if well enough to travel, which I fear is
doubtful" (*Letters*, p. 55). In the story, when the longed-for presence fails to materialize, Dhoya's moods worsen. He has fits of
solitary rage, "though there was no one but his own shadow to rave
against" (*JS&D*, p. 116). His gigantic size and his association with
the ugliest animals, "outcasts from they knew not what" (*JS&D*, p.
116), seem to represent the monstrousness of his frustration and
the guilt it arouses.[25]

Finally, after Dhoya burns a sacrifice to the moon, the dream
presence in another aspect, he hears a voice calling him from a
precipice and sees "the form of a beautiful woman" (*JS&D*, p. 118).
His happiness with the spirit woman, who has left the Isles of the

[24] Yeats, *John Sherman & Dhoya*, ed. Richard J. Finneran (Detroit: Wayne
State University Press, 1969), p. 117; hereafter cited as *JS&D*.

[25] Similar subject matter and imagery are present in an early (1887) poem,
"The Madness of King Goll," stimulated by a portrait his father painted of
him as King Goll. Goll, originally a "mild, a kingly boy" (l. 8, variant) isolated
by "a whirling and a wandering fire" (l. 28), withdraws into the forest, where
he sings to "toads and every outlawed thing / . . . the song of outlaws and their
fear" (ll. 6, 64, variants). But what seems first to have been a terrifying isolation
will be turned by Yeats into a positive thing: the uniqueness of the poet, the
fire, passion, and sexual dream metamorphosed into the fire of inspiration and
purification. *Variorum Poems*, pp. 81–86.

Young for him, is described in terms of dreams and implied weakness: he is "happy and as full of dreams as an old man or an infant —for dreams wander nearest to the grave and the cradle" (*JS&D*, p. 120). Dhoya's childlike security is threatened by a stranger, "a man leaning on his spear-staff, on his head a small red cap" (*JS&D*, p. 121) and the Oedipal battle of *Oisin* is repeated. Dhoya attacks the man, they fight twice, and when Dhoya gets him down he disappears. Later, the stranger comes back to play chess. No matter what move Dhoya makes, the man makes a better and stronger one. He wins back the woman and returns to a land Dhoya cannot enter. Dhoya, helplessly furious, wounds a mare with his spear, then leaps on the back of a huge black stallion and urges him over a cliff into the sea. The stallion, like the stranger, is emphatically male; Dhoya identifies with his masculinity but expresses the hopelessness of the identification by suicide. At the same time, his plunge over the cliff into the sea symbolizes final reunion with the mother-goddess after death.

Our discussion of *Oisin* and *Dhoya* suggests that Yeats's passivity was a reaction to Oedipal conflict. After the symbolic battle with the father, the hero goes to sleep or commits suicide. Since Yeats regarded words as weapons, it is possible that *Oisin*, with its riddling symbolism to which he alone had the key and its many references to the mystical beliefs his father disapproved of, may have served a defensive-aggressive purpose in relation to Yeats's father. Book II was the one that gave Yeats most concern as he was preparing it for press. He worried that its symbolism was too obscure, and at the same time denied that it was consciously chosen—saying that all of Book II came to him as a vision: "I saw the second" (*Letters*, p. 87). This is, I think, the truth, and it links this Book with "The Cap and Bells" and *On Baile's Strand*. As we will see later, material for poems and plays directly connected with the Oedipal conflict and particularly its aggressive aspects often came to him in visions, a circumstance that both enhanced the value of the material and mitigated his responsibility for it.

The combination of conflict with his father and his mother's stroke seems to have posed particular difficulties. Because of his

identification with a mother who had been defeated by life, Yeats
could not achieve something without feeling he had betrayed her.
Completing a successful long poem while his mother was near
death must have made Yeats feel especially disloyal. The collapse
and vocal difficulty he reports at the end of *Oisin* ("When I had
finished it, I brought it round to my uncle George Pollexfen [his
mother's brother] and could hardly read, so collapsed I was. My
voice quite broken"; *Letters*, p. 87) may serve as a denial of his
verbal potency and show an identification with his mother's illness.[26]

The beginning of a new work seems always to have lifted Yeats
out of depression. After finishing *Oisin*, however, he did not start
anything new for several months, and did so then only after repeated urging by his father. He writes to Katharine Tynan that
he wants to be passive, to break through the "web" of thoughts
and see the world again. Passivity is connected here with the absence of fantasy and creative work. He wants instead "regular
work," which would give him peace of mind, shielding him against
anxiety and guilt. In the same letter he indicates that his feeling
of guilt comes in part from a sense of the preternatural importance
he gives to his dreams and to his work, which impedes his contact
with other things and other people. He writes, for example, that
the fate of one of his manuscripts means more to him than the
death of an acquaintance. But he immediately repudiates the feeling by blaming it all on the "web" that has come between him and
the world. The sense that the world is empty and meaningless increases. Since *Oisin* "I have grown more and more passive . . . everything seems a vision and nothing worth seeking after" (*Letters*, pp.
58, 82).

In some people, such a degree of passivity and depersonalization

---

26 Given the Pollexfen tendency toward depression, one would expect depressive reactions to illness or death. And indeed Yeats's sister Lily also seems
to have had a sympathetic illness after their mother's stroke; Yeats worries
about Lily's despondent temperament and hopes she will help herself by writing stories. According to Murphy, another Pollexfen became so "morbidly
depressed" after two family deaths that he had to be institutionalized for a
time. Murphy, *Yeats Family*, p. 35.

might be cause for alarm. Yeats, however, seems to have used periods of passivity to reduce conflict and gather energy for new efforts. In another letter, he apologizes for his bookishness, but explains that "other things at present for many reasons make me anxious and I bury my head in books as the ostrich does in the sand.... I cannot help being inhuman, as you call it, these times. On the rare occasions when I go to see anyone... I keep thinking that I ought to be at home trying to solve my problems" (*Letters*, p. 75). From behind his shield, he seems to have been gaining some insight into his "problems." He sees that so far his poems have all been "a flight into fairyland" from the real world, (*Letters*, p. 63), poems of complaint and longing, not of understanding.

Although his insight into his helplessness increased, the helplessness itself persisted. In April 1888 the family moved to a new house in Blenheim Road. Shortly after his mother and older sister came home, Yeats suffered a collapse so bad that he could only "speak with difficulty.... I was the same way, only worse, when finishing 'Oisin' " (*Letters*, p. 69). He reacted by staying home and planting a garden of sunflowers and love-lies-bleeding. The next month he started *John Sherman*, whose hero names the garden as one of the three most important things in his life.

Before discussing *John Sherman*, I should note that it was at this time Yeats expressed a wish to change his style. After a second severe collapse in December 1888, he writes Katharine Tynan a letter expressing his disapproval of retrospective art. Art should express the self. We need, he writes, "to substitute the feelings and longings of nature for those of art.... We should make poems on the familiar landscapes we love" (*Letters*, pp. 98–99). To illustrate what he means, he encloses two verses of his poem "Innisfree," and explains that in the novel he is writing (*John Sherman*), he makes one of the characters "whenever he is in trouble long to go away and live alone on that Island—an old daydream of my own" (*Letters*, p. 100). He contrasts the beloved landscape with the hated one, "horrid London," and says that his story will express his grievances toward that city. His difficulties are now expressed in terms of place.

Describing his shift in style in the *Autobiography* (p. 48), Yeats says that after *Oisin* he threw off Romantic color and sought an impression of "cold light and tumbling clouds." He continues, "I became as emotional as possible but with an emotion which I described to myself as cold. It is a natural conviction for a painter's son to believe that there may be a landscape that is symbolical of some spiritual condition and awakens a hunger such as cats feel for valerian."

"Cold" emotion and emotion directed toward a landscape rather than a person were characteristic of Yeats's mother. Yeats described her as "intense," yet unable to express this intensity except in love of Sligo and the natural phenomena she observed there. She was particularly delighted by "tumbling clouds" and by stories about fishing villages in the region—stories "Homer might have told." Ordinarily, however, she was reticent. When she saw people kissing at a railway station, she taught Yeats to "feel disgust at their lack of reserve" (*Autobiography*, pp. 37, 21). Since she disapproved of showing emotion she showed little to her children.[27] Lily, more forthright than her brother, described their mother as "grim and austere.... She asked no sympathy and gave none.... When we were children and were ill she always said, 'Grin and bear it.' "[28] This judgment is borne out by a somewhat baffled comment on Susan Yeats's character made by her husband:

There is a good deal of his mother in Willie. I often said to her these words: 'You know I have to take your affection for granted, for I never saw the slightest sign of it.' ... I knew and never doubted that, more than most wives, she was 'wrapt up' in her unworthy husband. She was not sympathetic. The feelings of people about her did not concern her. She was not aware of them. She was always in an island of her own."[29]

---

27 Murphy traces this coldness to Susan's own parents. John Butler Yeats wrote of them, "Their canons did not permit them to indulge in an affection for their children" (Murphy, *Yeats Family*, p. 25). Lily Yeats suggests the effect of the Pollexfen coldness on all the Yeats children when she writes, "I was never so happy before [as at Grandmama Yeats's house]. Grandmama Yeats was demonstrative, called me pet names, caressed me.... The Pollexfen grandparents' house—all was serious, silent.... There were no pet names or caresses" (*ibid.*, p. 22).

28 Murphy, *Yeats Family*, p. 53.

29 A. Norman Jeffares, *The Circus Animals: Essays on W. B. Yeats* (Stanford, Calif.: Stanford University Press, 1970), p. 127.

Yeats's presentation of his mother in his *Autobiography* is idealized, though his praise of her sincerity, "she pretended to nothing
she did not feel" (p. 37), probably contains a veiled reproach for
her lack of feeling. Similarly, his comment, "I can see now that
she had great depth of feeling" (*Autobiography*, p. 19), suggests
that he could not see it as a child. In his reconstruction of those
early days, he focuses on the strong emotion he did not feel in her
at the time and is now having difficulty feeling in his relationships
with others. It is this emotional intensity that he wants for his style,
but an unsentimental, reserved intensity that would seem cold.

Yeats was a long way from fulfilling these goals. His particular
need of a woman to act as a source of emotional sustenance can be
seen from his correspondence with Katharine Tynan, who was
quite probably the model for Mary Carton, John Sherman's childhood sweetheart. Yeats's relationship with Katharine Tynan fits
in with his imagery of the beloved landscape and the satisfactions
it promised. His letters to her from London express a constant
longing for the Irish countryside: "It is pleasant to think that this
letter will go away out of this horrid London and get to the
fields. . . . I wish I could fold myself up and go in it" (*Letters*, p. 61).
Twice he compares himself to Robinson Crusoe, marooned and
hungry for news. News seems to represent nourishment as well as
support and contact with the outside world. "When one is tired,
the *tendril* in one's nature asserts itself and one wants to hear about
one's friends" (*Letters*, p. 82).

Besides providing Yeats with emotional sustenance, Katharine
Tynan gave him infinite possibilities for self-revelation. When
feeling unwell he apologizes for being "full of myself," and compares his need to instinctive animal behavior: he is like "a sick
wasp or a cat going about looking for someone to rub itself against"
(*Letters*, p. 61). Here he expresses a desire for contact, however
primitive, but elsewhere he describes his letters to her as narcissistic
and self-exploratory: "I like to write to you," he observes, "as if
talking to myself" (*Letters*, p. 83).

John Sherman (1891) continues this dialogue with himself. It
has received little attention, perhaps because the degree of self-

revelation in the novel has not been clear and because it seems a realistic freak. Yet once we realize that the inner dynamics of the story are provided not by the clash between the dreamy John Sherman and the ambitious Reverend William Howard (as Ellmann and Richard Finneran maintain),[30] but by the triangular relations of Sherman, mother/childhood sweetheart, and uncle, the resemblance to *Dhoya* and *Oisin* is immediately apparent.

Since *John Sherman* is one of Yeats's least-known works, let me outline the plot. Sherman and Howard are two young men from the same small town, Ballah. Sherman wants nothing more than to stay and dream in Ballah. Howard, by contrast, is bored with the town and its inhabitants; he leaves for London. Sherman's idyllic life is interrupted by a letter from his uncle, who accuses him of "living on his mother" and suggests he come to London and work like a man. The suggestion is supported by Sherman's childhood friend Mary Carton, who feels he is stagnating at home. Sherman compromises by going to London but taking his mother along. There he works for his uncle and meets a beautiful, capricious rich girl, a prototype for the Player Queen, Margaret Leland. They become engaged because Sherman feels it is expected of him, but at the last moment he backs out, cleverly turning her over to Howard. He then returns home and is reconciled with Mary Carton.

In the early descriptions of Sherman in Ballah, Yeats portrays the familiar beloved landscape, the garden, in association with the beloved mother. Within the garden Sherman, like Yeats, gratifies a desire to create life. Although all of Sherman's happiness is contained in the maternal garden, the description of Mrs. Sherman herself is ambiguous. It recalls John Butler Yeats's judgment of his wife ("She was not sympathetic. The feelings of other people about her did not concern her"). "A spare, delicate-featured woman, with somewhat thin lips, tightly closed." Not giving easily of herself, she is also unaware of her child's emotions: "she never knew what went on inside her son's mind. . . . Blessed are the un-

---

[30] Ellmann, *Man and Masks*, p. 78; Finneran's discussion is in his introduction to *JS&D*, pp. 26–31.

sympathetic." Despite her deficiencies, Sherman feels he "cannot leave her" (*JS&D*, pp. 49–50, 103–4, 56).

Mary Carton is more sympathetic. Sherman confides his anxieties to her as Yeats did to Katharine Tynan. Here the anxieties are clearly about love. "Perfect love and perfect friendship are indeed incompatible; for the one is a battlefield where shadows war beside the combatants, and the other a placid country" (*JS&D*, pp. 54–55). The "placid country" refers not only to his relationship with Mary, but to his mother's garden and maternal love. Sherman reacts to his perception of love as a dangerous battlefield by not thinking about it, substituting for it the safe (because emotionally detached) idea of marrying for money.

Mary had pointed out that London offered opportunities as well as dangers. When John returns home, she reproaches him for irresponsibility. Unlike Mrs. Sherman, she wants what really would be good for him. Sherman, however, cannot relate to her on an adult level. He literally runs home to mother. Passing an ancient burial ground, he is "suddenly filled by the terror of the darkness children feel" (*JS&D*, p. 111). This is reminiscent, though less intense, of the end of Lawrence's *Sons and Lovers*: "Stars and sun, a few bright grains, went spinning round for terror . . . there in a darkness that outpassed them all, and left them tiny. . . . 'Mother!' he whimpered—'Mother!' "[31] But Sherman does not return to the bright city. He is reconciled with Mary on his own immature terms, and his last description of her shows her in the desired aspect of mother: "She looked upon him whom she loved as full of a helplessness that needed protection, a reverberation of the feeling of the mother for the child at the breast" (*JS&D*, p. 111).

Clearly there has been a regression from the Oedipal fantasies portrayed in *Oisin* to earlier fantasies of being a placid infant at the breast. The letters from Sherman's uncle, who represents the father in the pattern, symbolize, Sherman says, his "anxieties." Like her son, Mrs. Sherman resents these letters, "for she was afraid of her son going away." Throughout the book, Sherman seems a gifted child rather than a man. He is incapable of making any

[31] D. H. Lawrence, *Sons and Lovers* (New York: Modern Library, n.d.), p. 491.

deliberate choice. Even his desire to stay home is externalized: it is the river that "bade him who loved stay still and dream" (*JS&D*, pp. 51, 48).

As the appointed time for his marriage to Margaret comes closer, the thought of leaving home shakes Sherman's feeling of "personal identity." Marriage becomes linked in his mind with death. "How hard it was to submit to that decree which compels every step we take in life to be a death in the imagination" (*JS&D*, p. 68). Marriage at this point seems to be a variant of death on the seashore.

Sherman's anxieties are so strong that human consciousness becomes a burden: "it would be a good thing to be a little black cat" with no responsibilities (*JS&D*, p. 69). As the conflict intensifies, images come to his mind. "He was at that marchland between waking and dreaming where our thoughts begin to have a life of their own—the region where art is nurtured and inspiration born."[32] In this case conflict nurtures not art but an intensely practical idea: Sherman realizes he can resolve his dilemma by arranging for Howard to fall in love with Margaret. This is the first of several instances in Yeats's work of a triangular situation in which two men share a woman, a situation related to homosexual fantasies.

Howard "could think carefully and cleverly, . . . but never in such a way as to make his thoughts an allusion to something deeper than themselves. In this he was the reverse of poetical" (*JS&D*, p. 89). Yeats's hero, by contrast, thinks symbolically: "Delayed by a crush in the Strand, he heard a faint trickling of water . . . a little water-jet balanced a wooden ball upon its point." The sound reminds him of a cataract at Ballah, and of an old daydream (*JS&D*, p. 92):

The source of the river that passed his garden at home was a certain wood-bordered and islanded lake . . . At the further end was a little islet called Innisfree. Its rocky centre, covered with many bushes, rose some

---

[32] *JS&D*, p. 85. This is the earliest definition of what is for Yeats an important territory: the birthplace of thought. See Yeats's *Letters on Poetry to Dorothy Wellesley* (Oxford: Oxford University Press, 1964), p. 94, and Ursula Bridge, ed., *W. B. Yeats and T. Sturge Moore: Their Correspondence, 1901–1937* (London: Routledge, 1953), p. 146, for further discussions of this marchland.

forty feet above the lake. Often when life and its difficulties had seemed
to him like the lessons of some elder boy given to a younger by mistake,
it had seemed good to dream of going away.

This ingenious passage links images of water and an island refuge
to the maternal garden and to the "woody central hill" of *Oisin's*
Isle of Joy, which is thus confirmed as having a symbolic connection with the mother. *John Sherman* also adds to our certainty that
the "dark towers" of *Oisin* are indeed a symbolic representation
of London, and that the demon is the threatening father. *John
Sherman* is, in fact, a translation into prose of what was expressed
in terms of poetic myth in *Oisin*. And in the novel many of the
obscuring clouds are cleared away.

It is after Sherman's sudden vivid memory of the island that he
decides he loves Mary, the mother-substitute, waiting at home, and
will "live in his love and the day as it passed . . . [like] the saints
on the one hand, the animals on the other" (*JS&D*, p. 102). This
state, without memory or sense of guilt, is the closest Yeats could
come to representing the peaceful, conflictless state of the infant.

TWO

The Dreamer Dramatized

IN THE PRECEDING chapter we saw that intense Oedipal conflict, potentially highly dramatic, underlay the embroidered surface of such works as *The Wanderings of Oisin*. More significantly, we noted that Oedipal conflict in these works took a particularly self-defeating turn, with the hero—threatened by spellbinding woman or powerful father—paralyzed, regressed, and above all longing to escape. But whereas we had only hints of Yeats's childhood feelings of deprivation in memories and daydreams (and in *John Sherman*), his early plays dramatize these feelings fully, and enable us to see how Yeats's early emotional experiences influenced both the expression of his Oedipal conflict and his adult relationships with women.

The Countess Cathleen, the heroine of Yeats's first important play (1892), is, as we shall see, the prototype of the self-sacrificing mother who gives all she has to feed her hungry children. But Yeats characteristically makes his heroine represent a beloved figure in the present as well as an idealized one from the past. Cathleen the nurturing mother also represents Maud Gonne. When Yeats introduced the character Aleel to represent himself as Maud's lover in the revision of 1895, his feelings toward Cathleen as ideal mother undercut the intended dramatic contrast between Aleel's heroic attitude and Cathleen's escapist or self-destructive one; instead of expressing his love with courage or directness, Aleel, frightened and childlike, wants only to flee.

The Shadowy Waters (1900) continues the theme of oral deprivation within the framework of an incestuous quest. Forgael, unable to come to terms with the imperfections of ordinary human existence or with death, escapes from life through a quest for a perfect love unattainable in this world. In the early drafts of this play, Yeats projects the hunger and rage of the deprived child onto a set of eagle-headed creatures who seek to devour the questing hero and drink his blood. Yeats's sadistic fantasies of incorporation and mutilation naturally affect his portrayal of sexual love in the play. Again, as in *The Countess Cathleen*, the drafts show that Yeats was struggling to portray both infantile deprivation and aspects of his adult experience.

From the fantasy of a nurturing mother in *The Countess Cathleen* there appears to be a progression to much more intense and disturbing fantasies in early versions of *The Shadowy Waters*. After this buildup of feeling, Yeats suppressed most of the oral material in the drafts—perhaps as part of a general attempt to repress feelings he feared might overwhelm him—and in *The King's Threshold* (1904), both oral needs and rage are denied.

The King's Threshold was written just after Maud Gonne's marriage to John MacBride. Yeats reacted to this assault on his self-esteem by portraying his hero Seanchan as completely self-sufficient, a poet who no longer seeks the ideal mother because he has incorporated all her desired qualities. Seanchan thus represents the culmination of Yeats's continuous efforts during this period to build up the hero as poet, capable of nourishing himself with his own creations. Aleel and Seanchan are called poets even in the earliest versions of their respective plays, but in revision Yeats further emphasizes their poetic roles. In the 1901 revision of *The Countess Cathleen*, he puts Aleel under the patronage of the god Aengus. In revising *The Shadowy Waters*, also, Yeats stresses the connection between Aengus and the hero Forgael, and particularly Aengus's gift of the poetic harp. In *The King's Threshold* the hero Seanchan himself becomes a godlike figure, whose life and death are shaped by his concept of the bardic role.

At times in the poems of this period, Yeats seems to distinguish between the visionary and the poet. He begins to suggest that although the poet may temporarily withdraw from the real world into his dreams, he does so in order to contemplate reality from a higher vantage point and to incorporate it into his visions in a way that creates a new, more meaningful reality. The poet thus gains a creative, active, self-expressive role, but as yet Yeats rarely has the courage of his vision; most of his poems continue to express passivity and complaint.

In *Where There Is Nothing* (1902) and *The Unicorn from the Stars* (1907), plays we will discuss in the last part of this chapter, a second important theme joins oral deprivation: primal-scene fantasies, that is, fantasies of parents' intercourse reconstructed from early childhood memories or fantasies. These fantasies, obscured in *Where There Is Nothing* as the hero's visions of angels riding unicorns, become increasingly important. By the time of *The Player Queen* (1922), riding is clearly equated with intercourse, and the central event of that play is the coupling of Queen and Unicorn. In *Purgatory*, a play of Yeats's last year (to be discussed, along with *The Player Queen*, in Chapter 4), the original fantasy is plain: the protagonist watches through a lighted bedroom window while the ghosts of his father and mother have intercourse.

'The Countess Cathleen'

Yeats started thinking about the Countess Cathleen as a subject in November 1888, as *John Sherman* was nearing completion. He contrasts the psychic energy involved in starting the play to the soothing effects of "mechanical work." Art, he wrote, should never be mechanical or even "retrospective," but should struggle with expressing the artist's self. Thus, though he returned to the Gaelic legends on which he had based *Oisin*, this time choosing one from the Christian cycle, the story of the countess who sells her soul to save the starving peasantry was clearly intended to broaden his expression of "personal thought and feelings."[1]

Precise discussion of the "personal thought and feelings" reflected in the play is complicated by the fact that Yeats revised it repeatedly over a period of almost thirty years. As Peter Ure points out, the revisions show a progressive enlargement of the part of

[1] Cited in Peter Ure, *Yeats the Playwright: A Commentary on Character and Design in the Major Plays* (London: Routledge, 1963), p. 13.

Aleel, whom Yeats introduced between the first (1892) and second (1895) published versions, when he made his most extensive revisions.[2] Each successive revision gives Aleel an additional scene with Cathleen, a pattern that has naturally been interpreted as a reflection of Yeats's troubled love for Maud Gonne.[3] Yeats did in fact dedicate the play to Maud when he revised it for the third time, in 1912, and in his late poem "The Circus Animals' Desertion," in which he describes *The Countess Cathleen* as a "counter-truth" to *Oisin*, he explicitly links Cathleen and Maud:

> She, pity-crazed, had given her soul away,
> But masterful Heaven had intervened to save it.
> I thought my dear must her own soul destroy
> So did fanaticism and hate enslave it.[4]

By 1912, as drafts of *The Player Queen* also show, Yeats viewed self-sacrifice with decided hostility because he associated it with Maud's dedication to politics and rejection of him; and he continued to worry about Maud as though she were a child. It is hostility combined with paternal worry that shapes the misleading description of the Countess in Yeats's late poem, for, as Ure points out, "fanaticism and hate" have no place in the play.[5] We have to look elsewhere to understand Yeats's original feelings toward the folk heroine Ketty O'Donner who becomes his Countess.

The story of Ketty's sacrifice gratified Yeats's longing for an ideal mother who would satisfy his needs whatever the cost to herself. Yeats considered the story "one of the supreme parables of the world"; the only story remotely comparable, he says, involves a "woman who goes to hell for ten years to save her husband."[6] In her relations with the peasants Cathleen resembles a loving, nonpunitive mother. In the 1892 version, Cathleen even excuses the thieves, saying that "He who has no food, offending no way, / May

2 *Ibid.*, p. 24. Substantially revised versions also were published in 1901, 1912, and 1919.

3 T. R. Henn, *The Lonely Tower: Studies in the Poetry of W. B. Yeats* (London: Methuen, 1950), p. 24, and Hone, *W. B. Yeats*, pp. 87–88; cited in Ure, *Yeats the Playwright*, pp. 16–17.

4 *Variorum Poems*, pp. 629–30.

5 Ure, p. 17.

6 *Variorum Plays*, p. 170.

take his meat and bread from too-full larders" (ll. 282–83).[7] In this early version, the poet Kevin (later Aleel) is said to be crazed by love, and "loneliness and famine dwell with him" (ll. 188–89). The linking of a need for love with physical hunger, which occurs twice in *The Countess Cathleen* and is developed further in *The Shadowy Waters* and *The King's Threshold*, points to the deeper psychological meaning behind Yeats's affection for the Ketty O'Donner legend.

In later versions the maternal Cathleen is seen as extremely powerful and Aleel as a timid child:

> When one so great has spoken of love to one
> So little as I, though to deny him love,
> What can he but hold out beseeching hands,
> Then let them fall. . . .
>
>   (ll. 503–6)

It is an irony of the play's construction that only by identifying with the peasants, rather than the poet hero, could Yeats have felt himself the beneficiary of Cathleen's care. But identification with the peasants seems to have been precluded even in the 1892 version, where Yeats appears briefly as the poet Kevin. In dramatizing his ideal mother, Yeats also dramatized his disappointment in his real mother's lack of sympathy for him and her involvement with his siblings. This disappointment becomes increasingly clear in successive versions, in which the Countess provides the peasants with food while depriving the hero of love. Yeats emphasizes not only Aleel's smallness, but his exclusion from warmth and pleasure: he is like a fly "upon a window-pane in the winter," now that his beloved has found "something . . . to put her hand to" (ll. 449–51).

The sense of exclusion from love arises not only from Yeats's childhood but from his contemporary relationship with Maud Gonne, which in a sense forced him to relive earlier frustrations. On January 30, 1889, Yeats met Maud; *The Countess Cathleen*

---

[7] Except for citations from unpublished drafts in the National Library, Dublin, all citations of *The Countess Cathleen* are from *Variorum Plays*, pp. 5–169; line numbers given here for the second and subsequent published versions refer to the collated text on the recto pages of the variorum edition; the version of 1892, numbered separately, appears there on verso pp. 6–168.

was begun that March. He apparently tried to use an early draft of the play as a warning to Maud: in July 1891 Yeats read it to her, interpreting Cathleen "as a symbol of all souls that lose their peace, or their fineness . . . in political service."[8] Yeats seems not to have realized the self-interest that underlay his wishes for Maud. When he urged her to give up politics, he spoke only of concern for her peace: "Oh, why do you not give up politics and live a peaceful life? I could make such a perfect life for you."[9] Aleel expresses the same altruistic motives in his attempts to restore the peace of the Countess. He sees her as destroying her chances for both peace and love, without necessarily gaining anything more valuable in return.

Between the first major revision of the play in 1895 and the 1912 version, Aleel comes to represent not only Yeats as lover of Maud but subjective, self-realizing man as opposed to the objective, self-denying man whom Yeats associated with traditional Christianity. The "subjective" view of Cathleen as tragically self-denying runs directly counter to the original legend, which unambiguously exalted Ketty. Even in the 1892 version, however, Cathleen's activities are viewed with ambivalence, and there are hints in a dialogue between Cathleen and her nurse Oona, perhaps stemming from Yeats's early intuitions about Maud's character, that Cathleen's concern for the peasants is in part an effort to replace her own hunger for love with something acceptable to conscience.

Oona sees love, like hunger, as basic to the human condition. There is no way to escape, she says, but growing "old and full of sleep" (l. 168). This line echoes the line to Maud (October 1891), itself an echo of Ronsard, "When you are old and gray and full of sleep," in which Yeats warns her against rejecting his love. The parallel reinforces the suggestion that Cathleen is trying to escape from her own desires into pity for others. Oona recommends heroic gaiety, not pity, and transcendent love. She wants, in a draft of the 1892 version, to sing about Dermot and Grania, whose love

8 Hone, pp. 87–88; cited in Ure, pp. 16–17.
9 Hone, p. 157.

me the fear of death, and she chides Cathleen for her sor-
Thus the two characters embody conflicting attitudes that
w... to assume great importance for Yeats later on: heroic self-
possession tied to a capacity for passion and scorn for death on
the one hand, and self-sacrifice and a fear of love on the other.

In the 1892 version Yeats seems to have projected aspects of himself onto Cathleen, there being no more appropriate character for
him to identify with (the bard Kevin appears only for a moment
at the end). In this version, Cathleen is torn between feelings of
responsibility toward the victims of famine and a desire to escape
to the Sidhe, associated in her mind with love: young Adene and
"all those wicked [r]oads." And in an unpublished draft of the
1892 version, Yeats gives her his own island daydream, as he had
earlier given it to John Sherman.[10] (Yeats was to develop the same
theme in his next play, *The Land of Heart's Desire* [1894], in the
character of Mary Bruin, who seeks to escape from the demands
of mature sexuality by fleeing to the land of the fairies.) By 1901,
Cathleen's desire to escape has diminished, and the theme of escape has been partially taken over by Aleel, who comes to bid her
"leave this castle." Yeats's original projection of himself onto
Cathleen is thus shifted to a more appropriate (male) character.

Cathleen seems stronger and more adult after Aleel comes to
embody escapist tendencies—she is no longer lulled like a child
in her nurse's lap—and also, since escape is expressed in terms of
pagan Ireland, more definitely Christian. In 1892 her need to assume other men's burdens was derived from a sense of herself as
head of a great house. In the drafts of 1912 her speech has become
specifically Christian: "Sin or no sin—we have not the right to
judge." The underlying conflict, it seems to me, is not, as Ure
suggests,[11] one between dreams and responsibility, but between
sexual love and its repression, or the diversion of sexual energy
into other channels with a resultant deformation of the self. It is
in this sense that Cathleen is a "counter-truth to Oisin." Oisin
rejects St. Patrick and chooses the Fenians; Cathleen reverses the

10 The parallel lines in the published version of 1892 are 267–70.
11 Ure, p. 19.

choice.[12] The contrast is more subtle in the latter case. Cathleen, like St. Patrick, believes in guilt and lives "daily measuring [her] own sins,"[13] but whereas Patrick was a wrathful, thoroughly unattractive representative of the father-God, Cathleen is a female version of the self-sacrificing Christian, a character that fascinated Yeats almost as much as it repelled him.

Concern with the repression of impulse seems to have motivated Yeats's introduction of a short scene in the 1912 version (replacing Cathleen's dialogue with Oona) in which Aleel tells Cathleen about Queen Maeve. Maeve, who weeps because she cannot remember her lover's name, seems childish at best, and one tends to agree with Cathleen that "If she [Maeve] had better sense" (l. 304), she would be less distressed. The new scene is not effective, but it shows Yeats's serious concern with something that he calls memory, but that seems to have a more general meaning of conscience or sense of guilt.[14] Maeve's forgetfulness frees her emotionally to take another lover. This is implied in Aleel's question, "What's memory but the ash / That chokes our fires that have begun to sink?" (ll. 316–17). The fire metaphor recalls one that Yeats used in a letter about *The Player Queen*, in which he defined the sense of sin as "the remorse of the lamp when it begins to smoke."[15] In *The Player Queen*, begun in 1907 or 1908, Yeats is preoccupied with the choking of impulse—the Real Queen, with her obsessive desire for martyrdom, seems almost a parody of Cathleen—and this preoccupation seems to be reflected in the discussion of memory for the 1912 version of *The Countess Cathleen*. In *The Countess Cathleen*, however, Yeats obscures the opposition between impulse and repression by linking impulse with self-defeating escapism, instead of with the heroic acceptance of life.

[12] As Ure points out, p. 19.

[13] Unpublished draft, National Library, Dublin.

[14] In Yeats's later work, as we shall see, an inability to forget the ideal (incestuous) image makes it difficult to find normal love. A clear example of the inhibiting effect of memory occurs in connection with the incest motif of *The Shadowy Waters*. The hero, having killed the Queen's husband, sings away her memory of him. She is then free to love the hero.

[15] Unpublished letter to Mabel Dickinson, Bancroft Library, University of California, Berkeley.

Aleel's inhibitions and passivity (and the conflict between his passivity and his putative heroic role) are more understandable if we recall that his relationship with the Countess reflects not only Yeats's relationship with Maud Gonne but also fantasies about an all-powerful mother. Yeats's attraction toward the self-sacrificing Cathleen, along with his masochistic fantasies of being excluded from her love, made it difficult to create a strong hero, particularly a sexually assertive one. To be really effective, Aleel would have had to assert himself and his sexuality with strength and directness. Instead, he acts like a confused child, "so wrapped in dreams of terrors to come / That he can give no help" (ll. 89–90). Yeats indicates that Aleel's desperation results from the bottling up not only of love but of anger, in a song he introduces in his final revision of 1919: "Were I but crazy for love's sake / ... I know the heads that I should break" (ll. 122–24). But to supply Aleel's missing anger would probably have required writing a different play.

Yeats tried to strengthen Aleel in the revisions by developing his role as poet. In the 1901 version Aleel has a dream that turns into fire (a familiar Yeatsian symbol of sexuality and the poet's gift), and in the fire the god Aengus commands Aleel to escape with Cathleen to the hills. In reporting the command to Cathleen, Aleel tries to convince her that Aengus was "angelical." But Cathleen realizes immediately that Aleel is speaking for another set of values:

> No, not angelical, but of the old gods,
> Who wander about the world to waken the heart—
> The passionate, proud heart—that all the angels,
> Leaving nine heavens empty, would rock to sleep.
>
> (ll. 493–96)

It is in this scene that the conflict between energy and repression emerges most clearly, and as in *Oisin* it is seen as a conflict between the old gods and Christianity. Yeats is interested in Christianity primarily as a symbol of destructive or negative attitudes—attitudes, he suggests, that stem from repression. Not only does Cathleen see that the angels want to lull the passions, she sees herself as sterile. In a speech that anticipates the later Queen plays, she notes that

Queens have wed shepherds . . . ;
God's procreant waters flowing about your mind
Have made you more than kings or queens; and not you
But I am the empty pitcher.

(ll. 508–11)

As we have noted, however, Aleel fails to convey a sense of heroic or creative abundance and is almost as unable to love, or at least to express his love forcefully, as the Countess is. In the later plays when a poet woos a queen, he has the courage of his desire even though it results in death. He can express lust and cruelty in part because he sees the queen not as a real and frightening woman, but as his own creation—an image. Aleel, in contrast to the later heroes, is inhibited by the Countess's goodness, which makes him feel unworthy, and by fear of his own angry impulses. Yeats could not yet express the sadistic impulses that accompanied his need for masochistic abasement, as he later did in works with a pattern of aggression and retaliation.

Yeats's essays and letters discuss examples of the surfacing of repressed desires that are strikingly like Freud's "return of the repressed"—for instance, the pious lady who on her deathbed wants to run away with her lover.[16] The revival of repressed sexuality is portrayed symbolically—though perhaps not consciously—at the end of *The Countess Cathleen*, when the lascivious demon Orchil comes floating out of Hell to meet the damned Cathleen. This striking detail, added in the 1895 revision after Yeats had created similar clawed creatures in *The Shadowy Waters*, was never developed. Yeats, though he liked *The Countess Cathleen*, said in later years that he would now give the play a completely different ending. Cathleen after signing away her soul would "mock at all she has held holy," horrifying "the peasants in the midst of their temptations" (*Autobiography*, p. 252). In terms of the Blakean reversal of values Yeats was so fond of, which makes what men traditionally call evil good and vice versa, such a climactic scene would be an ironic indication that Cathleen realizes she has made the wrong choice—realizes it in a moment not of damnation, but of insight.

[16] "Anima Mundi," in *Mythologies*, p. 343.

'The Shadowy Waters'

In *The Shadowy Waters* (1900) Yeats develops further the fantasies hinted at in *The Countess Cathleen* by images of starvation,
nourishment, and sacrifice, fantasies that involve the deepest and
earliest levels of personality. With the aid of drafts of the play,
we can analyze these fantasies and their relationship to Yeats's
personal difficulties at the time, and in so doing help explain not
only certain specific obscurities in the play but also some of its
more puzzling general characteristics, such as the vagueness and
obscurity of the style at a time when Yeats was striving above all
for concreteness.

Before we turn to the drafts, let us consider for a moment the
plot of *The Shadowy Waters* as Yeats summarized it in 1906:

Once upon a time, when herons built their nests in old men's beards,
Forgael, a Sea-King of ancient Ireland, was promised by certain human-
headed birds love of a supernatural intensity and happiness. These birds
were the souls of the dead, and he followed them over seas towards the
sunset, where their final rest is. By means of a magic harp, he could call
them about him when he would and listen to their speech. His friend
Aibric, and the sailors of his ship, thought him mad, or that this mysterious happiness could come after death only, and that he and they were
being lured to destruction. Presently they captured a ship, and found a
beautiful woman upon it, and Forgael subdued her and his own rebellious sailors by the sound of his harp. The sailors fled upon the other ship,
and Forgael and the woman drifted on alone following the birds, awaiting death and what comes after, or some mysterious transformation of
the flesh.[17]

Yeats first had the idea for *The Shadowy Waters* at age eighteen.
The year before, he had experienced a surge of sexual feeling,
which he describes as descending on him "like the bursting of a
shell" (*Autobiography*, p. 38), and which quite probably prompted
the reawakening of Oedipal fantasies. The play's themes of escape
to an island of perfection and the search for perfect love, based
on incestuous fantasies, are familiar ones. But besides the Oedipal
fantasies that give the play its form, another set of fantasies that
concern eating, incorporation, and identity appear in full force

---

17 Yeats, *The Arrow*, No. 2, Nov. 24, 1906; cited in *Variorum Plays*, p. 340.

in the unpublished drafts of the play. The drafts of *The Shadowy Waters* are extensive: in the National Library, Dublin, there are thirty-one folders of them arranged in rough sequence, and other manuscript versions are held in the Huntington Library, California, and the Berg Collection of the New York Public Library. In spite of some problems in dating, certain general trends may be observed. As the drafts progress, new developmental themes are introduced. In the early drafts Yeats presents a picture of infantile rage, in the last drafts one of Oedipal conflict, and, temporarily, in certain intermediate drafts, a theme of sibling rivalry.

Also observable in the drafts are an earlier and a later way of dealing with orality. At first, Yeats attempts to deal with it by regression: the prototype for his dreams of perfect satisfaction is the infant's satisfaction at the breast. But gradually Yeats works a way out of his oral dilemma by creating a model with which to identify. This model, the bard or poet, whom Yeats associates with "hard" images such as the harp or the unicorn, gives him a sense of solidity. Identification with such images leads to a stronger style and lessened fear of close relationships to people.

Central to the vision of orality in the drafts is a fear of devouring or being devoured by a woman. This theme is linked with the question of the hero's identity, that is to say, whether he is the devourer or the devoured. If the woman is seen as weak, he fears that he will destroy her; if strong, that she will destroy him. The drafts show various combinations and degrees of these complementary fears.

The first nearly complete draft, written no later than 1894, and early fragments written between 1894 and 1896 show Yeats's attempt to rid himself of a sense of loss, or oral deprivation, by representing it symbolically in a set of nightmare, eagle-headed creatures called Seabar.[18] The Seabar deal with their frustrated hunger

18 I am accepting, with some reservations about individual manuscripts, the sequence and dating proposed by Michael J. Sidnell, George P. Mayhew, and David R. Clark in *Druid Craft: The Writing of* The Shadowy Waters (Amherst: University of Massachusetts Press, 1971). Although my discussion of the play is based on a careful reading of the drafts in the National Library, Dublin, I have checked my transcriptions against those given in *Druid Craft*, and for the read-

by sadistic violence, demanding from the hero—who expresses his
own frustration more passively—a constant supply of blood. Yeats
describes them looking into the water and raging (*DC*, p. 97):

> And rise . . .
>   . . . from pale sands
> Where you have torn your breasts with iron talons
> And shrieked at the drowned image of the moon.
>
>   .   .   .
>
> And still the rustling of the heavy plumes
> About your necks & your fierce cries for food.

Later, Yeats will use the image of a bird looking at its reflection
in water to express perfect beauty, subjectivity, and the creation
of poetry. This transformation of the image suggests that the mature Yeats felt less dependent on external sources of satisfaction
and better able to achieve gratification from his own resources—
narcissistically. The Seabar, by contrast, are completely dependent
on others for nourishment and love, and react to frustration with
violent rage.

The moon seen reflected in the water is a symbol of the care-
taking mother. When there is no longer a supply of nourishment,
the moon seems lost, "drowned." Desire then turns to hatred of
both moon and self: the Seabar shriek and tear their breasts; their
own blood becomes a substitute for the desired milk. In another
early fragment, the Seabar express an explicit desire to wound the
mother, saying that perhaps if they could tear Dectora's flesh, "the
great / mother herself [the goddess Danu] would be wounded because of her wounds" (*DC*, p. 84). In a later fragment Yeats makes
the connection between moon and milk explicit. Forgael is to have
a ship made of "milky stone" and take Dectora to "where the children of Aengus weave / A happy dance under a milk pale moon"
(*DC*, pp. 260, 262).

Like the Seabar, Forgael expresses hunger and despair, but
through him Yeats explores different ways of dealing with them.
Yeats introduces Forgael at a moment of choice, when he is about
to renounce the life of a sea pirate for a life of passivity and vision.

---

er's convenience will cite in the text the page numbers in that work (abbre-
viated *DC*) for quotations from the manuscripts.

His dissatisfaction with the material power given him by the Sea-bar—who make him the "master of white cities"—is expressed in terms of nourishment and emptiness: "I dreamed I had the fatness of the world / But it has changed into a windy hall" (*DC*, pp. 181, 165). Moreover, he feels bound to the instruments of his masculine power: "a bond man bound / To the wet tiller & the heavy sword" (*DC*, p. 83). Seemingly, nothing he can get satisfies him, and in his frustration he wishes to destroy the world itself and replace it with fantasy: "O eagle headed race . . . quench the world" (*DC*, p. 167). Visions are Forgael's means of achieving independence from external reality: they assert that what he desires exists. Also, they allow him to derogate his body; he does not need it to obtain gratification. He leaves his body behind as his spirit wanders joyfully through the isles of the blessed.

Reality is always intruding, however, to disturb both his visions and his waking search for perfect joy. A suitable love object is part of this "reality," and consequently when fate offers him Dectora, he views her with extreme ambivalence. Only death—including a fantasied reunion with the mother—seems to promise satisfaction. Yeats once described Forgael as having an "abyss-seeking desire for the waters of death."[19]

If, as suggested in Chapter 1, Yeats's mother was represented in an early memory as a scratched and mastless ship, with which Yeats identifies, it is no accident that from its earliest conception *The Shadowy Waters* takes place on a ship, or that the drafts show Yeats struggling with his problematic relationships with women. Under the name Dectora, Yeats was portraying aspects of two of his adult relationships: his love affair with Olivia Shakespear (called Diana Vernon throughout the *Memoirs*), and his unsatisfied passion for Maud Gonne. Several bursts of concentrated work on the play began around the time he met Olivia (about March of 1894; *DC*, pp. 41, 77), and the drafts clearly reflect fear and ambivalence toward such a friendship.

[19] In an unsigned program note written for the Abbey Theatre, July 1906; quoted in Richard Ellmann, *The Identity of Yeats* (New York: Oxford University Press, 1954), p. 81.

Relationships with women involved two dangers for Yeats: he identified with women in their weakness (as he had evidently done with his despondent mother) and this same weakness aroused his sadism.[20] There is evidence that even before his relationship with Olivia, he was wondering whether love would exacerbate his sense of weakness. In the mid-1880's he outlined for his friend George Russell (A.E.) the plot of a play he proposed to write (*The Shadowy Waters*) in which love turns out to be only a shadow of the hero who has been trying to escape from himself through it, and who therefore unrolls its spell and moves on to other, better worlds (*DC*, p. 4). The first fragments correspond to this description. In the first drafts Forgael has been trying to initiate the heroine into an occult "mystery." His motive is not lofty devotion to a mystical ideal but self-hatred and fear: "I preyed that / a refuge might be for an hour / from my self. [The gods] have sent me you" (*DC*, pp. 70–71). When the girl, finally consenting to go with him, throws herself down and kisses his feet, he reacts by thrusting her violently away with the explanation, "Your eyes are but / my eyes, your voice is but my voice" (*DC*, p. 72). He had hoped that she would help him to forget himself; instead she reminds him of his weakness. Horrified by her likeness to what he hates in himself, he decides to sacrifice her to the Seabar: "take her and tare her in pieces / For she too is but my self" (*DC*, p. 73).

Olivia, it seems, embodied what had previously existed in fantasy. Yeats once wrote that Olivia "seemed a part of myself," like "the mild heroines of my plays" (*Memoirs*, p. 86). In the drafts, when he sees the woman as gentle and pliable, he sees her as Olivia. The cloud-pale imagery that first appears in draft versions written

[20] In January 1909 Yeats wrote in his journal: "I begin to wonder whether I have and always have had some nervous weakness inherited from my mother. (I have noticed my own form of excitability in my sister Lolly, exaggerated in her by fits of prolonged gloom....)" He immediately associates this "nervous weakness" with feelings of frustrated rage that resemble those shown by the Seabar and later by Paul Ruttledge in *Where There Is Nothing*: "In Paris I felt that if the strain were but a little more I would hit the woman who irritated me.... The feeling is always the same: a consciousness of energy, of certainty, and of transforming power stopped by a wall, by something one must either submit to or rage against helplessly.... Is it the root of madness?" *Memoirs*, pp. 156–57. For the similar feelings of Paul Ruttledge, see pp. 71–81.

between November 1894 and August 1895[21] corresponds to the imagery in poems written for Olivia: "the winds were made / Before the world was made that they might sigh / About her heavy hair & lingering feet."[22] In this mild aspect of Olivia he also identifies with her; and since identification with a passive woman is dangerous, he must repudiate or destroy her.

Associated with Olivia's gentleness or passivity is what Yeats describes in the first draft of his autobiography as her "sensitive look of distinction" (*Memoirs*, p. 72). Her beauty is linked in his mind with a weariness of life. This weariness shows up in his poems to her, but does not accord with his final view of Dectora as a representative of the life force. He notes, too, that Olivia's beauty had "the nobility of defeated things," and adds: "how could it help but wring my heart?" (*Memoirs*, p. 85). Yeats saw that Olivia, unhappily married to a man much older than herself, was suffering, but he attributed her suffering to a promiscuous life. Her supposed interest in other men had the advantage, however, of making it less likely that she would engulf him. And Yeats could permit himself a desire to save her from her putative "evil life." It was this desire, along with protective pity for her spiritual condition, that seemingly propelled him, after a fortnight of indecision, into asking her to leave home and live with him, although as he concedes, "no doubt my excited senses had their share in the argument" (*Memoirs*, p. 85).

As he admits elsewhere, he "was tortured by sexual desire," which drove him to masturbation. Because of his feelings of guilt, masturbation had an abnormally deleterious effect on him: it "almost invariably left me with exhausted nerves," it "was plain ruin. It filled me with loathing of myself" (*Memoirs*, pp. 71–72). This passage in the autobiography is followed by a remark about his friends' mistresses and a description of his first meeting with Olivia. Apparently, then, not only did he wish to save Olivia from what he imagined to be her evil life, he also, though perhaps uncon-

---

21 *Druid Craft*, p. 118; for basis of dating, see *ibid.*, p. 109.

22 *Ibid.*, p. 187. The word I have transcribed as "sigh" was considered illegible by Clark.

sciously, sought relief from the self-loathing and physical exhaustion brought on by masturbation.

Probably late in 1894, then, Yeats asked Olivia to leave her husband and live with him. She agreed in principle, but they resolved to wait until her aged mother had died, and to meet as friends until then. They chose two women friends as "sponsors" to help them keep their resolve, and adhered to it for over a year, until their sponsors urged them simply to "live together without more ado." Clearly Yeats was very hesitant about committing himself to Olivia. In the fall of 1895 he took rooms for several months with Arthur Symons. One afternoon when Olivia and her sponsor were coming to tea, presumably to discuss the couple's future, Yeats forgot the key to his flat when he went out for cake and had to send a man crawling through an attic window to let him in. He spent that evening telling Symons about his frustrated passion for Maud Gonne. At the sponsors' urging, which seems to have been the equivalent of parental permission, Yeats finally took new lodgings at Woburn Buildings in early 1896, and he and Olivia became lovers at last. The liaison lasted about a year, interrupted by a trip of Olivia's to Italy and trips by Yeats to Ireland with Symons and to Paris to see Maud Gonne (*Memoirs*, pp. 85–89).

The first draft of *The Shadowy Waters* reflects Yeats's fantasies about a relationship with a woman perceived as "but myself," with the attendant fears and confusion manifested in his relationship with Olivia: was he going to avoid her or become involved with her? And, if she responded to him, was he going to destroy her? Forgael urges a girl to partake of "many coloured fruit" that would give her knowledge and remove her desire from the world (*DC*, p. 68). Mystical initiation seems to be a substitute for sexual initiation, a sphere in which Yeats was a novice. When the girl returns to the physical plane by kissing Forgael's feet, he violently thrusts her away.

In real life, Yeats sought to initiate the women he loved into mystical knowledge. He introduced Maud Gonne into the Order of the Golden Dawn, and acted with more success as a spiritual adviser to Olivia, and later to his wife. He admonished Olivia, for example, not to attempt certain visionary experiences that he considered dangerous for her. He could have imagined either Maud or Olivia as the girl who weeps "tears of joy" at her initiation. Once he had won Olivia, the problem still remained: what was he to do with her? Mature sexuality frightened him, and his sadistic impulses, represented in the drafts by Forgael's attempt to sacrifice Dectora, made him feel guilty. The alternative was flight.

Apparently Yeats's emotional difficulties were increased rather than diminished by the affair with Olivia. He wanted to make something of this relationship, but intimacy only drove him back to longing for Maud, the unattainable ideal. And Maud herself during this period made several efforts to win Yeats back to frustrated dependency on her (e.g. *Memoirs*, pp. 87, 89). In the summer of 1896, after he and Olivia had been lovers for only four or five months, Yeats left with Arthur Symons for an extended tour of the West of Ireland. While visiting Edward Martyn's castle in August, Yeats had a vision of a beautiful naked woman shooting a star (*Autobiography*, pp. 223–24). This vision, which he interpreted as the mother-goddess killing the star-son (*Autobiography*, pp. 343–44), suggests a reaction against a feeling of dangerous omnipotence in his relationship with Olivia. In his fantasy, he regresses to complete passivity, the position Forgael adopts in the drafts, and gratifies his wish to be victim instead of murderer.[23]

A few days later Yeats, still in this regressive mood, met Lady Gregory, who invited him to stay with her at Coole. Yeats accepted, and found in Lady Gregory the perfect embodiment of the mother-provider he desired. We next see Yeats in Paris in December 1896. Although it is not clear from the *Memoirs* whether the affair with Olivia ended before or after this trip, Yeats's own recollections of his stay in Paris leave little doubt where his first affections lay. His numerous encounters with Maud there were very disturbing. He tells of being obsessed with the notion that if he held his hand in the fire until it was badly burned, she might be

[23] In a version written probably in late 1896, Yeats explicitly links Forgael's death with that of the star-son in his archer vision. See *Druid Craft*, p. 145. For a fuller discussion of this vision and its personal significance for Yeats, see pp. 111–12 below; its final permutation is described on pp. 138–40.

persuaded of his devotion. In another masochistic fantasy, he imagined that his arm was broken (*Memoirs*, p. 105). Completely frustrated and close to nervous collapse, he returned to Coole in the
summer of 1897 to recuperate. At Coole Lady Gregory took complete care of him, even sending him hot broth in the mornings
because she knew that the act of dressing exhausted him. She
helped him plan his days and, at his request, rebuked him if he
failed to begin writing at the appointed time. His nervous exhaustion seems related to an upsurge in autoerotic activity that followed on the break with Olivia and the renewal of his frustrating
relationship with Maud:

> I was tortured by sexual desire and disappointed love.... When desire
> became an unendurable torture, I would masturbate, and that, no mat-
> ter how moderate I was, would make me ill. It never occurred to me to
> seek another love. I would repeat to myself again and again the last con-
> fession of Lancelot..., "I have loved a queen beyond measure and ex-
> ceeding long."... In the second as during the first visit [to Coole] my
> nervous system was worn out (*Memoirs*, pp. 125–26).

Yeats's inability to commit himself to Olivia seems to have left
him feeling depleted and with a deep need to be mothered. The
earlier trip to Ireland with Symons in 1896 reflects this sense of
depletion. He returned to the countryside of his childhood for
emotional renewal. As he set out he was told by a medium (Olivia)
that he must live near water; later he interprets this as a forecast
of the healing influence of Coole Lake and Lady Gregory: "At
moments I have believed or half believed . . . that she came in reply
to those evocations [of the moon], for are not the common people
and their wisdom under the moon, and her house is at the edge
of [a] lake.... I found at last what I had been seeking always"
(*Memoirs*, pp. 100, 101). As nearly as possible Yeats had returned
to the garden of his childhood.

So far as one can tell from his letters, Yeats stopped work on
The Shadowy Waters during the affair with Olivia. Now at Coole
again, he resumed work on the play. His return to his unrecipro-
cated love for Maud Gonne and his acceptance of Lady Gregory's
mothering care are perhaps reflected in Forgael's increasing rejection of the idea of human love in favor of immortal and perfect

love. Forgael comes to see that the real girl is totally unlike the perfect woman of his dreams. In an early fragment, Forgael wakes from a trance to find an immortal woman whom he had seen many times in dreams but only now remembers is his true love. Later he more explicitly and cruelly repudiates the live woman, Dectora, for one of his dreams (*DC*, p. 267):

> I turn from you for you are not my love
> Now I have seen my love. You are silver pale
> And have shadows of sleap amid your hair
> Begone.

Forgael's dedication to an immortal love is developed further in the first version of the play published in book form (in December 1900); even while accepting Dectora's decision to accompany him Forgael says, "I will have none of you. / My love shakes out her hair upon the streams / Where the world ends" (*DC*, p. 299). Ordinary reality, even at its most vital, paled beside Forgael's transcendent dreams.

It is clear from the drafts that while the "cloud-pale" Dectora is Olivia, Maud—the apple-blossom Dectora—was the one Yeats connected with the life force. In one early draft the girl is persuaded to crush apple blossoms (Maud's favorite flower) instead of eating enchanted fruit. In another, Forgael wakes from a trance with a memory of "apple blossoms" (*DC*, pp. 84, 82). The heroine-as-Maud comes closer to the image of perfection than the heroine-as-Olivia. Because of this and because of his guilt at wooing a woman only to sacrifice her, Yeats develops the plot in such a way as to make her sacrifice unnecessary. "Back, back. Her flesh is like / apple blossom in spring, she / shall not die." Instead, Forgael surrenders himself: "I am weary / I will no longer lay waste the / many vesseled sea. I myself / complete the sacrifice. Let me be scattered upon the winds & / dissolved" (*DC*, p. 73). What seems to be happening is an alternation between roles. First Forgael is strong and the girl is to be devoured; then she is strong and he must be devoured instead. The desire for passivity reflected in the alternation of roles gained supernatural sanction in Yeats's vision in the West of Ireland.

After Yeats's Irish trip, Forgael's dreams become increasingly solipsistic. Everything emanates from his heart or, as Yeats put it, his "infinite desires." Action at this point is equated with aggression and murder. Obviously it is extremely dangerous and must be avoided. More acceptable are the vague visionary dreams of satisfaction associated with the good gods, the Danae. But here, too, there is a problem. The good gods are also seen as death gods. Passivity may lead to death; certainly it puts Forgael in the position of a victim: "Wisdom [his visionary activity] has made him weak. / And he shall be the sacrificial flesh. / Let all your talons be plunged into his heart" (*DC*, p. 175). Yeats, however, had conflicting feelings about Forgael's sacrificial death and tried another solution. Dectora's previously unimportant lover, the poet Aleel, develops into an alter ego who absorbs some of the passive posture. His arrival on a ship (with Dectora) just when Forgael is about to be sacrificed and his acceptance as an alternative sacrifice are given new meaning here by the enlargement of his role. He is now a second, weaker self as well as a rival. Forgael and the Seabar are now also seen to be similar. Forgael's heart, full of "famished, desperate . . . flame," makes him like the literally "famished" Seabar—ready to kill (*DC*, pp. 214, 210).

With Aleel's assumption of an important role, and the linking of Forgael and the Seabar, there emerges the theme of sibling rivalry. Forgael and the Seabar hate Aleel because he has known satisfaction in love. The impotence of the Seabar when faced by the "chosen" or loved one—they can only shriek and flee—suggests a child's helpless rage at the birth of a sibling. Yeats, with two younger brothers described by John Butler Yeats as being more "robust" and openly affectionate than his eldest son,[24] must have had more than one occasion to wish them dead. In the play, Forgael is made to kill Aleel and feed the Seabar so they may lie down in peace.

In the revisions made for book publication in 1900, Yeats changes

[24] See, for example, J. B. Yeats, *Letters to His Son W. B. Yeats and Others, 1869–1922*, ed. Joseph Hone (New York: Dutton, 1946), p. 51, cited hereafter as J. B. Yeats, *Letters to His Son*; and A. Norman Jeffares, *W. B. Yeats: Man and Poet* (New Haven: Yale University Press, 1949), pp. 9–10, cited hereafter as Jeffares, *W. B. Yeats*.

Aleel into a powerful king and returns the dreamy aspects of Aleel's character to Forgael (*DC*, p. 298). Before this happens, however, there is an interesting meeting between the split selves. Yeats causes Aleel to long, as Forgael usually does, for the end of the world ("the hour when all things shall be folded up"), thus indicating that the two characters are essentially one (*DC*, p. 203). While Aleel prays to the light powers, however, Forgael prays to the dark. Forgael's prayer is granted, and, having mercilessly killed his weaker self, he seems reassured. He contrasts himself (a half-god who knows the music of creation) with Aleel (who, being only a man, knew fear) (*DC*, p. 217). When Yeats makes Aleel a king, the conflict shifts to another level. The king is a paternal figure, and when Forgael murders him and takes his wife he is enacting the Oedipal drama.

Yeats's problems of identity led him to seek an object to hate, so that he could avoid feeling helpless like his mother or diffusing his hatred in a wish for the end of the world: "there is no good hour but that great hour / That shall puff out demons and gods and men."[25] Thus Forgael prays that he may be sent either "some enemy or some / woman" (*DC*, p. 82). Hating his mother for his early frustrations could only lead to guilt on Yeats's part and, because he also felt himself to be like her, to confusion in his relationship with women. In order to deal with the dangers of sadism and self-destruction he felt inherent in close relationships with women, Yeats developed a new mechanism to enable him to feel separate.

The harp that here symbolizes the power of words is, like Aengus's scepter in *Oisin*, a transitional object, a precious object that is partly self and partly other.[26] The development of this symbol shows Yeats drawing away from his confused identifications with

25 *Druid Craft*, p. 211 (earlier variants on pp. 95, 106–7).
26 I am making use here of Winnicott's concept of the transitional object. In normal development the transitional object forms a bridge between infant and mother. It is something—teddy bear or blanket—that the infant has completely within his control and feels comfortable with, but at the same time is separate from him. See D. W. Winnicott, "Transitional Objects and Transitional Phenomena," *International Journal of Psychoanalysis*, 34 (1953): 89–97. In the 1900 version of the play, the harp strings were made of Aengus's hair, and so were actually part of the poet-god's body.

women, and gradually establishing a distinct sense of self. Whereas in his early verse he consistently portrays himself as a man who is like a woman, "the Knight of the Waterfall," he now becomes the man with the harp, the poet. And whereas he had once thought passive knowing the only alternative to violent aggression (as exemplified by the rage of the Seabar and Forgael's murder of Aleel), Yeats now saw a way to avoid being either passive victim or murderous assailant. The poet is not merely the passive recipient of vision, but actively incorporates and digests the raw material of experience, including desire and its objects, and re-creates them in his verse. In the process of making the experience manageable for artistic purposes, he also gains control over it. The incorporating and digesting of material has the added advantage of symbolically satisfying oral needs.

In the version published in 1900, there is increasing emphasis on the harp and the power of poetry. Forgael wants the love that "is made / Imperishable fire under the boughs / Of chrysoberyl."[27] This transformation under a jeweled tree is a symbol not only of fulfilled desire but of passion being changed to poetry.[28] In the play, however, desire can be fulfilled only by death—and poetry, by stimulating desire, serves death. Yeats speaks of this danger in his essays, and in his story of 1897, "The Tables of the Law": "the beautiful arts were sent into the world to overthrow nations, and finally life herself, by sowing everywhere unlimited desires." Art fuels men's desires for perfection and death by dealing with "an absolute emotion."[29] Aleel hints of this view in a song that praises

---

[27] *Variorum Poems*, p. 765, ll. 355–57.

[28] Jewels were associated with Maud: "Sometimes, when I had gone to sleep with the endeavour to send my soul to that of Maud Gonne, ... I would wake dreaming of a shower of precious stones. ... I thought we became one in a world of emotion ..., and that this world had for its symbol precious stones." Although Yeats says that "no physical sensation" ever accompanied such dreams, and that he never dared ask Maud to come to him in a sexual dream, in the same passage in the autobiography he relates another dream in which his bedroom (or possibly the foot of his bed; the text is ambiguous) changes into "precious stones" and he wakes having "emitted seed." The sexual jeweled-room image is then associated with a childhood memory suggesting oral gratification: "these stones had a familiar look—they reminded me of the raised glass fruit on the bottles of lime-juice in my childhood. As so often in Yeats's imagery, womb and breast are conflated. *Memoirs*, pp. 127–28.

[29] *Mythologies*, pp. 294, 295.

the Island of the Gods because there beauty and song *do not awaken desire and unquiet.* Eventually Yeats will create the image of another kind of poetry and another kind of poet. The ancient bards, to be discussed in Chapter 3, became a model for creation from joy and from immersion in reality: no thought of another life "ever [troubled] their delight in one another."

In *The Shadowy Waters,* the destructive possibilities of poetry are symbolically represented by the effects of the harp. It belongs to the god Aengus and, played by his messenger the Fool, casts a spell on all who hear it. Once having heard it, Forgael becomes discontented with all life and isolated from the world about him. But though poetry here is in the service of death, Yeats suggests that it can have other functions. In a draft of 1899 Dectora taunts Forgael because of his ugly and misshapen body (*DC*, p. 276), but the power of the harp enables him to make her love him. This wish that poetry might bring him love did not work out in the way Yeats hoped, but through his conception of the great value of the poetic harp he came to have a kinder vision of himself as its master.

Yeats's confusion about his identity and role is evident not only in the play's content, as we have seen, but in its vague, dreamy style, which corresponds to his perception of himself as weak and womanish. His emphasis on the style's spellbinding or magical effects is in part an attempt to cover this weakness, just as Forgael's emphasis on his mystic knowledge covered a fear of sexuality.

Even in the mid-1890's Yeats wanted his style to be concrete, not vague (*Letters*, p. 236). But afraid to be too real or too hard, he continually substituted obscuring symbolic detail for the things or processes that would have given concreteness to his verse. In the later drafts and again in the revisions made between 1900 and 1906 he worked on this problem, cutting down on symbolic detail and building up some sense of a real world as a counter to the world of dream. The grotesque Seabar, part of a personal nightmare vision of infantile frustration, are superseded by sailors whose frustrations are more readily understandable. In part they represent adult reality. They are real human beings who resent being denied ordinary satisfactions in order to follow Forgael's dream of perfection. Behind their attempt to kill Forgael is their craving for women and drink, and there is a tension built up between reality, the senses, and life on the one hand, and dream and death on the other.

As noted above, in February 1888 after finishing *The Wanderings of Oisin*, Yeats complained to Katharine Tynan that the web between him and the world was so thick that "An accident to one of my MSS ... would seem of more importance" than the death of an acquaintance. "Yet I do not think I am an egotist. ... It is all the web" (*Letters*, p. 58). His self-sufficiency and self-importance made him feel guilty, and he repudiated them by blaming the web. In a subsequent letter he apologized, explaining that he had been "tired" and "somewhat unwell" (*Letters*, p. 61). This stance of illness and confusion is parallel to his collapse after the affair with Olivia. When he had done something he might be expected to be proud of—gained the love of a beautiful woman or finished an important poem—he reacted by feeling helpless. Pride in himself was apparently experienced as a betrayal of his mother.

One of the ways he lessened the guilt of such betrayals was to feel pride indirectly, by identifying with an image that represented the poet—the scepter, harp, or unicorn—or with a figure such as the bard. In a roundabout fashion, making his images and work concrete also added to his own sense of solidity and made him less afraid of being devoured or castrated. Like his later invention, the mask, his mature work presented a hard, clear surface.

In the 1890's, however, his struggle against the abstract both in his work and in his personal relationships was far from over. To be concrete would be to show too much authority; he was vague and withdrawn. Impersonality and denial of the physical are reflected in the style of Yeats's early poems and plays, a style that strives for musical effects divorced from content, or for the incantatory effects of magic. It is a disembodied style and hence, like the visionary activities on which he embarked in this period, an attempt to deny the body. Repudiation of the body would take extreme form in Yeats's next play, *The King's Threshold*.

'The King's Threshold'

The King's Threshold (1903) opens with Seanchan fasting at the King's doorstep to protest his banishment from the council. A stream of visitors tries to get him to break his fast. He refuses them one by one and dies cursing the leprous moon. Seanchan's repudiation of figures like the Mayor, the Monk, and the Chancellor in the first part of the play seems a rational criticism of corrupt society (Bushrui calls it "magnificent satire"),[30] but his rejection of his sweetheart Fedelm and the Princesses in the second part is so outlandish that Ure attributes it to delirium.[31] A reasonable suggestion, until we grasp the psychological unity underlying the entire play.

The sequence of repudiations serves to make the hero completely independent of external reality. He no longer needs to eat or to express anger. His violent denial of his sweetheart represents the ultimate independence. The play was completed in August 1903, six months after Maud Gonne's marriage to John MacBride. Seanchan's independence reflects Yeats's wish for a similar self-sufficiency, and is a denial of vulnerability and hurt. Seanchan's death is experienced as a triumph—a masochistic victory—because he has shown that he can do without his sweetheart and also because his death presumably causes her some sorrow. The unconscious idea seems to be: I don't need Maud Gonne, but when I am dead she will be sorry.

From the beginning of the play when Seanchan talks to his pupils, he radiates strength and independence—unlike Yeats's earlier dreamer-poets—which seem to derive from identification with his craft. As he says to the Chamberlain, it was not

> that I was driven
> From the great council. You have driven away
> The images of them that weave a dance
> By the four rivers in the mountain garden.
> (ll. 507–10)

---

[30] S. B. Bushrui, *Yeats's Verse-Plays: The Revisions, 1900–1910* (Oxford: Clarendon Press, 1965), p. 74.

[31] Ure, p. 40.

The Chamberlain answers: "You mean we have driven poetry away."

The poet's role, as Seanchan sees it, is to hang

> Images of the life that was in Eden
> About the child-bed of the world, that it,
> Looking upon those images, might bear
> Triumphant children.
>
> (ll. 129–32)

The unformed infant is shaped by what the mother looks at: mothers will take me (my images) and produce children like me, "triumphant children." "Triumphant" is again used to describe Seanchan's state of mind at his death. It also describes the music of the horn at his funeral. "Yet make triumphant music; . . . O silver trumpets be you lifted up / And cry to the great race that is to come." Again triumphant music calls forth triumphant children. The King's opening speech suggests the additional association of triumph with maleness:

> I welcome you that have the mastery
> Of the two kinds of Music: the one kind
> Being like a woman, the other like a man.
> Both you that understand stringed instruments,
> And how to mingle words and notes together
> So artfully that all the Art's but Speech
>   . . . and you that carry
> The twisted horn.
>
> (ll. 1–8)

The poet, the bearer of the twisted horn, influences the birth of triumphant, apparently male, children. In contrast, a world without his influence "would be like a woman / That, looking on the cloven lips of a hare, / Brings forth a harelipped child" (ll. 137–39).

Recognizable here is a common process in symbol formation: displacement of essential qualities from below the waist upward onto the head. The harelipped child, then, is female. The harelip suggests also a difficulty in taking nourishment. The image seems to represent, as did the monstrous Seabar, Yeats's feelings about his infant self as helpless and unable to get proper nourishment—feelings that were reinforced by the recent wound of Maud's marriage and that he repudiated by projecting them onto the hare-

lipped child and the Cripples. At the same time, by making
Seanchan self-sufficient and needed, he reverses the real infantile
position of helpless dependency.

Seanchan describes his role in terms appropriate to a woman in
childbirth, as

> labouring
> For some that shall be born in the nick o' time
> And find sweet nurture, that they may have voices,
> Even in anger, like the strings of harps.
>
> (ll. 167–70)

The children nurtured on his words will be poets, and like Seanchan they will transform their anger into beauty. Yeats was conscious of his own need to turn anger into beauty as a way of coping
with feelings of rage that threatened to overwhelm him. In January
1909 he wrote in his journal (*Memoirs*, p. 157):

In one way [my tendency to frustrated rage] has helped me, for the
knowledge of it has forced me to make my writings sweet-tempered and,
I think, gracious. There was a time when they were threatened by it; I
had to subdue a kind of Jacobin rage. I escaped from it all as a writer
through my sense of style. Is not one's art made out of the struggle in
one's soul? Is not beauty a victory over oneself?

In *The Shadowy Waters* the image of the eagle-headed birds
shrieking at the reflected moon expressed complete dependence
on others for need gratification. The crane to which the Oldest
Pupil compares Seanchan is simply looking at his image in the
water, not screaming like the Seabar, but Seanchan's fear of his
shadow and the moon's reflection may express the mortal needs
that he is trying to suppress:

> Hunger has made you dream of roasting flesh;
> And though I all but weep to think of it,
> The hunger of the crane, that starves himself
> At the full moon because he is afraid
> Of his own shadow, and the glittering water,
> Seems to me little more fantastical
> Than this of yours.
>
> (ll. 99–105)

Throughout *The King's Threshold*, the independent poet is contrasted with the servile, dependent, greedy minor characters. Just
as the Cripples represent the infantile hunger and rage Seanchan

repudiates, the Mayor and his followers represent anal need, the need, that is, to hoard, gain, be practical. They value words primarily as bargaining counters. They have no understanding of the way their world is—as Seanchan would see it—dependent on the poet.

> Cry out that the King's money would not buy,
> Nor the high circle consecrate his head,
> If poets had never christened gold, . . .
>   . . .
>   . . . cry out that not a man alive
>   Would ride among the arrows with high heart,
>   . . . had not
> Our heady craft commended wasteful virtues.
>   (ll. 520–27)

Not only has the poet achieved independence from external reality, but reality has become dependent on him—a magical (albeit narcissistic) reversal similar to Forgael's claims of superhuman power in *The Shadowy Waters*. Here, however, the poet is not only supremely powerful, he is also supremely good, his virtues contrasting directly with the vices of the other characters. The Cripples think only of their stomachs; Seanchan, with his words and his life, gives nourishment. The Cripples vent their anger by beating the Mayor; the poet sublimates his anger and produces poetry. The Mayor is practical and retentive; Seanchan exemplifies the "wasteful virtues." The key word is "give": on both the oral and the anal levels, Seanchan is a giver. His extreme independence and altruism are incorporated into his view of himself as a parent. We noted that he saw his function as producing triumphant children, nurturing them, and enabling them to become poets. He is in effect a parent, and in the climactic lines "O my chicks, my chicks! / That I have nourished underneath my wings" (ll. 846–47), a mother.

Yeats's female identification has been discussed earlier in relation to the Oedipal quest. In *The King's Threshold* there is no quest for a perfect woman because Seanchan himself possesses her attributes. This is why Yeats, although adopting other elements of Edwin Ellis's verse drama *Sancan The Bard*, rejects the ending, in which Bard and Girl find they embody each other's ideal. He had not, as Ure suggests, temporarily exhausted this theme,[32] but rather was at the moment violently rejecting it. In the play, Yeats reverses a crucial action: writing in the months after Maud Gonne had definitively rejected him, Yeats has Seanchan cast Fedelm off like "an old torn cap, / A broken shoe, a glove without a finger" (ll. 792–93). The choice of mutilated objects to represent Fedelm leads back to Yeats's memory of a scratched and mastless boat that leaves him feeling desolate as it moves away. In the memory as in the adult experience, Yeats was helpless. In the play Yeats both expresses past helplessness and disappointment and tries to correct it (defend himself) by incorporating into himself as poet all the nurturing, life-giving qualities of a good mother, and projecting onto the moon and associated characters those of a bad mother.

Seanchan's diatribes against the moon are foreshadowed by a short scene between him and a Soldier. Here Yeats touches briefly on the theme of sibling rivalry, and the poet, heretofore seen as provider, is seen as a child. The Soldier, urged by two girls, reluctantly offers Seanchan food: "Snuff it, old hedgehog, and unroll yourself!" (l. 475). Seanchan seizes the image and develops it in a way that suggests both an unborn infant—"I lie rolled up ... / I am out of life" (ll. 478, 482)—and a rebellious child—"yet, / Hedgehog although I am, I'll not unroll / For you, King's dog!" (ll. 482–84). The sharp spines of the hedgehog symbolize the way an essentially passive posture, like Seanchan's in the play, can be used defensively.

As a child, Yeats was similarly withdrawn. His father wrote when Yeats was seven, "I am continually anxious about Willy. He is almost never out of my thoughts. I believe him to be intensely affectionate, but from shyness, sensitiveness, and nervousness, very difficult to win." His father adds that unlike his brother Robert, Yeats was "very easily rebuffed and continually afraid of being rebuffed."[33]

In the play, poetry is described as being so fragile that it dies "at an insult" (l. 158). It might be noted here that the rebuff to

---

[32] *Ibid.*, p. 33.

[33] William Murphy, "Father and Son: the Early Education of William Butler Yeats," *Review of English Literature*, 8 (Oct. 1967): 85.

the poet in both the 1904 and 1906 versions of the play consisted simply in being sent from the King's table to a lower table, not, as in the 1922 revision, in banishment from the council of state. The poet's reaction to the insult—refusal to move or eat—embarrasses the figures of authority as does a child's similar refusal. More significantly, the Soldier responds to the poet's withdrawal as though it were the act of a spoiled child. In line with the Soldier's treatment of the poet as a spoiled child or sibling is his anger against the girls for urging him to be nice. His anger at female fickleness prepares for Seanchan's later accusations against Fedelm, and for his dying contest with the moon.

The last part of the play is pervaded by the moon's image. The leprous moon sheds poison that contaminates food, in contrast to the poet, who provides "sweet nurture." Through the motif of a leper's blessing hand, the moon is connected with the play's important female characters. When the young Princesses bring Seanchan food, he tells how a leper once blessed their mother's hand. The he asks:

> Hold out your hands;
> I will find out if they are contaminated,
>
> . . .
>
> You are all lepers! There is leprosy
> Among the plates and dishes that you have carried.
> (ll. 639–40, 650–51)

Ellis had a similar passage in *Sancan The Bard*, but Yeats goes further and connects the disease with the moon, who becomes the original leper, blessing with leprosy. When Fedelm comes he dreamily asks:

> Is this your hand, Fedelm?
> I have been looking at another hand
> That is up yonder.
> (ll. 691–93)

She, too, it seems, is contaminated.

The theme of repudiation continues, but now it is sex rather than food that is spurned. Fedelm tempts Seanchan with their marriage (sexual union). He counters with a vision of a union of joyful stars and clods of dirt—to Yeats spirit and matter—that will

produce a "great race," with the qualities that Seanchan has associated with himself as poet: pride, generosity, and the ability to
laugh. As in his vision in the West of Ireland, Yeats sees himself
as a star, this time tempted by the idea that a sexual union between
himself as Seanchan and Fedelm-Maud will produce triumphant
children. Just as Seanchan expresses a complementary or higher
aspect of the drives of the Mayor and the Cripples, giving instead
of retaining, nourishing instead of demanding food, so here on the
sexual level (seen in terms of anality), he is pure (a star) whereas
others, particularly Fedelm, are dirty. She wants him as a husband
to satisfy natural desires; he would consider union only to further
the ideal of a great race. The greediness of love—which carries
with it the danger of being devoured—is stressed in an earlier passage in which sexual hunger is displaced upward: "They'd little
ears as thirsty as your ears / For many love songs. Go to the young
men" (ll. 602–3).

Seanchan starts to go with Fedelm but is stopped by the memory
of Adam's paradise, where hunger is perfectly appeased:

> . . . spirits in the images of birds
> > . . .
> > . . . dig in the fruit
> With so much gluttony, and are so drunk
> With that harsh wholesome savour, that their feathers
> Are clinging one to another with the juice.
> > (ll. 749–54)

Yeats moves from Fedelm's temptation of Seanchan to the poet's
counter-vision of sexuality, the engendering of a Nietzschean super-
race, to Seanchan's final rejection of Fedelm, all the more bitter
because her hopes have been gradually raised only to be dashed at
the end. Yeats's underlying fantasy seems to be: I don't want you
(Maud); I have something better—in this case an imagined paradise of perfect oral satisfaction.

Having rejected Fedelm, Seanchan begins to speak with a para-
noid intensity. Turning her away, he stresses her worthless (castrated) quality in the series of images quoted earlier: she is "an
old torn cap, / A broken shoe, a glove without a finger, / A crooked
penny; whatever is most worthless" (ll. 792–94). The last object,

a "crooked penny," by its shape a distorted circle, connects her again with the original mother image. Both the moon-mother and the later sexual object, Maud, are found lacking. And his enumeration of woman's deformities reflects not only devaluation of a longed-for object but also fear of losing his identity in the beloved woman's, fear of his own castration.

I have said that Seanchan takes to himself all the qualities of the ideal woman. How can we reconcile this with a feared loss of masculinity? The answer, I think, is that Seanchan is bisexual—he is both a man (the triumphant bearer of the twisted horn) and a woman. He corresponds to the young child's conception of a mother with a phallus, formed at a time when the child cannot imagine that his all-powerful mother lacks that important organ.[34]

Seanchan's dying speech is devoted to his triumphant contest with the moon. He reminds his pupils of the selflessness with which he has mothered them, and ends:

> O my chicks, my chicks!
> That I have nourished underneath my wings
> And fed upon my soul.
>
> (ll. 846–48)

He then refers to himself in terms that connect the selfless mothering bird with the dying Christ (like the pelican, long a Christ symbol, who tears her breast to feed her young). Finally, the poet mocks the moon as an "evil picture" in the sky, and dies "outfacing it," his heart bursting with some "triumphant thought."

Such, at any rate, was the ending Yeats gave the play in 1922. In the versions of 1904 and 1906 the poet returned to life and love, an ending that did considerable violence to the play's inner logic. But in 1904 and 1906 Yeats had an immediate reason for a happy ending: if the play was to negate Maud's rejection of him, it should be a triumphant play. Or, as Yeats explains, if Seanchan "had not risen up from the death that threatened him, the ending would not have been . . . joyful enough to be . . . proclaimed in the mouths

---

[34] Such a hermaphroditic image once appeared to Yeats in a waking dream: "Sometimes when I lay in bed . . . I would see forms at my bedside: once a fair woman who said she was Aedain, and both man and woman." He goes on to say he saw "my mother holding a cup in her hand" (*Memoirs*, p. 127).

of trumpets."[35] The happy ending thus served as a double denial: "You [Maud] can neither feed me nor make me sad."

In the revision of 1922 artistry prevailed, and Yeats gave the play an ending consistent with the underlying masochistic fantasy. It is also possible that so long as he was still smarting from Maud's defection, victory was essential, whereas later, when he had achieved more distance, he could take satisfaction in the artifact alone.

'Where There Is Nothing' and 'The Unicorn from the Stars'

The Unicorn from the Stars, a play of 1907, is the next to deal with the dreamer, this time as mystic rather than poet. Since it is a reworking of an earlier play, *Where There Is Nothing* (1902), its main theme—the consuming thirst for destruction—belongs to the period before Maud Gonne's marriage. The symbolic Unicorn that dominates the later play is, however, connected with more positive efforts at forging a new identity, efforts that continue in *The Player Queen*. In this sense, *The Unicorn from the Stars* provides a link between two stages in Yeats's development. The earlier version, *Where There Is Nothing*, repays consideration here because it shows the symbolic unicorn in the process of formation, and also because—thanks to the speed with which it was written— it is rich in unelaborated psychic material.

Where There Is Nothing falls into two parts (a structure lost in revision), which correspond to a pattern Yeats often repeated: a quest for the ideal woman followed by punishment and reunion in death. In the late dance plays, *The King of the Great Clock Tower* and *A Full Moon in March*, attention is focused on the Oedipal crime. In this earlier play Oedipal desires are present, but Yeats also portrays developmentally earlier material: desire for satisfaction at the breast and concomitant rage against sibling rivals and the mother herself when she fails to satisfy.

In the first part Paul Ruttledge, a country gentleman haunted by dreams of destruction, joins a group of tinkers to seek the

[35] *Variorum Plays*, p. 313.

natural pleasures of "mother earth." He marries a tinker, Sabina, and gives free drink to the celebrating peasants. This causes an uproar in the countryside, which the magistrates intervene to stop. Paul captures them, and the first part ends with the magistrates' humiliation at a mock trial. With the opening of Act IV, there is an abrupt change in Paul. Falling sick, he joins a monastery, where he punishes his body, sees visions, and preaches heretical doctrines. Finally he is banished, and dies joyfully at the hands of an angry mob.

In his last speech Paul expresses eagerness to descend into the earth, which, like Yeats's early island images, symbolizes the mother's body. The drive toward union with the beloved gives the play its structure, but within that structure the key images are of hunger and rage.[36] Oral desires and accompanying sadistic urges are evident in the hero's conflicting ideas of heaven as a place of drinking and of fighting. In Paul's first description, heaven is drunkenness and ecstasy, and the Latin phrase chosen to represent it, "Et calix meus inebrians quam praeclarus est" (How splendid is the cup of my drunkenness), is repeated rhythmically throughout the play. To celebrate his marriage Paul gives drink to the impoverished peasants so they can share his pleasure. In the second part of the play, however, Paul denies his oral desires. He refuses food as Seanchan does in *The King's Threshold*, and the same image of the entranced crane is used to describe him: "You haven't much more flesh on you than a crane in moolight" (V, 172–73). Toward the end of the play, then, Paul has reached Seanchan's position. He has overcome his own hunger and wishes only to give others drink. Both Paul and Seanchan deal with orality by moving from passive receptiveness to the active nourishing of others. This was the period of Yeats's active involvement in the Irish theater, work that may for him have served as an opportunity to provide his compatriots with nourishing words.

[36] This division is similar to that observed by Norman Holland in his work on Shakespeare. He suggests that "for Shakespeare, perhaps for all writers, the larger chunks of action—plot, conflict, character, configuration—come from the phallic or oedipal stage of childhood.... The details of language and characterization seem to come from the earlier oral and anal stages." Holland, *Psychoanalysis and Shakespeare* (New York: McGraw-Hill, 1964), p. 130.

Paul's alternative view of heaven is "the continual clashing of swords" (II, 278). Or, as he says at another point: "I want the happiness of men who fight, who are hit and hit back" (II, 261–62). This desire is reminiscent of the process by which the developing child establishes his first sense of separateness and individuality through aggressive and destructive actions. Certainly fighting becomes at times for Yeats the ideal relationship between men and the supreme expression of the individual self. But there are differences between the ideal of fighting and wanton destruction.

Paul's urge to destroy, the "kind of Jacobin rage" Yeats saw in himself, is overwhelming, and is unjustified by his avowed moral purpose to destroy falsehood. He is plagued by dreams in which he is a destructive beast: "Sometimes I dream I am pulling down my own house, and sometimes it is the whole world that I am pulling down. I would like to have great iron claws . . . and to pull and pull till everything fell into pieces" (I, 144–48). His desire is double. He wants to pull down everything covering the earth, or, as in his following speech, pull down towers topping a castle, while at the same time he wants to reestablish contact with the uncovered earth or "put a crowbar under the gates" (l. 146, variant) of the castle and force entry. Desire to enter a house is a recurrent theme in Yeats. In *The Green Helmet*, only Cuchulain is worthy to enter the house called "Ireland"; in "The Cap and Bells" the disappointed lover enters only after death, in a disembodied form. In *Purgatory*, the meaning of "entry" is clarified, as an old man watches his mother "open the door" to his father and then watches their ghostly intercourse. In *Where There Is Nothing*, the earth and its buildings are joined in symbolic intercourse, and the hero has to destroy the projections, the paternal phallus, before he can reenter the mother's body. Similar fantasies have been recorded in children.[37]

Alongside Paul's desire to enter the earth or house, Yeats portrays the earlier desire to be in symbiotic union with the mother, to be a nursing infant. When Paul is asked what would be gained by the wholesale destruction he proposes, he answers: "we would

[37] Melanie Klein, *The Psychoanalysis of Children* (London: Hogarth, 1959), pp. 45, 91, and 191.

have more room to get drunk in, to drink contentedly out of the cup of life" (II, 151–52). When thirst is unsatisfied, rage is directed against the mother, who is both desired and hated. As Paul says: "I only know that I want to upset everything about me ... and whether it comes from love or hate I don't know, they are so mixed together here" (I, 156–60).

In an early scene, Paul's destructive urge is attributed to jealousy of his brother's children. In a revealing letter, Yeats enlarges on the importance of the children (*Letters*, p. 405):

Those children were not Paul's but his brother's, in fact the fools that he begot. ... I have tried to suggest, without saying it straight out, that Paul finds himself unnecessary in his own house, and therefore the more inclined to take to the roads. ... I see the perambulator on the middle of the stage, or rather I cannot see it, for everyone is standing round it, stooping over with their backs to me.

The sudden materialization of the scene and Yeats's shift into the first person suggest the emergence of a childhood memory. In the memory, parents and friends turn their backs on the child, their attention centered on the baby.

In the play, Yeats reverses this: the hero is "bored" by his "father's friends" and annoyed with his brother's wife, the mother figure, who doesn't "understand [him] in the least" (I, 41k). Paul's wandering, however, far from being motivated by boredom, represents flight from a situation of intolerable conflict: love and hate of the mother and desire to reestablish contact as it was before the intrusion. Ironically, earth does not prove to be a kind mother; Paul calls her "my hard mother, Earth" (V, 97). And like her prototype, she rejects him in favor of a preferred sibling.[38] The

[38] Recent research by William Murphy suggests that Yeats actually experienced such a rejection by his mother. John Butler Yeats wrote to Lily of the time when Yeats was twelve: "When I used to spend those miserable weeks at Burnham Beeches and came back every Saturday, I was no sooner in the house than I had to listen to dreadful complaints of everybody and everything and *especially of Willie*. It was always of Willie." William M. Murphy, "The Ancestry of William Butler Yeats," *Yeats Studies: An International Journal*, No. 1 (1971), p. 13. (Italics in original.) In his memoirs Yeats's father describes his son as the family's problem child: "Though he had always the best intentions he was rather a trial. ... Willie used to get blamed for everything, and he could not deny he was generally the cause of whatever went wrong." Cited by Murphy in "Father and Son," p. 89.

only difference is that the favored one, the tinker Charlie Ward, tries to help Paul. But it does no good; Charlie "is her good child and she loves him" (V, 97–98). Paul never has a chance.

Here it might be helpful to look at the events behind Yeats's decision to write the play, particularly his rivalry with George Moore over ownership of the plot. Yeats and Moore had been not only collaborating on a play, *Diarmuid and Grania*, but living together at Tillyra Castle. There seems to have been a fairly equal balance between them at first, with Moore ruling in construction, Yeats in style. In giving Moore the final say in dramatic construction, which he himself equates with "the masculine element,"[39] Yeats may have felt himself threatened with a passive role. Having the last word on style meant that he could actively incorporate the aspects of Moore he needed and turn them into his own substance. But Moore apparently resisted assimilation, and the partnership collapsed. The quarrel with Moore, initiated by Yeats's withdrawal from future collaboration, may, like the fighting in *Where There Is Nothing*, represent a repudiation of passivity. The infuriated Moore threatened to turn Yeats's plot into a novel. To forestall this move, Yeats dictated the entire play to Lady Gregory in two weeks, and angrily wrote A.E., "Tell Moore to write his story and be hanged" (*Letters*, p. 381). In 1904, when Moore was trying to get back into the theater, Yeats wrote the actor Frank Fay (*Letters*, p. 443):

Moore's return to the theatre is out of the question. If there were not other reasons, and there are very sufficient ones, it is enough that he represents a rival tradition of the stage and would upset your brother's plans at every turn. He is very jealous of the success of the theatre and has been laying pipe to get into it, for months past.

The theater, like the house called Ireland in *The Green Helmet*, has become a place that only the worthiest may enter, and the jealous rival is rigorously excluded. The feud, with its attendant rivalry over possession not only of the plot but of the theater itself, seems to have reactivated childhood conflicts and triggered Yeats's portrayal of Paul's destructive rage.

Yeats's brother Jack had married young, as Yeats himself did not

---

39 Yeats, *Plays and Controversies* (London: Macmillan, 1923), pp. 186–87.

feel free to do, and at times failed to take his elder brother seriously, as when he said about Yeats's theory of masks: "Oh Masks, such a lot of talk about Masks—every one knows about Masks being just about the last thing but three."[40] Their father, moreover, compared his sons in ways that could hardly avoid annoying Yeats. He wrote, for instance, that he had high hopes of Jack's drama. Jack, he said, was audacious, "careless as to his reputation," whereas his eldest son was oversensitive and overcritical.[41] Moreover, J. B. Yeats attributed Yeats's constant revision to indolence, the besetting sin, in his opinion, of his son's early life.

In *Where There Is Nothing* a great deal of aggression is directed against figures of authority, who, though perhaps connected with an attack on Moore's advocacy of dramatic "realism"—they are practical, everyday figures who fail to appreciate the hero's idealism—ultimately derive from Yeats's father. Paul, after ridiculing his "father's friends" mercilessly, takes the Colonel's cloak (III, 293). This act links the play to *On Baile's Strand*, a drama on the father-and-son theme, written in 1901. There, the cloak was given to Cuchulain by his father, who had risen from the sea to challenge him. In *Where There Is Nothing*, Paul's taking of the cloak is the final term of the Colonel's humiliation. Both instances suggest highly ambivalent, if not hostile, father-son relationships.

At first glance, it is hard to see anything of Yeats's father in the pompous, preachy Colonel, but Yeats's *Autobiography* contains the following striking passage: "The only lessons I had ever learned were those my father taught me, for *he terrified me by descriptions of my moral degradation* and *he humiliated me* by my likeness to disagreeable people."[42] The trial scene in the play gave Yeats considerable trouble. Later he said he disliked it because of its passivistic commonplaces, which are, incidentally, out of key with the hero's destructive frenzy, but it seems more plausible that he disliked it because of the openness of Paul's hostility.

[40] Quoted in Robin Skelton, " 'Unarrangeable Reality': The Paintings and Writings of Jack B. Yeats," in Robin Skelton and Ann Saddlemyer, eds., *The World of W. B. Yeats*, rev. ed. (Seattle: University of Washington Press, 1967), p. 229.

[41] J. B. Yeats, *Letters to His Son*, p. 68.

[42] *Autobiography*, p. 19 (my italics).

As a young child Yeats had difficulty in learning to read, and later had difficulty studying. When he was past seven, according to his father's memoirs, "it was with the greatest difficulty he mastered the English alphabet. His teachers, which consisted of the whole household, said he would never learn it. And afterwards we had to teach him to read, and though I retained a hopeful belief, most thought he would never read, that is, properly."[43] Yeats's father, though later asserting that young poets must be left "to themselves and to chance" (*Autobiography*, p. 94), had little sympathy for his son's waywardness. Yeats describes him in his *Autobiography* as an "angry and impatient teacher," who "flung the reading book at my head" (p. 86).

The elder Yeats was particularly distressed by Yeats's slowness and what he later considered his "indolence" because he associated it with the mental imbalances of the Pollexfen family, which he feared the boy might have inherited through his mother. In a revealing letter to his daughter Lily, John Butler Yeats writes, "Willie seemed to me as if he might become victim to that apathy and mental sloth which has made all the Pollexfens to be failures in spite of their fine natural qualities."[44] In two letters to his brother Isaac, he is even more explicit: "I think sometimes that all the Pollexfens are mad. Agnes [Yeats's mother's sister] . . . really had a big brain. But she was mad from her cradle." And again, "Lollie [Yeats's other sister] . . . has Pollexfen traits, a distinct tendency to what the doctors call depressive mania. . . . She is too much like poor unhappy Agnes."[45] He especially recommended that his son be kept away from Agnes, but he was probably not thinking only of her. William Pollexfen, Yeats's grandfather, "was a troubled man whom only his wife could manage."[46] One of Susan Yeats's brothers, William Middleton Pollexfen, died in a mental home in 1913, "after decades of hopeless insanity,"[47] and two other

43 Cited in Murphy, "Father and Son," p. 87.
44 Murphy, "Ancestry of Yeats," p. 17n.
45 Murphy, "Father and Son," pp. 85n–86n. Lollie "cracked under the strain of her life and showed the classic symptoms of persecution complex, mania, and depression from about 1910 until 1915." Murphy, *Yeats Family*, p. 34.
46 Murphy, "Ancestry of Yeats," p. 16.
47 William M. Murphy, " 'In Memory of Alfred Pollexfen': W. B. Yeats and the Theme of Family," *Irish University Review*, 1 (Autumn 1970): 45.

members of the Pollexfen family had to be institutionalized for depression.[48]

At any rate, Yeats was dreadfully unhappy because of his "indolence." "It made me wretched to be idle but one couldn't help it" (*Autobiography*, p. 17). Perhaps he guessed what his idleness meant to his father, who in spite of his son's misery insisted that he work and humiliated him when he did not: "I worried him a good deal about his lessons. Subconsciously I resolved that he should be a distinguished man, and I think he caught the infection from me, so that his anxieties became my anxieties."[49]

In *Where There Is Nothing*, the tables are turned. Yeats-as-Paul becomes the teacher, humiliating his unwilling pupils with their failure to be good Christians, i.e., their moral degradation. In the first draft of his autobiography Yeats says he went through a period of preoccupation with abstract morality that enraged his father. At one point, when his father tried to draw him away from impersonal argument to physical confrontation, Yeats refused, saying he could not fight his own father. As the autobiography shows, however, Yeats's moral zeal covered a hostility toward his father that influenced his conception of Paul Ruttledge. After describing his father's attempt to box with him Yeats goes on to talk about his walks through London during this period. He was oppressed by the size of the buildings, particularly the New Law Court: "what could the most powerful soul do against weight and size? Then I called up to the mind's eye a London full of moss and grass, and a sort of preaching friar far off among fields, and I said to myself, 'the right voice could empty London again'" (*Memoirs*, pp. 19–20). Paul's was to be such a voice. Interestingly enough, Yeats later realized that Paul "did rather ram his ideas down people's throats."[50] In the revision hostility would be cloaked in dreams.

In expressing hatred of established authority, Yeats may also have hoped to win sympathy from Maud Gonne and the young nationalists around her. As he writes to Lady Gregory at the time of Victoria's Jubilee: "I have found a greatly increased friendliness

[48] Murphy, *Yeats Family*, p. 35.
[49] Murphy, "Father and Son," p. 94.
[50] Reproduced in *Variorum Plays*, p. 1166.

on the part of some of the young men here. In a battle, like Ireland's, which is one of poverty against wealth, one must prove one's sincerity, by making oneself unpopular to wealth. One must accept the baptism of the gutter. Have not all teachers done the like?" (*Letters*, p. 339). This appears to be a deliberate confutation of Maud's view that writers returned from Coole "seemed less passionately interested in the national struggle than in their own lack of money."[51] Paul's repudiation of a gentleman's life would then serve as a denial of Yeats's intimacy with Lady Gregory and a rejection of her money and aristocratic values. In trying to convince Maud of his sincerity, he may have been preparing for still another proposal of marriage. Yet his feelings about Maud were clearly ambivalent. Sabina worries that after their marriage Paul will beat her. The Player Queen, who is clearly derived from Maud, would later express the same fear. Such fears are a projection of this ambivalence and Yeats's dread of his own sadism.

Ambivalence, indeed, is one of the play's major themes. Paul's mingling of love and hate is a clear example, but perhaps its major expression is the terrible laughing beast Paul is searching for. The beast is at first identified with Paul and expresses Paul's destructive urges toward his mother, father, brothers, rivals, and the world. When the beast is externalized and attacks the hero, it represents the castrating, devouring mother who arises in retaliation for the child's sadistic urges. This early image of the mother is related to a developmentally somewhat later image of the mother having intercourse with the father. When Paul starts on his wanderings he expresses the desire "to be a witch, and to ride through the air on a white horse" (I, 328–29). This image goes through many permutations — from witch/horse to Queen/Unicorn to aristocratic mother / beastly father — the successive variants evoking, with increasing clarity, a primal scene. At its first appearance the image suggests Paul's desire to imitate the mother's act (witch and broom or horse having long been recognized by psychoanalysts as having the unconscious significance of intercourse),[52] his ambiv-

---

[51] Quoted in Hone, *W. B. Yeats*, pp. 173–74.
[52] See, for example, Ernest Jones, *On the Nightmare* (New York: Grove Press, 1931), pp. 204–6.

alence toward the mother who is seen as a witch, and, finally, his inability to perform. He is unable to "find a broomstick that will turn itself into a white horse" (I, 337–38); i.e., he is impotent, unable to "fly." Instead, Paul walks the roads. This, as he himself says, is a means of making contact with "mother earth," and symbolizes a regressive attempt to reenter her body. His new occupation, that of a tinker, whose task it is to fix holes, hints at repairing damage or possibly undoing castration. This, together with Paul's desire to be the witch and his lack of a broomstick, suggests a confusion of identity; it is unclear whether Paul identifies with the father, the mother being made love to by the father, or a composite mother-father.

The beast Paul says he is seeking, unlike the witch on the white horse, is unambiguously male, and through it Paul struggles toward a masculine identity. Paul tells Sabina he is looking for a beast who can root up towers and spires. As he describes the beast, he obviously identifies with it: according to the stage directions, he "holds out his hands and moves them like claws" (II, 380–81). Paul later asks his bride if she would like to see a beast with eyes that are "hard" and "blue, like sapphires" (II, 382–83). These are the eyes of the Unicorn. The destructive beast with whom Paul identifies is now seen as a bridegroom, and Paul's marriage to Sabina is symbolically related to the witch and her white horse. Paul will reenact the primal scene in a definitely masculine role. It is now that the beast is identified with laughter, greatest of the enemies of God—the God, that is, of St. Patrick and of guilt. Laughter expresses triumph over anxiety, and it also serves to cover destructive rage.

After Paul joins the monastery, his inner rage prompts dreams of retaliation, terrible nightmares of birds and beasts attacking him. In further punishment for destructive urges, Paul mortifies his body to the point that even his friend Father Jerome is dismayed. It is after this voluntary mortification that Paul has a climactic vision of bright light and angels riding unicorns, an exalted or purified version of the witch on her broom-horse, parental intercourse in a "good" form. The vision becomes more explicit in the poem "Ribh at the Tomb of Baile and Aillin" (1934), in which a monk, after years of mortification, is rewarded by the sight of angelic intercourse.

After his vision Paul returns to the tinkers, where he expresses a desire for death: "at death the soul comes into possession of itself, and returns to the joy that made it" (V, 393–94). Union with the beloved mother in death is not a new idea for Yeats—we recall Dhoya's suicidal leap into the sea—but perhaps because of his mother's recent death (in 1900) the theme is more pervasive here. As Paul dies he sees himself gathered to the beast: "Take me down —down to that field under the earth, under the roots of the grave" (V, 458–60). This is an early version of what became in *A Vision* Christ ascending into the abstract sky, Oedipus descending into the center of the earth. Though Paul says he is looking for his father in heaven after searching in vain "for the favour of my hard Mother, Earth" (V, 97), after his penance his desire for contact with her is stronger than ever. After his vision of angels and unicorns, he sees that "we are going back to the joy of the green earth" (IV, 278–79). Paul's death returns him to "the source of joy." And Yeats forges images of rage, hate, and frustrated desire into the joyful Unicorn, symbol of the poet and father of the New Dispensation.

In *The Unicorn from the Stars* (1907), the revised version of *Where There Is Nothing*, written with Lady Gregory's help, the main conflict is between Martin Hearne, the epileptic hero, and his practical uncle Thomas, who functions dramatically as his father. Thomas Hearne, like the "father's friends" in *Where There Is Nothing*, believes in work. "Work must go on and coachbuilding must go on, and they will not go on the time there is too much attention given to dreams" (I, 72–74). Thomas wants to remake Martin to his specifications. Speaking of the coaches he has shaped, he says: "What I can do with wood and iron, why would I not be able to do it with flesh and blood?" (I, 107–8).

Under Lady Gregory's hand, Thomas has become a strong and believable opponent. The hero, too, has changed. After *Where There Is Nothing* had been performed, Yeats realized that audiences found Paul unsympathetic. He had to have "some humil-ity,"[53] and his urge to destroy must appear as a supernatural com-mand. Martin is not an angry young man like Paul, but a victim of epileptic seizures during which he sees visions and is commanded to destroy. Destructive impulses are thus projected outward and appear as something foreign to the hero, a mechanism by which Yeats often absolved himself of responsibility and guilt.

Martin's visionary activities represent two ways of coping with anxiety: facing it and fighting, or fleeing. On the one hand, the visions provide an escape from the uncle's pressure. Martin's vision is described as an open "window into eternity" (I, 483) that his uncle would very much like to shut. Oisin, we recall, rode from his father and the lands of time to the timeless land of eternal youth under the aegis of the goddess-mother. Martin's vision may stand for the forbidden union itself, appropriately accompanied by a convulsive seizure.

Martin's vision, however, is also a source of strength. After pro-jecting his sexual and destructive impulses onto the figure of the Unicorn, Martin identifies with it and feels new energy. He "knew something was going to happen or to be said, something that would make my whole life strong and beautiful like the rushing of the unicorns" (I, 505–8). The Unicorn's command to destroy all sources of authority enables Martin to stand up to his uncle, just as Yeats gained assurance in his relationship with his father after he began his mystical studies.

The vision itself is similar to the climactic vision in *Where There Is Nothing*, except that it is dynamic rather than static and Martin participates in it. Thrown into a trance by flashing light on the coach's symbolic unicorn, he has a vision of white horses. Suddenly he is pulled up on one and the horses sprout horns and become unicorns. The image thus condenses the change we observed in the previous play, from broomstick-horse to Unicorn. The Unicorn as developed there combined a desire for masculinity with fantasies of a primal scene. In *The Unicorn from the Stars*, the Unicorn is not only strong and phallic, but also virginal and pure. The accu-

53 *Variorum Plays*, p. 708.

sations of impurity made against it are vestiges of the original, primal-scene fantasy.

In the earlier play, the theme of contented drinking represented one view of heaven: the peaceful union of mother and nursing child. This ideal was quite distinct from the other, predominantly active, view of heaven as a battleground. Here, the two views merge. The masculine Unicorn has entered the vineyard of Eden and is crushing the grapes. Martin's friend, the priest Father John, associates the flowing wine with the line from *Where There Is Nothing*, "How splendid is the cup of my drunkenness." But here the life-giving fluid—milk, wine, and blood are all related, wine being the "blood of the grape"—can only be released by violence against the body that contains it; paradoxically, "destruction is the life-giver" (I, 560). Moreover, the fluid is not under the giver's control, but forced out by masculine activity. And the whole process becomes symbolic of the poetic act. What seems to be happening in part is a shift from orality to sexuality, with a corresponding emphasis on violent masculine activity.

The second part of Martin's vision is the most destructive and, in line with Yeats's wish to disguise hostility, extremely hard for Martin to remember. Gradually, his dream comes back to him, in much the same way as dreams are actually remembered, with the most significant feature hinted at in various ways but never completely recalled. The sight of a beggar crashing down a bag of money and saying, "Destruction on us all," makes Martin remember the crucial feature of his vision; the figure he saw was (I, 553–60)

a bright many-changing figure; it was holding up a shining vessel; then the vessel fell and was broken with a great crash; then I saw the unicorns trampling it. They were breaking the world to pieces—when I saw the cracks coming I shouted for joy! And I heard the command, "Destroy, destroy, destruction is the life-giver! destroy!"

The world-vessel goes back to mother earth, and her "cup of life" from which Paul in *Where There Is Nothing* wanted to drink. Here, like the grape, it is being destroyed. The figure has taken over the images and language Yeats used to describe the vessel of the Fool of the Forth in his *Celtic Twilight*: the Fool throws it at a boy who has killed a man. The Fool is a figure of vast, untamed energy somehow connected with poetic inspiration. Being touched by him means death or madness, but also divine or poetic frenzy: Yeats interpreted the Fool's chalice as the dreams that drive men mad.[54] In Martin's vision the chalice is not thrown in punishment, but is itself broken, and license is thereby given to the hero's wish to destroy.

In *Where There Is Nothing* destruction was balanced by Paul's desire to "drink contentedly from the cup of life"; accordingly, heaven was imagined as drunkenness and God was equated with the green earth. In *The Unicorn from the Stars* the theme of renewed contact with mother earth is, except for one reference, dropped, and heaven is imagined as figures on unicorns doing battle with flashing swords. At one point Martin has a vision of paradise where all the people do is but an overflowing of their idleness, and life is a perpetual "dance bred of the secret frenzy of their hearts" (II, 413–15). But even here, as "frenzy" suggests, the emphasis is on violent activity rather than quiet union. Intensity is the key quality, and man must move "from exaltation to exaltation" (II, 422–23). Martin's vision also expresses the need for intensity. He rebels against all authority—King George, the Law, the Church—so that "all life will become like a flame of fire, like a burning eye" (II, 363–64).

This flame is paradoxically both the fire of passionate joy, like the flame in *Oisin* flaming against the God of St. Patrick and the laws of the weak, and the annihilation of passion. The flame that originated as an image of sexual passion comes to stand for the purging away of passion. This fire, Father John points out, does not sound like the light of God. "There is another kind of inspiration, or rather an obsession or possession. A diabolical power comes into one's body, or overshadows it" (II, 18–21).

We have already suggested that Yeats disguised sexual and aggressive impulses by projecting them outward. Martin's vision presents him with the masculine image he needs—the Unicorn (a symbol also of the "manful energy" Yeats was seeking at the time

[54] *Mythologies*, pp. 114–15.

he was working on *Unicorn*). There is also another defense at work. Aggression and sexuality are not only projected outward, but mysticized, a process that accounts for the play's many paradoxes. One, mentioned above, is that the flame of passionate joy is also the annihilation of passion. Another paradox, which also links flesh and spirit, concerns the Unicorn. The Unicorn, as we have seen, represents masculine or phallic activity, but it is also a traditional symbol of the soul; as Yeats sees it, particularly the subjective man's soul. The destruction of church and law stands for the soul's rejection of all accusations external to itself. It takes its own burden of "sin" and correspondingly grows "strong and hard." The Unicorn, a symbol of masculinity, takes on meanings that imply mastery of sexual impulses.

Yeats was hampered in his efforts to present a masculine ideal at this point by his association of masculinity with destructiveness. In fact, in the play there is a triad of joy represented by the laughing beast, destruction, and masculine activity. The same association of masculinity and destruction in *The Shadowy Waters* resulted in the hero's renouncing masculine activity and adopting the passive posture of victim. Yeats would gradually shift masculinity into a new triad: joy, sexual energy, creativity. The poet's sexuality is thus linked to his creativity: when others destroy things, in the words of Yeats's late poem "Lapis Lazuli," poets "build them again" and "are gay." In *Unicorn from the Stars*, however, there is only increasingly frenzied destructive activity, until the hero's dying vision of the vineyards of Eden puts an end to the action. Before Martin dies he has a moment of insight. He sees that (III, 361–65)

I was mistaken when I set out to destroy Church and Law. The battle we have to fight is fought out in our mind. There is a fiery moment, perhaps once in a lifetime, and in that moment we see the only thing that matters.

This is the moment Yeats writes of in his essays when the ordinary self is joined to the buried, subconscious self—the moment of genius or truth.

THREE

Dream, Vision, and the Poet

IN THE PREVIOUS chapter, we saw Paul Ruttledge, the hero of *Where There Is Nothing*, engage in a frenzy of destructive activity ending in death. We saw, too, the origins of the symbolic Unicorn, foreshadowing Yeats's later use of the mask. But though the Unicorn indicates new elements of strength and hardness in Yeats's view of himself, in *Where There Is Nothing* it is intimately linked with destruction. The stories of *Rosa Alchemica*, written a few years earlier, in 1896, are perhaps more characteristic of the early Yeats; they show characters who withdraw from reality completely or who seek another reality through mystical experience. And although they, too, present a destructive vision—the vision of an ideal world that incites a desire to destroy the actual world—they also present the beginning of Yeats's shift from the basically destructive position of his early aesthetes and visionaries to a more constructive one based on a new acceptance of the body and ordinary reality. In this sense the stories can be seen as important transitional works.

The three stories of *Rosa Alchemica* are perhaps the first works in which Yeats shows a clear dissatisfaction with his earlier self, as evidenced in the detached and ironic portrayal of the aesthete narrator of the title story, "Rosa Alchemica."[1] What is more, Yeats seems here and in the other two stories to be taking provisional steps toward an ultimately more satisfying position. Each of the

---

[1] Although many critics have confused the narrator with the author as he was in the 1890's, as Whitaker points out there is both critical distance and "some irony" in Yeats's treatment of the narrator and his ideal of mirror-like detachment. Thomas R. Whitaker, *Swan and Shadow: Yeats's Dialogue with History* (Chapel Hill: University of North Carolina Press, 1964), p. 39.

three stories may be seen as an attempt to find a path to personal satisfaction. In the first two stories, the title story and "The Tables of the Law," the central characters experiment with the free expression of impulse, and become frightened or disillusioned. In the title story, however, there emerges an important mechanism for controlling frightening events or impulses— the talismanic object. At the end of "Rosa Alchemica," the narrator clutches a rosary to still his inner turmoil. Yeats's increasingly bold use of such talismanic objects constitutes a defensive shift that replaces the previous retreat from reality and minimizes the risk of being overcome by unconscious impulses.

The unnamed narrator of "Rosa Alchemica," holding himself "apart, individual, indissoluble, a mirror of polished steel" (*Mythologies*, p. 268), represents an extreme of detachment. The art objects with which he surrounds himself fail to satisfy him, and he longs for an intense mystical experience he describes as ecstasy. Frustrated, he comes to have the apocalyptic wish for the dissolution of his body and, by extension, the world. Not only does the narrator's isolation fail to provide lasting satisfaction, it fails to offer any defenses against his fears. His imperishable and beautiful possessions increase his obsession with his own death, and his repudiation of human love and sexuality make him easy prey for Robartes and his offers of mystical union. The narrator's wishes for apocalypse, dissolution of his body, and mystical union disguise— as his subsequent vision shows—regressive sexual fantasies. When he finally attains the (orgasmic) sense of dissolution he longed for, he is terribly frightened by it. He retreats to the external control of Catholicism, and when he feels threatened by "the indefinite world," he drives off his fears by pressing his rosary to his neck.

So, too, did the early Yeats try to escape from the real world and contact with people in daydream and fantasy, and so, too, did he find that fantasy ultimately increased his fears of castration, dissolution, and death. Yeats worked his way out of this dilemma by hardening his style, a change that gave him a feeling of new strength and clear identity; like the narrator of "Rosa Alchemica," he drew comfort from talismanic objects and emotional sustenance from a structured belief system—notably, in Yeats's case, *Anima Mundi* and related concepts. Yeats came to see that the man who loses himself completely is no more able to create than the man who remains completely detached. The solution Yeats found toward the end of his life was a precarious balance between self-control and an acceptance of inner forces that are at once a danger and a source of power. As he wrote to Dorothy Wellesley, great art is a struggle to keep something down, "violence or madness—'down Hysterica passio.' All depends on the completeness of the holding down, on the stirring of the beast underneath."[2]

The narrator of "Rosa Alchemica" is a man fascinated by alchemy, who has decided that the effort to transform lead into gold is part of a general desire to transmute all things into a divine substance. He himself longs for a world of essences, and he has written a book on the transmutation of life into art. He is surrounded by innumerable paintings that elicit the ecstasy of Christianity without its "rule and custom"—an ecstasy of joy and freedom. But this joy, though free, is not limitless; he cannot rid himself of death's bitterness, and he can never know limitless energy. All the pure art around him, then, keeps reminding him of his failure to transform all matter into spirit, a failure that leads him to sympathize "with the consuming thirst for destruction which made the alchemist veil under his symbols . . . a search for an essence which would dissolve all mortal things." The fire of the alchemist is compared to the Last Day: "all must be dissolved before the divine substance . . . awake." The narrator had succeeded at times in dissolving the mortal world "but had obtained no miraculous ecstasy" (*Mythologies*, pp. 269–70).

Michael Robartes breaks suddenly into the narrator's isolation like an eruption from his unconscious of the impulses his mirror-like surface conceals. Robartes is magnetic and sensual; he brings with him an incense made of a purple flower that made Christ cry out against his destiny: a temptation of the sensual life. Robartes

2 Yeats, *Letters on Poetry to Dorothy Wellesley* (Oxford: Oxford University Press, 1964), p. 94.

offers not ascetic Christianity, but erotically tinged mystical union. He argues that the more of an artist a man is, the more he communes with many gods. The vision Robartes then induces in the narrator presents images presumably from the racial memory, creations of man's passion and reverence: Lear and Beatrice, Aphrodite and Mary.

These images have significance in Yeats's developing mythology. Lear, the raging old man, who Yeats said reminded him of his grandfather, came to be associated in *A Vision* with Oedipus (the new god) and Oedipus in turn with poetic genius.[3] Beatrice represents the image or muse who sets in motion the poetic process (*Letters*, p. 731). Lear and Beatrice thus represent two figures in Yeats's version of the Oedipal myth: the aged Oedipus and the object of desire or incestuous image. These figures are followed in the narrator's vision by Aphrodite and Mary, representing the pagan and the Christian views of love so important in Yeats's cyclical view of history.

The vision, then, hints at the nature of the narrator's submerged passions, which it is suggested will somehow be gratified in mystical union. His fear of losing control is fear of abandonment to his own impulses. Through his terror he hears a voice, a disciple of the Arab doctor and mystic Avicenna, telling him that "all life proceeds out of corruption" (*Mythologies*, p. 276), an idea Yeats will develop further in "Crazy Jane Talks with the Bishop." In "Rosa Alchemica," however, the idea that corruption is inevitable and necessary is too much for the narrator. He sinks immediately into a trance: his objective mirror breaks, he feels conquered by vision, sinks into a deep sea that becomes fire and sweeps him away, sees pale hands and faces, hears caressing voices, and finally sees death—"Beauty herself"—and falls like "a drop of molten gold" back into the world. He comments that he has "felt fixed habits and principles dissolving before a power, which was hysterical passion or sheer madness," a power so overwhelming that it makes him tremble. He then projects his own fear of

[3] Yeats, *A Vision* (New York: Macmillan, 1961), p. 28.

dissolution onto the world, which he feels is "about to plunge . . .
into a night as obscure as that which followed the downfall of the
classical world" (*Mythologies*, pp. 277, 278, 280).

The vision reveals turbulent material from the narrator's unconscious. The sea of flame, the caressing hands, the narrator's
sensation of melting and falling back to earth as a drop of molten
gold—all these represent the sexual process from initial excitation
to emission.[4] The connection of this vision with personages from
Yeats's version of the Oedipal drama, Lear and Beatrice, suggests
some awareness on Yeats's part that the vision is related to an
incestuous fantasy. The narrator experiences the vision not as
enlightenment, but as a disturbing, fundamentally sexual experience. He is not completely put off by his first try, however, and
goes on to experience a more specific vision. While awaiting initiation into the Order of the Alchemical Rose, he sees a woman and
describes her as follows: "her cheeks were hollowed by what I
would have held, had I seen her anywhere else, an excitement of
the flesh and a thirst for pleasure, instead of which it doubtless
was an excitement of the imagination and a thirst for beauty"
(*Mythologies*, pp. 282–83). This description focuses our attention
on the sexual elements and juxtaposes sexual and spiritual excitement in a way that would become characteristic of the later Yeats.

After learning an intricate antique dance, the narrator passes
into a room where alchemy has apparently yielded gold (or spirit).
He is surrounded by dancing men and women and a mosaic depicting a battle between gray Christian angels and an array of glimmering pagan gods. Robartes thus seems to be making good on his
promise to bring the narrator into communion with the gods,
whose radiant individuality, as contrasted with the colorless same-
ness of the angels, links them to the hero and the poet.

All the gods have dancers for partners except Eros, who moves
alone and seems to be the presiding spirit. The narrator sees "the
brightness of uttermost desire" in the eyes of the dancers, "as

---

[4] The alchemical ritual, itself full of sexual parallels, from which Yeats
derived much of his imagery for this story is particularly suited to a representation of Yeats's fantasies.

though they had found at length, after unreckonable wandering, the lost love of their youth" (i.e., the ideal love, the incestuous image). A Voice speaks: "into the dance, into the dance, that the gods may make them bodies out of the substance of our hearts" (*Mythologies*, p. 289). The narrator is suddenly swept by a "mysterious wave of passion," and finds himself dancing with a woman with black lilies in her hair. He recoils from her in the horrified realization that she is "drinking up" his soul; she is a vampire woman of the sort Aleel saw among the demon-conspirators of *Cathleen*. As he recovers he presses his rosary to his heart, "and then the war that rages within me at other times is still, and I am at peace" (*Mythologies*, p. 292).

Yeats seems to be representing here his own fear of being harmed by close contact with a woman. As in *The Shadowy Waters*, the metaphor is oral—the vampire woman drinks the narrator's soul "as an ox drinks up a wayside pool" (*Mythologies*, p. 290). It suggests an early fantasy of injuring the mother by sucking her dry, which is reflected in the regressive fantasy that the same will be done to him. Robartes releases images from the narrator's unconscious without providing any support for his ego; hence the narrator panics when he loses his mirror-like surface and is threatened by fusion and dissolution. The narrator's turning to the talismanic rosary reflects Yeats's own way of mastering fright. In Yeats's case, however, talismanic objects brought a freedom and courage in investigating the unconscious that is not shown by the narrator, who simply becomes unimaginatively and defensively rigid.[5]

Yeats continues his investigation of unlimited spiritual desire and its turbulent sensual subsurface in "The Tables of the Law." The story's central figure, Owen Aherne, is a heretical Catholic who is tempted by the same images Robartes worships. His story

[5] Whitaker, approaching the story from a Jungian viewpoint, also sees the visions as a "projection of [the narrator's] own darker longings." Whitaker, however, while implying that the narrator should have faced "the responsibility of meeting and assimilating Robartes, his shadow-self," instead of retreating to a "timid Christian moralism," neglects the psychologically crucial talismanic object. *Swan and Shadow*, p. 42.

starts in much the same way as "Rosa Alchemica," with a discussion of unlimited desire: the narrator links Aherne's face with the image of "a man holding a flame in his naked hand" (*Mythologies*, p. 293), explaining that Aherne seems to him a superior type, the man who has risen above the practical toward unbounded desires. He has a "fanciful hatred of all life" (*Mythologies*, p. 294), expressed in the paradox that the beautiful arts will overthrow life by sowing unlimited and thus insatiable desire. Like the narrator in the previous story, Aherne is surrounded by paintings, all of which give evidence of "absolute emotion."

The narrator of "Rosa Alchemica" moved from his aesthete's retreat into an abyss of unconscious impulses. Aherne's progress is similar, but whereas the fantasy behind the narrator's visions in "Rosa Alchemica" seems to be one of fusion with the mother, the central fantasy in "The Tables of the Law"—from a later stage of development—is one of rebellion against the father. Things are correspondingly more under control in Aherne's story than in the previous one. Instead of seeing his impulses manifest as vision, Aherne discovers a prophet, Joachim de Flora, whose writings announce the triumph of spirit over law. The fact that the impulsive material is presented in a book already distances it, but Yeats goes further: the book, embossed and illustrated by famous Renaissance artists, is itself contained in a box made by Cellini. The book and box together—works of art—constitute a talismanic object that contains and binds dangerous impulses. Yeats describes the book as he would later describe his prized Japanese sword (another talismanic object), as having been passed on "from generation to generation" (*Mythologies*, p. 297).

Aherne, after showing the narrator box and book, tells him about the doctrine it contains. As Aherne interprets Joachim's doctrine, it resembles Blake's notion that energy is divine. Spirit includes all impulses, which become the highest law. Aherne, stressing the Blakean aspects of Joachim, names poets and wits who have broken the commandments and suggests that breaking the law is itself of value. The theme is a familiar one from the time of Yeats's *Oisin*: a rebellion against the father-God Urizen in the name of impulse.

Yeats goes on to make explicit the connection between the artist and Joachim, who considers himself elected "to reveal that hidden substance of God which is color and music and softness and a sweet odour." The holy prophet like the artist is in a realm beyond good and evil; he accepts no law and admits "no father but the Holy Spirit. Just as poets and painters and musicians labour at their works, building them with lawless and lawful things alike, so long as they embody the beauty that is beyond the grave" (*Mythologies*, p. 300). Aherne himself wants to emulate Joachim. He has had tiny ivory tablets made to replace the broken tables of the law, and wishes to write there "my secret law . . . just as poets and romance-writers have written the principles of their art in prefaces" (*Mythologies*, p. 301).

The narrator, sensing the destructiveness behind Aherne's self-glorification, stands up for orthodoxy. Ten years later, the narrator sees Aherne again. This time Aherne not only admits that his doctrine is dangerous, but explains that it has led to his damnation. To be united to God one must first feel separated from Him. "God has made a simple and an arbitrary law that we may sin and repent!" (*Mythologies*, p. 305). Since Aherne, following only the laws of his own self-development, no longer believes in external law or sin, he can never achieve union with God. At the end of "The Tables of the Law" Aherne takes the submissive posture of a child before God and his representatives, the angels. It is all right, he says, for the angels, who have pure bodies, to follow their impulses and "thirst for the immortal element in hope, in desire, in dreams; but we whose hearts perish every moment, and whose bodies melt away . . . must bow and obey!" (*Mythologies*, p. 305).

Both "Rosa Alchemica" and "The Tables of the Law" contain elements of undoing or reversal, which suggests that though Yeats can conceive of tolerating his impulses, he is not yet secure about expressing them. In "Rosa Alchemica," the narrator retreats from his orgiastic vision to the shelter of Catholicism. Aherne, too, first follows his impulses and then surrenders to self-doubt. Yeats admits that a similar self-distrust, expressed in obsessive rumination, characterized his own relation to his instincts[6] and kept him from acting spontaneously. Joachim's command to obey spirit, to find holiness in one's desires, may represent an attempt on Yeats's part to overcome paralyzing, obsessive thoughts. In both stories, Yeats seems to be trying out ways to tolerate his instincts without being overcome by them.

Although Yeats's position vacillates (he undoes), there are some signs of progress toward the double aim of freer expression and more ego-syntonic control. In the first story impulse is first denied and then completely out of control. By the end of his story, the narrator ceases to deny the existence of a turbulent inner world, but consciously uses his talismanic rosary as protection against further involvement. "The Tables of the Law" is a more intellectual and distanced story. Though impulses are symbolically bound in box and book, Aherne's task, which is essentially to be his own god and write "the secret law of my own being," is too much for him. Aherne relinquishes his freedom and rebinds himself through obsessive reasoning about his wickedness and alienation. This type of reasoning, like the denial of impulse by the narrator of "Rosa Alchemica," does not master impulse but thwarts it or blots it out. The narrator, failing to come to terms with his emotions, is extremely unhappy. He feels dirty, "leprous," and guilty, full of "boundless wickedness" even when he has turned away from forbidden impulses and become a priest.

The third story, "The Adoration of the Magi," suggests the advent of a new era, in which the values of Christianity are reversed. This Apocalypse, however, lacks force. Although Yeats hints at the arrival of a new pagan god—"another Leda would open her knees to the swan"[7]—he has difficulty describing him. In early versions of the story, he avoids the problem by naming over the sacred talismans of Celtic Ireland—Cauldron, Whetstone, Sword, and

[6] Letter to Robert Gregory, cited in Ellmann, *Man and Masks*, pp. 174–75.
[7] *Ibid.*, p. 241.

Spear. By the final version, however, he has arrived at the arresting dynamism of the Unicorn-god. Perhaps Yeats's hesitancy in imaginatively representing his new god spurred his development of the symbolic unicorn in *Where There Is Nothing* and *The Unicorn from the Stars.* In the later play, the beast has the same qualities of self-sufficiency, coldness, and passion that it will have in the final version of "The Adoration of the Magi." In a letter of 1908 to the publisher A. H. Bullen, Yeats implies that the play makes explicit the vague hints of the earlier story: "I planned out *The Unicorn* [*from the Stars*] to carry to a more complete realization the central idea of the stories in *The Secret Rose*" (*Letters,* p. 503). He apparently considered rewriting the story then, to make it, too, more explicit (probably by introducing the figure of the unicorn). In his diary of 1908–9, Yeats explored the idea of revising the story to accord with the concepts of self and mask that he was to develop in *The Player Queen* (*Memoirs,* p. 138). Much later, in 1925, Yeats did in fact revise his story, using the symbol he had developed earlier to striking effect. The story has become a parable of self-sufficiency, the mask achieved.

"The Adoration of the Magi" also presents a solution to the problem of freely expressed impulse. The poet may give expression to his impulses without guilt by transforming them into art. The birth of the unicorn from a prostitute symbolizes this transformation. The cold, self-sufficient artifact is rooted in passion, "so malevolent a flame" (*Mythologies,* p. 311). Even the timid narrator realizes that writing down something that involves forbidden impulses binds it and deprives it of its potential to harm: "I have grown to believe that there is no dangerous idea which does not become less dangerous when written out in sincere and careful English" (*Mythologies,* p. 309). The unicorn is not only the god of a new era, but, along with the poem, the poet's mask. He is the "most unlike man of all living things, being cold, hard and virginal" (*Mythologies,* p. 312). In terms of the binding of impulse through mask and talisman, the unicorn's coldness and hardness are particularly important. Impulse as expressed in the finished work is impulse refined and no longer dangerous. Later, when speaking of the artist Aubrey Beardsley, Yeats asks: "Does not all art come when a nature, that never ceases to judge itself, exhausts personal emotion in action or desire so completely that something impersonal, something that has nothing to do with action or desire, suddenly starts into its place?" (*Autobiography*, p. 200).

After representing, and implicitly criticizing, both his early aesthetic self and the destructive vision of uncontrolled impulses in "Rosa Alchemica" and "The Tables of the Law," and hinting at the advent of a new era in "The Adoration of the Magi," Yeats began to find ways to synthesize destructive elements with more creative ones, and to present a new, more creative vision. This vision, shown as an ideal realized by the bards of old, was first expressed in two essays jointly titled "Thoughts on Lady Gregory's Translations" (1903), which introduced her work.

The distinctive thing about the ancient Irish story-tellers and bards, Yeats tells us, is that they could respect and love life because they were not frustrated in their longing for miracle. Because of their closeness to nature and their still unspoiled sense of wonder, they believed "in the historical reality of even their wildest imaginations."[8] Thus their lives were, in a sense, perpetual vision, and in this they have a distinct advantage over the narrator of "Rosa Alchemica," who is continually striving for vision. And though the bard's vision of a promised land took on a highly elaborated form, it did not lead him to wish for the destruction of life, but enhanced his enjoyment of it—a key difference between his visions and those of Aherne and Robartes. Though the bard continually "reshaped the world according to his heart's desire" (*Agate*, p. 6), he did not reject it. He rearranged and intensified elements of it to create new patterns. His imagination, moreover, was fed by a full life of the senses, and his most faithful presentations were always of the human emotions of love, terror, and friendship. In the past, as Yeats sees it, the bards were very much

[8] Yeats, *The Cutting of An Agate* (New York: Macmillan, 1912), p. 3; hereafter cited in the text as *Agate*. (The two essays on Lady Gregory's work were omitted from later editions of this collection.)

like the heroes they sang of. Only their proverbial blindness made them celebrants of heroic action rather than heroes themselves. Inhabitants of Eden, constantly engaged in joyous activity, they sought only love and companionship, and let no thought of another life "ever [trouble] their delight in one another" (*Agate*, p. 23) (as it troubled Forgael).

In this vision of harmony Yeats thus postulates a time when dream and reality were enough alike that the poet could create out of a love of life, not a denial of it: "their [the bards'] invisible life is but the life about them made more perfect and more lasting" (*Agate*, p. 25). The bard who feels complete and in harmony with the world because he has everything he needs exemplifies the self-sufficiency Yeats wished for. Psychologically, such an image is perhaps closest to the Eden of the nursing child, for whom desire would simply be for an increase of the good already experienced. By 1906 Yeats seems aware that his ideal of physical wholeness and satisfaction is derived from memories of early childhood: "I am orthodox and pray for a resurrection of the body, and am certain that a man should find his Holy Land where he first crept upon the floor."[9] Yeats's vision is of an essentially unfallen existence, and emphasizes the importance of the body as a source of both emotional satisfaction and creativity.

One cannot discuss Yeats's model of the bard and his efforts to simplify and solidify his work in the early 1900's without discussing his relationship with Lady Gregory. When Yeats met her she was already working "to add dignity to Ireland,"[10] and he was badly in need of self-respect and self-sufficiency. Although the considerable popular success of his early poetry undoubtedly made Yeats feel more confident and freer to experiment, it failed to give him the sense of self-sufficiency and power he desired. Reading over the proofs of his first book of poetry, he perceived that it was "a flight into fairyland" (*Letters*, p. 63). The self-criticism implicit in this judgment and in the irony with which he presents the narrator in

[9] *Ibid.*, p. 115. "The Holy Places."
[10] Elizabeth Coxhead, *Lady Gregory: A Literary Portrait* (New York: Harcourt, Brace, 1961), p. 62.

"Rosa Alchemica" suggests that it was his own negative feelings about his poetry "of longing and complaint" (*Letters*, p. 63) that urged him in a new direction. But he might never have gone so far in that direction without the support of Lady Gregory.

Lady Gregory's relationship to Yeats had a very special function: it gave Yeats a chance to repeat or re-experience parts of his childhood in a more positive way. She became the educating and nurturing mother in a variety of aspects extending over the whole area of early mother-child relationships. She encouraged Yeats to acknowledge his bodily needs. She concerned herself with his physical and mental health. She taught him "real" speech. And, finally, she provided him with models that he later incorporated into his own identity. In all these roles, Lady Gregory often counteracted the influence of Yeats's own mother. For example, Susan Yeats, as we have seen, was disgusted by physical facts, and Yeats may sometimes have felt that she would have preferred him without a body. Lady Gregory, by contrast, though she was extremely proper, even asexual, in her conduct, and eschewed explicit scatological and sexual detail in her writings, clearly delighted in the earthy stories of the Irish heroes and gave them new life in her translations.

An important aspect of Lady Gregory's mothering consisted in showing Yeats (and future generations of Irishmen) how to be healthy. Praising her works, Yeats stresses their special appropriateness for Irish youth, which "would make me give them before all other books to young men and girls in Ireland."[11] With the ancient heroes as models, the new generation will grow up in their likeness, clean and strong. (Compare *The King's Threshold*, where children grow up crippled and diseased because they have listened to the wrong poets.) Yeats recounts Lady Gregory's prescribed treatment for his own case: "Finding that I could not work, and thinking the open air salutary, Lady Gregory brought me from cottage to cottage collecting folklore" (*Autobiography*, p. 242). When he recovered, Yeats made sure that Lady Gregory continued

11 Cited in Bushrui, *Yeats's Verse-Plays*, p. 46.

in her maternal role; she was now to occupy herself with his mental health: "When I was in good health again, I found myself indolent . . . and asked her to send me to my work every day . . . , rating me with idleness if need be, and I doubt if I should have done much with my life but for her firmness and her care."[12]

As an embodiment of what he called in 1901 "the Great Memory" (*Anima Mundi*), Lady Gregory both provided Yeats with images and gave him the confidence to use them. Her involvement with Ireland's dignity enabled him to see that "to assume the mask of some other self"[13] was a sacred duty—an example of the way images could work to raise a totally new generation of Irishmen. Yeats freely used Lady Gregory's work as a quarry for his own. His first long play written after meeting her, *On Baile's Strand*, is founded on an incident in her *Cuchulain of Murithemne*, and he speaks of her *Cuchulain* as being "the substantial origin of my own art."[14] As we shall see in Chapter 4, this play represents Yeats's first important attempt to deal openly with his father conflict. By providing the source, Lady Gregory partly relieved him of responsibility for what he was writing.

She also collaborated actively in the writing of the plays themselves. Yeats writes in the dedication to *Kathleen Ni Houlihan*: "We turned my dream into [this] little play, and when we . . . found that the working people liked it, you helped me put my other dramatic fables into speech."[15] And in 1904 Yeats wrote about *The Pot of Broth*: "I hardly know how much of the play is my work, for Lady Gregory helped me as she has helped in every play of mine where there is dialect. . . . I had no mastery of speech that purported to be of real life."[16] In a way, then, Lady Gregory taught Yeats to talk.

Yeats's introduction to common speech was only one element of this literary collaboration. Lady Gregory also stimulated the

12 Jeffares, *W. B. Yeats*, p. 120.
13 1909 diary, cited in Ellmann, *Man and Masks*, p. 174.
14 Cited in Bushrui, p. 41.
15 Coxhead, *Lady Gregory*, pp. 67–68.
16 *Ibid.*, pp. 105–6.

development of his theories of tragicomedy, first applied in *On Baile's Strand*.[17] Here, the characters of Fool and Blind Man—the comic types Lady Gregory delighted to help Yeats with—are the "shadows" of the tragic protagonists on a lower plane. Yeats explains this in a letter of 1904 to Frank Fay. Cuchulain, he writes, "is the fool—wandering, passive, houseless and almost loveless. Concobhar is reason that is blind because it can only reason because it is cold" (*Letters*, p. 425). The division into tragic hero and comic double is important, because through it Yeats externalizes and so distances the distinction between high and low that he felt in himself. Although the collaboration between Yeats and Lady Gregory did not produce great art, it began a psychological process that allowed him to feel more self-sufficient and capable. At this stage he got permission to be earthy and "real" from a specific mother figure who functioned as a sort of alter ego, and as a comic mask he used to enlarge the boundaries of self; in his late poems with Crazy Jane and the wild, wicked old man, earthiness has been integrated with the self.

Having taken as a model the bard whose creativity was rooted in the body, Yeats criticizes not only his own early work, but previous models he now felt neglected the body. He is particularly critical of Shelley (Bloom shows how much Yeats distorted Shelley in the process of turning away from him),[18] giving him as an example of the poet who could not move the ordinary man because he split the soul from the body. There are two choices, Yeats tells us elsewhere: "upward, into ever-growing subtlety" (the art surrounding Robartes and Aherne), "or downward, taking the soul with us until all is simplified and solidified again" (*Agate*, p. 59). Yeats's criticism of Shelley as a poet of the upper way (of "infinite desire") should be seen as part of his own struggle against the desire to take flight permanently, like so many of his contemporaries, into the vaporous pre-Raphaelite world.

An important tenet of Yeats's new position was that heterosexual intercourse was necessary not only for one's art, but for one's san-

---

17 Bushrui, p. 42.
18 Bloom, *Yeats*, pp. 53–63, esp. 61–62.

ity. The full extent of Yeats's fears about celibacy and (as the first draft of his autobiography shows) masturbation is revealed in *The Words Upon the Window-Pane*, a play about Jonathan Swift that Yeats wrote in 1930. Yeats had long been preoccupied with Swift's life. He wrote in the introduction to the play, "Swift haunts me; he is always just round the next corner."[19] In the play, Vanessa pleads with Swift to marry her, to gratify his "strong passions." Her blood, she says, will overcome his hereditary taint and make their children healthy. He refuses because he is afraid of passing madness on. Swift's eventual end as a "dirty old man," his "brain gone," his face covered with boils, serves as a terrible warning to those who abuse the body. Yeats seems to have viewed Swift's madness and certain scatological aspects of his writing as an eruption in unclean form of sexual thoughts, a frighteningly possible alternative to Yeats's new acceptance of sexuality. In a letter written in 1933 he says, "The man who ignores the poetry of sex, let us say, finds the bare facts written upon the walls of a privy, or is himself compelled to write them there."[20]

This idea is explicit later in his portraits of his friends in the section of his *Autobiography* called "The Trembling of the Veil" (1922). He shows how Lionel Johnson, a man of the highest visionary ambitions, exhausts his strength trying to repress his sensuality, refusing to concede anything to the claims of the body. This effort of will is ultimately self-destructive because each resurgence of natural desire leads him to a despair that yields only to drink. Yeats relates how, after he had drunk a great deal, Johnson praised a father of the church "who freed himself from sexual passion by a surgical operation" (*Autobiography*, p. 135). Castration, self-imposed or otherwise, both haunted and fascinated Yeats throughout

19 *Variorum Plays*, p. 958.
20 *Letters*, pp. 818–19. The strength of Yeats's belief in sexual intercourse as a prophylactic measure can be inferred from his response in March 1937 to an invitation to lecture in India. He had to refuse, he explained, because the tour would require him to repress the sexual desire his Steinach operation had revived. "I believe," he wrote, "that if I repressed this for any long period I would break down under the strain." Cited in Roger McHugh, ed., *Ah, Sweet Dancer: W. B. Yeats–Margot Ruddock, A Correspondence* (London: Macmillan, 1970), p. 117.

his life. Masochistic imagery involving self-castration, as we shall see, informs "The Cap and Bells," and castration is a major theme of the late dance plays. The self-torture Yeats portrays in his friends and fellow poets relates to the masochism he himself is struggling to repudiate—a struggle that lasted as long as his life.

Yeats's early model of harmony, the bard, is indicative of his struggle to accept his body and to repudiate his masochism, but it was just one stroke in a battle waged on many fronts. Yeats also evolved a new theory of poetry—which might be described as a poetics of incarnation—to accompany his views about the importance of the body. Preoccupied with the dangers of formlessness, in 1903 he conceptualized his preoccupation as an opposition between boundlessness (emotion, the moon) and the controlling poet (form, the sun). The folk or race "thirsts to escape out of bounds, to lose itself in some unbounded tidal stream" (*Agate*, p. 29). Folk art expresses basic emotions in an essentially loose way. It becomes the poet's task, therefore, to give such emotions precise individual shape or body. In his discussion of the bards, Yeats emphasized that "because they were as much excited as a monk over his prayers, they did not think sufficiently about the shape of the poem and the story" (*Agate*, pp. 1–2). Yeats later identified this common emotion with *Anima Mundi*. As we have seen, the prototype of the physical form of *Anima Mundi* was the womb-like cavern from which Oisin receives help. Thus Yeats's fear of dispersion and loss of substance, like his aversion to formlessness in literature, is closely related to his fear of the female body. This fear is dealt with explicitly in late poems like "A Dialogue of Self and Soul," where woman is symbolized by a "fecund ditch." "A Dialogue" also illustrates Yeats's use of hard talismanic objects—the ancestral sword—to enable him to face his impulses (and a woman's body) with less fear of dissolution. It is only with the protective sword across his knees that the "I" is able to contemplate formless and frightening life.[21]

His new emphasis on form is thus crucial in distinguishing between the earlier poet-mystic and the bard. In a letter transmitting *Ideas of Good and Evil* to A.E. in May 1903, Yeats wrote: "I feel

21 *Variorum Poems*, pp. 477–79.

about me and in me an impulse to create form, to carry the realization of beauty as far as possible. The Greeks said that the Dionysiac enthusiasm preceded the Apollonic and that the Dionysiac was sad and desirous, but that the Apollonic was joyful and self-sufficient" (*Letters*, p. 402). Much later, Yeats explained why he "could not" use free verse: "I would lose myself, become joyless."[22] Joy requires having a clear-cut, precise outline; as Yeats says, "the very essence of genius is precision." Here, Yeats himself relates the need for definite form to his fear of dispersion (I would lose myself) and dissolution: "all that is personal soon rots; it must be packed in ice or salt."[23] Hard images and concrete diction are as necessary as precise form. "Adam's Curse" (1902), Yeats's first poem to show a new naturalness of style and diction, gives solidity to the idea of writing poetry by comparing it to hard labor:

> I said: 'A line will take us hours maybe;
> Yet if it does not seem a moment's thought,
> Our stitching and unstitching has been naught.
> Better go down upon your marrow-bones
> And scrub a kitchen pavement, or break stones
> Like an old pauper, in all kinds of weather;
> For to articulate sweet sounds together
> Is to work harder than all these. . . .'[24]

Apollonic discipline is not only difficult, but "joyous and self-sufficient." Aherne and the uncreative narrator of "Rosa Alchemica" failed to achieve either control or self-sufficiency. Seven years later in his introduction to Lady Gregory's translations, Yeats identifies Adam with the creative self. The bard resembles Adam, "who created all things out of himself by nothing more important than an unflagging fancy"—an interpretation that makes naming things the real creative act, and in the interests of self-sufficiency leaves out God the Father (*Agate*, p. 21). During this same period, as we have seen, Yeats portrayed a completely self-sufficient hero in *The King's Threshold,* out of a need to deny the hurt inflicted by Maud Gonne.

In a sense, then, Yeats's insistence on self-sufficiency originated

---

22 Yeats, *Essays and Introductions* (London: Macmillan, 1961), pp. 522–23.
23 *Ibid*, p. 522.
24 Yeats, *Variorum Poems*, pp. 204–5.

as a defensive maneuver. In his prose, Yeats speaks of several ways of compensating for defects in the real world through fantasy. One way is unspecific; art appears as a superior form of daydream. In the story "Anima Hominis" (1917) art is described as a compensating dream; there are certain men whose art is "a compensation for some accident of health or circumstance" (*Mythologies*, p. 327). In *Ego Dominus Tuus* Yeats cites the example of Keats, who "poor, ailing and ignorant" wrote "luxuriant song" (*Mythologies*, p. 323). A more specific sort of compensation and one more relevant to Yeats's own work is what he calls, in discussing Dante, the re-creation of a lost, precious object. This object is ultimately an incestuous one, symbolized later by an equally unattainable woman.

Yeats painstakingly demonstrated in his later work the ways in which this "daimon" influenced the poet's work. What his view amounts to, finally, is that the poet can never achieve his object in reality—though he may re-create it in words. In re-creating the object in words, the poet becomes independent of everything outside himself; he becomes self-sufficient. Though life as Yeats saw it is tragic, there is compensation in the workings of imagination, a purely inner joy that "is in the arrangement of events as in the words, and in that touch of extravagance, of irony, of surprise, which is set there after the desire of logic has been satisfied . . . and that leaves one, not in the circling necessity, but caught up into the freedom of self-delight." It is this joy "of making and mastering," that "remains in the hands and tongue of the artist," while with his eyes he contemplates "the great irremediable things" (*Agate*, pp. 129–30). Art thus gives the artist the power to experience deprivation, to contemplate frightening events without being overwhelmed. Satisfactions from outside almost cease to matter: "Our minds, being sufficient to themselves, do not wish for victory, but are content to elaborate our extravagance" (*Agate*, p. 190).

Yeats's desire for self-sufficiency is reflected in new attitudes toward substance that are connected with the way he experiences himself, i.e., as a unity of mind, body, and ordinary personality. He describes the change in an essay in the *Discoveries* section of *The Cutting of An Agate* called "The Tree of Life," in which he

explains that the poet must find a place midway on the tree between essence and physical fact. At one time, he says, he cared only
for the upper region, "states of mind, lyrical moments, intellectual
essences"—i.e. "impersonal beauty." He wanted to put himself
into his poetry, but he understood this self as the stuff of his visions,
the immortal part or essence. Though these visions originated in
his mind, he experienced them as abstracted from him and projected them outward.

> As I imagined the visions outside myself my imagination became full of
> decorative landscape and of still life. I thought of myself as something
> unmoving and silent living in the middle of my own mind and body, a
> grain of sand ... that Satan's watch-fiends cannot find. Then one day I
> understood quite suddenly ... that I was seeking something unchanging
> and unmixed and always outside myself, a Stone or an Elixir that was
> always out of reach, and that I myself was the fleeting thing that held out
> its hand.

In recognizing that he himself was a suitable object for poetry, he
was making obvious progress toward solidity. Hereafter, he says,
"I entered into myself and pictured myself and not some essence"
(*Agate*, pp. 68–69). The shift in emphasis from perfect ethereal
visions sought outside the self to the "personality as a whole" is
precisely put in a letter to Yeats's father in 1913: "Of recent years
instead of 'vision,' meaning by vision the intense realization of a
state of ecstatic emotion symbolized in a definite imagined region,
I have tried for more self-portraiture" (*Letters*, p. 583).

Yeats's increasing talk in later years about the importance of
the self and its emotions was somewhat deceptive. The move from
"vision" to self-portraiture was a real one, but the self in question
was always a highly dramatized and so nonsubjective one, always
seen through mask and image. Yeats's concept of mask was first
fully dramatized in *The Player Queen*, begun in 1907 or 1908, in
which the characters all seek their anti-selves or masks. The play,
with its actress heroine who becomes a queen, illustrates the way
Yeats tried to exploit his models of bard and hero as anti-selves
that must somehow be joined to the self, to use the mask to assimilate a whole new set of qualities to the self, which is the real subject of poetry. More than just the social self, or the discrepancy

between the self and other people's view of it, the mask supplies the qualities that creatively oppose or are missing from the poet's personality, what Yeats calls in "Anima Hominis" an "opposing virtue." "Every passionate man," Yeats felt, was somehow linked "to another age, historical or imaginary, where alone he finds images that rouse his energy" (*Autobiography*, p. 93). The difficulty of achieving bardic (or heroic) unity of being makes it appropriate for a mask which, Yeats tells us, should be "of all things not impossible, the most difficult." Yeats's later heroes, particularly Cuchulain, are in a sense the poet's masks, which like the bard express confidence and spontaneous joy.

The mask of spontaneity is important as a defense against obsessive thinking. In 1910 Yeats quarreled with Lady Gregory when Edmund Gosse, an old friend of Yeats's, wrote Lady Gregory an insulting letter and Yeats failed to condemn him as quickly as the Gregorys expected. Yeats's letter of explanation to Lady Gregory's son Robert shows his awareness of the mask as a means of recapturing spontaneity (*Memoirs*, pp. 252–53):

My Dear Robert: I want you to understand that I have no instincts in personal life. I have reasoned them all away, and reason acts very slowly and with difficulty and has to exhaust every side of the subject. Above all, I have destroyed in myself, by analysis, instinctive indignation.... As I look back, I see occasion after occasion on which I have been prevented from doing what was a natural and sometimes the right thing either because analysis of the emotion or action of another, or self-distrustful analysis of my own emotion destroyed impulse.... All last week the moment that my impulse told me I should demand with indignation an apology from Gosse, my analysis said,... "You want to do a passionate thing because it stirs your pride."... In impersonal and public things, because there this distrust of myself does not come in, I have impulse.... I even do my writing by self-distrusting reasons. I thought to write this note in the same way as I write the others. And then I said, "I am really explaining myself to Robert Gregory. I am afraid to write to him directly or speak to him directly, and so I am writing this note thinking that some chance may show it to him. So I will write it as if to him." Since then, while writing it, I have thought this an insincerity, for I have understood that I am trying to put myself right with myself even more than with you....

All my moral endeavor for many years has been an attempt to re-create practical instinct in myself. I can only conceive of it as of a kind of acting [i.e., as mask-wearing].

A few days after writing this letter, as Ellmann notes, Yeats wrote his poem "The Mask" (his first explicit use of the word).[25]

In a fascinating passage in "Anima Hominis," Yeats explains that he achieves his mask or at least the sensation of an "heroic condition" while creating: "I begin to dream of eyelids that do not quiver before the bayonet: all my thoughts have ease and joy, I am all virtue and confidence" (*Mythologies*, p. 325). Tragic art, as opposed to "happy art," will express not only the poet's vision of joy (or heroism), but will suggest the ways in which this vision arose from the poet's need, "the poverty or the exasperation that set its maker to the work." True art is the result not only of struggle against the world but of inner warfare: "the division of a mind within itself." When the artist refuses this struggle, the joy he presents seems unconvincing, a "hollow image of fulfilled desire."

The ultimate test of the genuine poetic vision consists in its revelation of man's most profound desires. It must be "a vision of reality which satisfies the whole being." Yeats attempts a systematic albeit obscure revelation of man's most profound desires in *A Vision*, where he sets up Oedipus as the new God to replace Christ and makes the basically incestuous quest for the image his sacred equivalent of the search for the holy grail. Man's most urgent desires in Yeats's system as in Freud's are incestuous. But whereas analytic theory seeks to establish incestuous and other desires as general facts, Yeats mythologizes his conflict and gives it the dignity of a religion. Yeats's mythologizing of incestuous desire, though it runs through *A Vision*, is perhaps nowhere more strikingly evident than in the relationship it propounds between the man and his daimon. Bloom, after reflecting that this is the "darkest yet most vital of *A Vision*'s complexities," refers to it as Yeats's version of the Oedipus complex, of the encounter between libido and imago.[26] The daimon—in some sense, a poetic muse—is the incestuous image that stimulates the poet, makes him quest, and ultimately leads him to the discovery of his mask. His destiny can only be fulfilled through sexual love for a beautiful woman, a sub-

---

25 Ellmann, *Man and Masks*, p. 176.
26 Bloom, *Yeats*, p. 231.

stitute for the idealized image of the mother.[27] This is what Yeats seems to mean when he says "the relation of man and woman ... becomes an element where man and Daimon sport, pursue one another, and do one another good or evil."[28]

In a way now familiar to us, Yeats found supernatural sanction for the necessity of a frustrating relationship between poet and sweetheart (or daimon). The characteristic manner in which Yeats obtained supernatural reinforcement for tendencies within himself can be seen in the following episode, which concerns poet and sweetheart.

In 1927, in a letter to Olivia Shakespear, Yeats described a trip to a London medium. The medium gave him a book test: a shelf and page number that would lead him to a book in his study. He arrives at the Dante designs of Blake. The two plates are of Dante entering the holy fire and the serpent attacking Vanni Fucci. He comments: "The medium was the most stupid I know and certainly the knowledge was not in my head.... Certainly we suck always at the eternal dugs. How well too it puts my own mood between spiritual excitement, and the sexual torture and the knowledge that they are somehow inseparable!" Yeats goes on to say that earthly passion impelled Dante to purification: "it is the eyes of the Earthly Beatrice—she has not yet put on her divinity—that makes Dante risk the fire 'like a child that is offered an apple.' Immediately after comes the Earthly Paradise and the Heavenly Beatrice (*Letters*, p. 731).

This episode shows Yeats finding a double sanction for his own condition of mind during creativity. He sees it corresponding to a similar state of mind in Dante, and he sees the correspondence as pointed out to him by the supernatural. Sexual passion impelled Dante into the fire as it impelled Yeats to begin the creative process; as the purifying fire leads to heavenly vision, the creative

---

[27] Morton Seiden's interpretation is similar: Yeats "appears to believe, without committing himself, that a man may search for his Daimon in a beautiful woman, that this quest is a sublimation of incestuous desire, and that such desire as this can be fulfilled in dreams." *William Butler Yeats: The Poet as a Mythmaker, 1865–1939* (Lansing: Michigan State University Press, 1962), p. 69.

[28] The *A* version of *A Vision*, cited in Bloom, *Yeats*, p. 234.

process leads to the poetic vision or poem. A further comparison between himself and Dante is implicit in a rewritten poem about the Countess Cathleen that Yeats includes in his letter to Olivia. In this poem Cathleen (who as we have seen represents the depriving mother as well as the sweetheart) is transfigured and becomes "heaven itself." In *A Vision*, moreover, Yeats puts Dante in the same phase as himself (phase 17) and gives him the same frustrating muse.

The sequence of psychological events which Yeats was observing in himself, and for which he sought sanction in Dante and the supernatural, might be reconstructed as follows: "Sexual torture" set the creative process in motion. Sexual torture occurred because he was aroused to his utmost only by a woman he considered unattainable (the "daimon" of Yeats's personal mythology, the Oedipal mother). By their nature such desires could not be satisfied in reality and generated guilt and self-hatred. These feelings impelled Yeats to creation as a restitutive act: not only would he "re-create" the lost object in his work, but by creating good poems he would prove himself worthy of the woman he could not possess. The change in his state of mind would color his picture of the woman: she would become heavenly or "heaven itself," befitting Yeats's purified desire for her. The flame of passion becomes the flame of heavenly vision.

Elsewhere, Yeats deals with the role of sexual frustration in creativity in less metaphorical terms. Thus, in "Anima Hominis," he considers the importance of "purifying discouragement" as a means of transforming hopeless passion into art. Purifying discouragement involves commitment to a passion one knows to be hopeless, and the renunciation of all hope of satisfaction in real life. The passion then becomes vision, and the vision is transmuted into art. "The passions, when we know that they cannot find fulfillment, become vision; and a vision . . . prolongs its power by rhythm and pattern" (*Mythologies*, p. 341).

Yeats relates purifying discouragement to the psychoanalytic concepts of repression and the return of the repressed: "The doctors of medicine have discovered that certain dreams of the night . . . are the day's unfulfilled desire, and that our terror of desires condemned by the conscience has distorted and disturbed our dreams. They have only studied the breaking into dreams of elements that have remained unsatisfied without purifying discouragement."[29] Unrepressed, such elements can lead to madness, hysteria, or obsessional thinking. When repressed passion enters a dream, we must "break the logic that had given it the capacity of action and throw it into chaos again" (*Mythologies*, p. 341). In "Anima Mundi," another story of 1917, Yeats tells a cautionary tale about a lady, in a story by Balzac, who is not sufficiently conscious of her erotic wishes for purifying discouragement to free her of her obsessions. This lady, after a pious life, plans on her deathbed to flee with her renounced lover. "After death a dream, a desire she had perhaps ceased to believe in, perhaps ceased almost to remember, must have recurred again and again" (*Mythologies*, p. 353). A psychoanalyst would describe a recurrent dream as the repeated eruption into consciousness of ego-destroying impulses.

Thus far, Yeats's ideas approximate psychoanalytic concepts. But he does not see these ideas as useful in the same way a psychoanalyst would. He tells us in his *Autobiography* that "elaborate modern psychology sounds egotistical, I thought, when it speaks in the first person, but not those simple emotions which resemble the more, the more powerful they are, everybody's emotions" (*Autobiography*, p. 93). For Yeats, petty, egotistical emotions acquired importance and dignity by being transmuted via purifying discouragement into vision, myth, or works of art.

Yeats emphasizes that an active focusing of attention is essential to the mastery of unsatisfiable passion. One should try to hold this material "in the intellectual light where time gallops, and so keep it from slipping down into the sluggish vehicle" (*Mythologies*, p. 353). This active marshalling of one's thoughts contrasts with the passive experiences of the supernatural that, as we have seen, were so important to Yeats. Having an obsessive character, Yeats needed

---

[29] As Seiden points out (*Poet as Mythmaker*, p. 70), according to the Freudian theory of dreams as wish fulfillment, the desire "condemned by the conscience" would be incestuous desire.

to invoke reciprocally corrective active and passive experiences. The passive experiences brought him a sense of maternal support; the active experiences undid the danger of loss of autonomy and dissolution implicit in the passive experiences. The concept of *Anima Mundi* carried with it the frightening threat of "victimage": "all my proof that mind flows into mind, and that we cannot separate mind and body, drives me to accept the thought of victimage in many complex forms" (*Autobiography*, p. 199). But if a man took active measures to fend off the danger of victimage, he could safely immerse himself in *Anima Mundi*. The supremely pleasurable creative act, with its affirmation of both fusion and autonomy, was identified by Yeats with the joys of the afterlife: after death, as in creation, a man will be able to face his true feelings and become free of them, will see his life in "harmonies, symbols, and patterns, as though all were being refashioned by an artist" (*Mythologies*, p. 356).

Yeats sometimes used *Anima Mundi* to help resolve psychological stalemates. Shortly before Yeats broke off his relationship with Olivia Shakespear (as we saw in our discussion of *The Shadowy Waters*), he had a vision that sanctioned his desire to make the break and return to his hopeless passion for Maud Gonne. As reported in the *Autobiography* (p. 223), the vision was of a "naked woman of incredible beauty, standing upon a pedestal and shooting an arrow at a star." The vision corresponds to Yeats's view of Maud Gonne as goddess or queen. The archery image recurs in his descriptions of her "beauty like a tightened bow ... / ... high and solitary and most stern,"[30] and again in the portrait of Aoife in *On Baile's Strand*, which was derived from Maud Gonne: "that high, laughing, turbulent head / Thrown backward, and the bowstring at her ear."[31] Yeats does not refer to the personal significance the vision undoubtedly had for him, but stresses instead its archetypal meaning, which broadens personal emotion into myth. The mythic parallel, he says, is "the Mother-Goddess whose representative priestess shot the arrow at the child [star-son]" (*Autobiogra-*

30 Yeats, "No Second Troy," *Variorum Poems*, pp. 256–57.
31 *Variorum Plays*, p. 487.

phy, p. 343). The vision had all the greater authority for being shared by Arthur Symons and others, who, Yeats reports, had similar dreams the same night.

A year or so before he had this vision, in 1894, Yeats had a dream with a similar theme (also related to his desire to submit to Maud Gonne), which resulted in the poem "The Cap and Bells."[32] He says, in fact, that the "dream was more a vision than a dream, for it was beautiful and coherent, and gave me the sense of illumination and exaltation. . . . Blake would have said, 'The Authors are in eternity,' and I am quite sure they can be questioned only in dreams."[33] Yeats prized the poem above many of his others, though its meaning continually changed for him.

The cap and bells of the title belong to a jester. Poets in ancient times were often jugglers and jesters as well as bards; in Yeats's own work the fool in *A Vision* is associated with childlike innocence and wisdom. The jester in this poem is both child and poet. The cap and bells are symbols of his special skill in creating poems, and also of his sexual organs. The jester is in the same position as the poet-swineherd hero of *A Full Moon in March*; he is courting an unresponsive queen. The setting for the poem is a garden, a garden having typically Yeatsian Eden-mother associations. The garden has "fallen still," and the jester sends his soul to stand on the queen's windowsill. A window is a female image, and the line "He bade his soul rise upward" can be read as referring to an erection. In the first version Yeats had his soul rise in a "long and straight" blue garment; it has as its particular attribute a wise tongue, which it has gotten by thinking about the queen's footfall. The tongue is an appropriate member to be singled out in a poem about a poet; it can also have phallic significance. The queen will not listen, however, and rising in her nightgown, pushes down the latches. The poet-jester then tells his heart to go to her "In a red and quivering garment"—having the attributes of flame, phallus, and tongue. It had, in fact, "grown sweet-tongued by dreaming / Of a flutter of flower-like hair." At the end of the poem the queen's

---

[32] *Variorum Poems*, pp. 159–61.
[33] *Ibid.*, p. 808.

hair becomes the flower of joy, a beautiful image that fits perfectly with the garden, and in an early version, with the night that smelled "rich with June."

The jester, crushed by his second defeat, decides to send her his cap and bells and die. The loss of the cap and bells is the same—has the same effect—as the decapitation suffered by the later heroes of *King of the Great Clock Tower* and *A Full Moon in March*: it causes death and it is a symbolic castration. The queen, like her counterpart in the plays, accepts the offering, places it under her hair, and with her "red lips" sings it a love song "Till stars grow out of the air." The image of growth fits with the other images, and moreover makes the queen the mother of the star-child. *A Full Moon in March* contains a song about a drop of blood from a slain lover-enemy that impregnated a queen, and in this poem, although there is no blood and the head has been replaced by the symbolic cap, the idea is essentially the same. Holding the hat on her bosom like a child, she sings a love song.[34] When the dead lover-son is reborn as the star-child, she opens both door and window and is united with the heart and soul, now disembodied and purified.

The strong mood of peaceful joy evoked by the poem's last stanza echoes the joy Yeats derived from the dream experience itself. The joy of union described in the poem, the submissive escape from responsibility, corresponds to the pleasurable closeness of mother and child, and to the joy of direct contact with the Eternal Authors, *Anima Mundi*. Throughout Yeats's middle and later years, he continued to use *Anima Mundi* for support and creative stimulation—particularly in times of illness or stress. Its nourishing fluidity was the complementary aspect of his new hardness and self-confidence. The stronger he felt, the better able he was to use *Anima Mundi* without fear of dissolution.

[34] In the first version of the poem, recently published by Richard Londraville, there is a stronger sense of physical excitement ("She took them into her chamber / Her breast began to heave / She laid them upon her white breast") akin to the excitement shown later by the Queen in *A Full Moon in March* (quoted from *Ariel* [Calgary], 3 [July 1972], Plate 3 following p. 68). Yeats probably changed these lines not only for the obvious aesthetic reason, but because they disturbed the ethereal, asexual surface of the poem.

FOUR

The Dreamer Recast: Late Plays

THE IDEAL POET, as Yeats came to see him, observes reality truthfully and creates a pattern out of its harshness and discords. The destructive aspects of the poet's desire for perfection, along with other potentially dangerous wishes and emotions, are held in check by discipline and dedication to art.

Although the poet is a man "living in the presence of certain ideas,"[1] ideas are always subordinated to form and to emotion, for the poet speaks primarily to man's feelings. To speak to them effectively, he must simplify his own personality and project himself as the embodiment of a single emotion, the emotion felt by "lover or saint, sage or sensualist·(*Autobiography*, p. 53). And because, in Yeats's view, only impersonal emotion is persuasive, the poet must speak through mask or image, or offer us dreams and visions from beyond the self.

Yeats first incorporated his theories about discipline and emotion, mask and image, into *The Player Queen*. Because the play went through so many drafts during a particularly eventful period in Yeats's life (1907–8 to 1919), studying it will help us see both the varied uses of the mask and its relation to personal conflict. The play also shows Yeats attempting to clarify the relation of sexual energy to creativity. In this chapter, after examining in detail the way Yeats develops his ideas in *The Player Queen*, we will discuss a group of late ritual plays in which the central themes of *The Player Queen* are further explored.

The Player Queen concerns two lowly players who both assume exalted masks. Decima, longing to command, becomes a true queen.

---

[1] Yeats, as quoted by Ellmann, *Identity*, p. 43.

Septimus, inspired, is united with the pure Unicorn who heralds the end of the Christian Era. The story is as follows. A group of players has been invited to the Queen's palace to present "The Tragical History of Noah's Deluge." The imperious chief player, Decima, has run away to avoid playing the degraded part of Noah's wife and has locked out Septimus, her poet husband. Lying drunk in the street, Septimus hears a mob threaten to kill the Queen because she is reputedly a witch who couples nightly with a Unicorn. Septimus, roused by mention of the Unicorn, defends him, and comes to feel that he shares the Unicorn's divinity and purity. An old beggar enters who is known to go into a trance and bray like a donkey when the crown is about to change hands. He feels a trance approaching. Recognizing the beggar as inspired like himself, Septimus goes off with him as the first act ends. In the second act, the Real Queen appears, nun-like and drab, hoping for martyrdom. Decima is discovered by Nona, another actress in the troupe, hiding under the Queen's throne. In the ensuing argument between Nona and Decima, Decima learns that Nona has become Septimus's mistress. Septimus enters to announce that a New Dispensation is come, and that the Unicorn is the new Adam, whom Septimus will arouse with sensual music so that he may beget a new race. Decima asks Septimus to return to her. When he refuses she changes places with the Real Queen, who flees to a convent. Decima regally confronts the submissive mob and announces she will marry the Prime Minister. The play ends as she banishes the players.

The plot of *The Player Queen*, as one critic has remarked, is easy to distort in the retelling.[2] For one thing, it follows no apparent logic. One is uncertain whether such key events as the coupling of Real Queen and Unicorn are "true" or imagined. Moreover, the play is loaded with private meaning not available through a careful reading of the text. The incomplete merger of character portrayal and private myth leaves some rough edges (which, however, provide important clues to the psychological wellsprings of

2 Helen Hennessy Vendler, *Yeats's Vision and the Later Plays* (Cambridge, Mass.: Harvard University Press, 1963), p. 125.

the play). It is difficult, for example, to assimilate Decima the ambitious, self-realizing woman to her mythic role as harlot-Eve of the New Dispensation—a role, as we shall see, that does not develop from the character presented in the play, but is imposed by Yeats as an expression of fantasies and wishes. Besides the confusion caused by imperfectly integrated levels of meaning, the play suffers from inadequate development of the second, mythical theme. Decima's role as Eve, introduced late in the drafts, is only obscurely hinted at, whereas her ambitious character is explicit and pervasive.

Yeats's initial interest was not in the Unicorn but in the Player Queen, toward whom he seems always to have been deeply ambivalent. The contrast between her power and her lover's helplessness involves a masochism that obviously attracted Yeats, but that he apparently was fighting: he parodies the masochism of the Real Queen. Side by side with the masochistic desire to be humiliated by an all-powerful woman is the desire to identify with her power and be like her. There is no doubt that Yeats identified with his Player Queen. He wrote, for instance, of wanting "to lose myself in my Player Queen's life."[3] Decima had the energy Yeats believed necessary to a creative person, who must strive to become what he wants to be. This is related to Yeats's theory of the mask, as we shall see later.

If the fantasies underlying *The Player Queen* were the masochistic wish for humiliation by a powerful woman and the contrary wish to identify with her, Yeats also put much personal experience into the character of Decima and her relationship to the hero. He first mentions the play in an unpublished letter of June 11, 1908, to the masseuse Mabel Dickinson, his gymnastics teacher and friend. "I spent Monday evening with Mrs. Campbell and told her the story of *The Player Queen*. She seemed delighted and [asked] to buy it. . . . I would not agree. . . . I knew that if I had to think of pleasing anybody I could not write at all."[4] Yeats seems anxious to maintain his independence from the actress who has

---

[3] Unpublished letter to Mabel Dickinson, University of California, Berkeley.
[4] *Ibid.*

just triumphed in his *Deirdre,* and determined that the thought be entirely his and not changed to please a woman; it may not be entirely coincidental that in the drafts Yeats explores the question of the poet's control of his own dreams against the wishes of his leading lady, who wants to use them as a mask to glorify herself. By September, however, he had changed his mind and was writing with the actress "at my elbow." It seems likely from his description of Mrs. Campbell's "soul of fiery light" that, as Ure suggests, he first saw Decima, with her "energy of soul," as the successor to Deirdre in Mrs. Campbell's repertoire.[5] But as the character of Decima developed, Yeats poured into it his more complex feelings about Maud Gonne.

Yeats's initial work on the play coincided with a particularly difficult period in his relationship with Maud. In the letter of June 11, 1908, he says his nerves "are rather on the stretch just now but I expect to go to Paris [i.e., to see Maud] on Saturday." What Yeats expected from this trip is not clear. Perhaps he hoped that Maud, permanently estranged from John MacBride, would seek an annulment; her conversion to Catholicism made divorce impossible. He disappointedly wrote Miss Dickinson from Paris that Maud seemed content with her ambiguous status. He is weary, he writes, of "modern mystery and romance," and wants only "clear light, strong bodies, bodies having all the measure of manhood." This wish is particularly striking because he and Maud had just initiated a "spiritual marriage," abjuring physical love and striving for union only on the "astral plane."[6]

Yeats apparently tried to abide by this agreement, though according to his journal he feared his visions of union would only intensify physical desire.[7] Understandably he describes his "strange bewildered summer" to Mabel as one that "has set my nerves tight as a violin string but not one that makes sweet music." "I have," he explained, "an impossible problem without and much religion within," and adds with unusual candor, "I am only religious when

5 Ure, *Yeats the Playwright,* p. 145.

6 Virginia Moore, *The Unicorn: William Butler Yeats's Search for Reality* (New York: Macmillan, 1954), pp. 197–98.

7 *Ibid.,* p. 200.

my own wisdom fails me." The "religion within" was not one of Christian resignation, as Maud would have liked, but rather one of harmony between spirit and body. The letter continues: "Nothing has ever interested me but harmonic life. Sometimes I think of it in another world, the kingdom of fairy or sometimes on earth, more on earth lately. Yet it is always to the other world I go [to get decisions, and] when I cannot get them I am sunk in gloom." Thus Yeats explicitly assigns to "the other world" (*Anima Mundi*) the role of a wise and comforting parent.

A few years later Yeats even sought predictions from mediums about his future relationship with Maud.[8] Given Yeats's difficulties, his obsession at this time with the idea that a New Dispensation would shortly replace Christianity is not surprising. His struggle with Maud reawakened his own guilty fear of the body just when he had tentatively accepted it.

Yeats's next letter to Mabel reveals a preoccupation with sin and a Blakean desire to redefine good and evil. First, Yeats defines virtues as "energies, not observances." Then he connects the lack of pure energy with a sense of sin; it is like the "remorse of the lamp" when it begins to smoke. In a metaphor that suggests choked fire he compares himself to damp (and therefore not vital) barley, thus implying that his sense of sin arises from feelings of impotence and a lack of vital energy. Clearly the energy in question is in part sexual: the fuel that feeds the flame. When energy is abundant, as it is in Mrs. Campbell and Decima, the flame exists without recrimination. But when energy is low, as it is in the Real Queen, a sense of sin arises that is in part sorrow at one's own impotence.

Maud's insistence on "spiritual" union has intensified Yeats's feeling of impotence; he fears he is becoming more "intellect" than "soul" (soul here has the meaning, later attached to "heart," of passion and sexuality). He appeals to another woman to reverse this feeling about himself, asking Mabel to "really judge me and tell me what I am . . . the question is whether I am [a soul and not an intellect] for the arts know nothing else." It was at this time that Yeats felt so strongly the persecution of the abstract and wrote

8 *Ibid.*, p. 232.

his father that he needed a "separate channel" for his philosophic thought (*Letters*, p. 533), which otherwise obsessed him and ruined his work on *The Player Queen*.

In a way then *The Player Queen*, and particularly Decima with her burning energy, offered a direct contrast to Yeats's life, an imaginative saturnalia that blotted out reality. As he writes, "I have been [melancholy] for two months but taken refuge every morning in the only modern play I have ever written . . . gay and exuberant . . . full of the sound of trumpets."[9] Gaiety and the sound of trumpets take us back to the exuberant masculine music of *The King's Threshold*, and from there to the "laughing Fenian horn" of *Oisin*, the symbol of Yeats's rejection of sin and guilt and his exaltation of male energy.

Although Decima represents the joyous energy Yeats coveted, she also represents both Maud and his efforts to dictate Maud's role. Yeats emphasizes Decima's beauty and cruelty, her tendency to arouse extreme desire without satisfying it. According to Virginia Moore, he wrote in a journal of 1908–9 that Maud "would be cruel if she were not a child."[10] Maud's ingenuous harshness thus differed from Decima's deliberate cruelty, but its effects on the unfortunate lover were similar. The triangle of Decima, Septimus, and Nona—set up by the third scenario—represents an important aspect of Yeats's life at the time. Frustrated by Maud, Yeats was driven to several casual affairs. He wrote in the diary of 1908–9 quoted by Moore, "I was never more deeply in love, but my [physical] desires must go elsewhere, if I would escape their poison." "What end will it all have?" he asks. "I am in continual terror of some entanglement."[11] He attempts to cope with this terror, typically, by compartmentalizing his life: just as abstract thought must have a "separate channel," sexuality must be diverted so it does not poison him. We will see another instance of this splitting in the clean-dirty dichotomy introduced by Septimus's defense of

[9] Unpublished letter to Mabel Dickinson.

[10] V. Moore, *Unicorn*, p. 203. The journal she refers to is apparently not the journal reproduced in *Memoirs*, since the passages Moore cites do not appear in the published version.

[11] *Ibid.*, p. 202.

the Unicorn. With the mask, Yeats at once describes and aims to transcend his obsessive splitting: a man initially degraded and split can achieve unity and strength by adopting an exalted mask.

Worn by the artist, the mask enables him to create by releasing his deepest energies. The role of queen enables the Player Queen to triumph over her degraded self—a ditch-born drab—and fully develop her genius. The Real Queen, by contrast, wants to lose what little self she has, to become less and less. Like all "objective" men, she flees her mask. And as we shall see (in Chapter 5), the mask is really only available to the subjective man, the artist. Decima hopes "to grow greater and greater," or, as Yeats writes to his father (*Letters*, p. 534):

> Queens that have laughed to set the world at ease,
> Kings that have cried, "I am great Alexander
> Or Caesar come again" but stir our wonder
> That they may stir their own and grow at length
> Almost alike to that unlikely strength
> And those that will not make deliberate choice
> Are nothing.

In *Per Amica Silentia Lunae* Yeats similarly affirms: "All happiness depends on the energy to assume the mask of some other life, on a re-birth as something not one's self" (*Mythologies*, p. 334). *The Player Queen* was written to give flesh to this idea.

I began in, I think, 1907, a verse tragedy, but at that time the thought I have set forth in *Per Amica Silentia Lunae* was coming into my head, and I found examples of it everywhere. I wasted the best working months of several years in an attempt to write a poetical play where every character became an example of the finding or not finding of what I have called the Antithetical Self; and because passion and not thought makes tragedy, what I made had neither simplicity nor life. At last it came into my head all of a sudden that I could get rid of the play if I turned it into a farce.[12]

Similarly, Yeats writes elsewhere that he tried to escape from allegory by "mocking in a comedy my own thought" (*Mythologies*, p. 334). Why did he find early versions of the play so unsatisfactory? A possible reason is that because of Maud's rebuff he felt degraded, and found himself portraying a humiliated hero he

12 *Variorum Plays*, p. 761.

could not happily identify with. Turning the play into a comedy was, in effect, a confession of failure. This change alone, however, would probably not have allowed him to complete the play if he had not eventually devised a suitably exalted mask for his hero Septimus. But whereas Yeats had many difficulties with Septimus's mask, he never had any problem finding a mask for Decima.

The earliest scenarios deal with Decima's role-playing—and the attendant "lack of heart" attributable to her genius. As Yeats wrote of Synge, he had "that egotism of the man of genius which Nietzsche compares to the egotism of a woman with child," a complete absorption in his own dream (*Autobiography*, p. 311). Yeats wished to identify with the Player Queen's self-involvement, but because of Maud's continued influence and what he calls "business," he has difficulty losing himself in his work. "I can never absorb myself in my own dream (with business ever knocking at the door). If I could only lose myself in my Player Queen's life I would show the world such a dream as would make my enemies nothing."[13]

The Player Queen's character is fairly well developed in the early scenarios and remains constant throughout the revisions. The character of the hero, however, changes enormously. Though it is difficult to pin down, the force behind the changes seems to be a conflict between the desire to give the hero a mask as valuable as Decima's and the masochistic need to present a degraded male protagonist. In the first versions the hero's humiliation was too extreme even for Yeats, but his masochistic tendencies were so ingrained that the struggle was hard and the results slow to appear.

When the hero first appears in the scenarios, he seems to lack a mask altogether. Though described as a poet, he is without dignity, and as the Player Queen's lover he is shoved aside when he tries to prevent her from showing herself to the crowd.[14] By changing places with the Real Queen, Decima rids herself both of her

[13] Yeats, letter to Mabel Dickinson.
[14] Maud's ability to captivate a crowd with her beauty and majesty is well known. During the Jubilee riots of 1897 Yeats prevented her from joining a crowd the police were battering. She angrily blamed him for what she considered the only cowardly deed of her life. *Memoirs*, p. 113.

lover and of the despised part of Noah's wife (Septimus was to play Noah). With regal calm she drains a cup of poison, and the poet is forced to admit that she is indeed suited to a great role. His position, in contrast, is primarily negative and inferior to hers.

Yeats's subsequent portrayal of the hero as the stage-manager Martin—"stupid, completely commonplace, calculating and business-like"—seems an attempt to disassociate himself from the hero, who now represents the realistic drama Yeats disliked. Martin says he wants his wife to play Noah's wife rather than queen, because ordinary people want plays that resemble ordinary life. In Yeats's words, "he puts the point of view of the ordinary people against the artist." Martin finally denounces the Player Queen, who represents ideal drama, as no wife for a sensible man. This version, though consistent, left Yeats without a figure to represent himself, except perhaps the Player Queen.

In what appears to be the first complete prose version,[15] Yeats turns Martin back into a passionate lover—with whom he can identify—and the hero's failure is seen as his inability to wear a mask. The mask in question, unlike the noble mask of queen, is merely a façade of cool indifference. Worn by the lover, the mask prevents him from being sucked in and destroyed. As one of the players remarks, "True love makes one a slave / Less than a man." While protecting its wearer, the mask seduces the beloved by its enigmatic coldness and beauty: "It is the mask of burning gold, / It is the mask with emerald eyes, / That makes your heart beat so quickly." At this point the hero admits his own dreams of queens and the heroic life—thus indicating that he aspires to the heroic mask as well as the mask of coldness. But though he has not the energy to embody his dreams himself, he refuses to let the Player Queen embody them.[16] Martin and the

---

[15] The drafts in the National Library, Dublin, are undated and often in incorrect order. The draft in question is in a folder marked "3 ms. versions of complete scenario," but seems instead to be a rather fully worked out draft.

[16] We know that Yeats tried many times to mold Maud's dreams, first through his Golden Dawn activities and then through attempts to found an Irish heroic order. He envisioned Maud acting as his seer, as his wife was to do later: "I, who could not influence [Maud's] actions, could dominate her inner being. I could therefore use her clairvoyance to produce forms that would arise from

Player Queen now seem to be struggling over the possession of a single heroic mask. One must have the mask, the other must submit.

In creating this situation, Yeats is alluding to his relationship with Maud, a relationship in which his feeling of being demeaned by an overpowering woman existed alongside a desire to force her submission. The paradoxical situation of artist suppressing artist arises because Martin, like Yeats, is not only a poet but a possessive lover, and the Player Queen refuses to submit to him either by playing a demeaning role on the stage[17] or by being his wife. He is threatened by the Player Queen's ability to assume a mask that provides her with the coolness and independence he cannot achieve. His only recourse is to treat her cruelly. Martin's ostensible gentleness in this version covers such an impulse to cruelty. He "timidly" tries to lure the Player Queen from her hiding place by saying that although as Noah he must beat her, he will be careful never to hurt her. The beatings that "don't hurt" are clearly related both to Maud's "dread of physical love," which Yeats mentions in a journal of 1909,[18] and to Yeats's own tendency to see sex as a form of aggression.

In the final version, the protagonists achieve the capacity to co-exist, though not entirely peacefully (and at the cost of their love). Septimus now has something at least as good as the Player Queen's crown: his relationship with the magnificent Unicorn. This god-beast far outshines Decima in nobility and coldness. In addition, by incorporating Decima's chosen role in his scheme of the New Dispensation, Yeats had found a way to control her and it. She becomes a Queen as she had wished, but she is also the harlot-Eve. Moreover, this is Yeats-Septimus's idea, not hers, and ultimately conflicts with her desire for self-exaltation.

---

both minds, though mainly seen by one" (*Memoirs*, p. 124). But Maud's self-image was always substantially different from the one Yeats hoped to create for her. In art, the case was different, and Martin takes credit for providing the heroine with her image.

[17] During the Middle Ages the play of Noah's ark was a mainstay of the antifeminist repertoire. The shrewish wife who is beaten with a big stick provided comic relief from the Flood.

[18] V. Moore, *Unicorn*, p. 202.

As Yeats struggled with his hero, he discovered that the Real
Queen was a suitable vehicle for his masochism. Whereas the early
scenarios dealt primarily with Decima and her relationship with
the hero, the drafts, written after the spiritual marriage with
Maud ended, also develop the character of the Real Queen. Her
exaggerated religiosity reflects Yeats's feelings about Maud, and
perhaps represents an attempt to devalue her in order to cure himself of his remaining attachment. He writes in the unpublished
1909 journal:

We are divided by [Maud's] religious ideas, a Catholicism which has
grown on her. . . . In addition to this the old dread of physical love has
[re]awakened in her. This dread has probably spoiled all her life, check-
ing natural and instinctive selection, and leaving fantastic duties free to
take its place. It is what philosophy is to me, a daily rooter-out of instinct
and guiding joy.[19]

In the first drafts, the Real Queen is simply an austere and repressive Catholic. In succeeding drafts, she becomes fixated on martyrdom, longing to follow the example of her patron saint: "Was it
not St. Winifred . . . who said 'Better all life should perish than
one sin be committed'?" Her Chancellor replies, "A little wearing
of the mask is all I ask of you." But she refuses even his request
that she dress and walk regally, lamenting, "The flesh full of original sin is covered with embroidery as though it were some precious
thing."

These traits of the Real Queen would seem to derive from the
prudery and asceticism Maud demonstrated in decrying Yeats's
Land of Heart's Desire as insulting to her religion, and in resign-
ing from the Abbey Theatre at the "further insult to Irish Woman-
hood" implied in "The Shadow of the Glen." Just as Yeats saw
the suppression of sex as stunting Maud's personality, he saw suppression of sexual impulses as stifling creativity in literature and
politics. He later wrote of the modern poet: "Whether we have
chosen chisel, pen or brush, / We are but critics, or but half create, / Timid, entangled, empty and abashed."[20] Of Irish politi-

19 *Ibid.*
20 "Ego Dominus Tuus," *Variorum Poems*, p. 368.

cians, he said: "The political class...have suffered through the cultivation of hatred as the one energy of their movement, a deprivation which is the intellectual equivalent to a certain surgical operation" (*Autobiography*, p. 295). The crowd in *The Player Queen*, which wants to kill the Queen for imagined sexual excesses, embodies the relationship Yeats saw between "fanatical hatred" and repressed sexuality.

It was the "energy and abundance" he saw in Synge that provided Yeats with a balance to sterility in both literature and politics. Yeats wrote a poem comparing Synge to Don Juan and his critics to eunuchs, when Synge's comedy about parricide, *Playboy of the Western World*, was attacked.[21] His further defense of Synge defined the arts as beyond "good and evil"—a place where both lust and hostility may be freely expressed.[22]

Tied to the idea that the arts must freely express energy, particularly sexual energy, was the idea that this energy was somehow the essence of the self, and that capturing this essence in art conferred immortality. The idea, by no means original, that man's essence survives in his work, offered Yeats considerable consolation in the face of Synge's death. In May 1908 he wrote Mabel Dickinson:

Synge's illness, and the almost measurable stopping of a mind I have been so near to has [been unbelievable] . . . , but not a little to my wonder [considering how intimate we have been] it was the death to his imagination that set me sorrowing. Will you take this as proof that I have no heart? *Deirdre* has been in my thoughts and now that he will finish that half the sorrow of loss is over.

Yeats's feelings about Synge's death are reflected in the Player Queen's insistence that as long as she can fulfill her creative potentialities, she can face death. Yeats may even have thought of finishing *Deirdre* for Synge. In his *Autobiography* (p. 296) he records a visit to the dying man: "I did not like to ask more ques-

21 "On those that hated 'The Playboy of the Western World,' 1907," *Variorum Poems*, p. 294. Yeats's anger at Synge's detractors made him wonder momentarily "if I have been right to shape my style to sweetness and serenity.... Perhaps the always gracious thought was only right in old days when one had a dumb sword to carry one's ungraciousness." *Memoirs*, p. 161.

22 Yeats, *Plays and Controversies* (London: Macmillan, 1923), p. 192.

tions lest he should understand that I wished to know if another could complete the work if he died." Perhaps Yeats's *Celtic Twilight* and descriptions of beloved landscapes, written during his mother's illness and after her death, reflect a similar attempt to capture and immortalize a vanished spirit and thus attenuate feelings of emptiness and loss.

Early in 1909 three traumatic events occurred that involved or threatened the loss of a beloved person: the spiritual marriage with Maud ended, Lady Gregory fell seriously ill, and Synge died. By the time of Synge's death on March 24, Yeats had had a breakdown reminiscent of his collapse on finishing *Oisin* after his mother's first stroke (*Letters*, p. 526). His journal entries for February 1909 include several references to the "stopping of my faculties," headache, and palpitations. These occurred after the initial breakdown (*Memoirs*, pp. 157, 160, 171). After the earlier collapse he had sought "routine work" and halted creative production. Similarly, in a letter of early March 1909, he writes: "I am afraid I must put *Player Queen* off for a time, as to do work of this kind amid all these distractions is a great strain.... I must do work that will bring in a little money" (*Letters*, p. 526). Lady Gregory fell ill in February. The shock occasioned a transient break with reality. Yeats thought he was learning of his mother's death (*Autobiography*, p. 290):

This morning I got a letter telling me of [Lady Gregory's] illness. I did not recognize her son's writing at first, and my mind wandered.... I thought my mother was ill and that my sister was asking me to come at once: then I remembered that my mother died years ago and that more than kin was at stake. She has been to me mother, friend, sister and brother. I cannot realize the world without her.... All the day the thought of losing her is like a conflagration in the rafters. Friendship is all the house I have.

Only when he was again in Lady Gregory's sheltering house did he resume work on the play.

Yeats's creative energy seems often to have been dependent on his feeling in contact with a nurturing spirit, whether a real person like Lady Gregory or an abstraction like *Anima Mundi*. He frequently suggests a relationship between creativity and a craving for mothering. Drunkenness, trance, and some form of dreaming represent both the craving and a preamble to its satisfaction, i.e., the acquisition of spiritual sustenance from the supernatural. In *Where There Is Nothing*, as we have seen, the "blessed cup of intoxication" was related to regressive wishes. In *The Unicorn from the Stars*, Martin when he awoke from trance was as helpless as a little child.

In the final, published version of *The Player Queen* (1922), Septimus has lost all managerial qualities and become a drunken poet. Because Septimus is drunk, he is as vulnerable as a child and "therefore in need of protection" (Scene I, ll. 350–51). Because of his bad wife, he is exposed to indignities: "left to lie down in the open street . . . drenched with cold water," liable "to be eaten by dogs" (I, ll. 68–72). Septimus's exaggerated rhetoric, "Robbed, so to speak; naked, so to speak—bleeding, so to speak— and they pass by on the other side of the street" (I, ll. 104–6), encourages us to laugh at an essentially self-debasing series of images.

Unmoved by Septimus's appeals for sympathy and his claims to be a great poet, the mob rolls him to the side of the street, where he hears them discuss the Queen. The extraordinarily violent and hysterical crowd embodies the relationship Yeats saw between repressed sexuality and fanatical hatred. As Ure points out, the scene is too ugly to be funny.[23] The Real Queen has not appeared in public since her father's death. The mob convinces itself that she is a witch who, it is implied, like other witches consorts with the dead. More specifically, she is accused of coupling with a Unicorn.

Yeats, who had originally set the play in Spain, probably had the Inquisition in mind as he had when he set *Mosada* there; the Queen coupling with a Unicorn recalls the union of witch and devil, which, as Ernest Jones has shown, is basically an incestuous fantasy.[24] The situation in *The Player Queen*—someone looks

23 Ure, *Yeats the Playwright*, p. 138.
24 Jones, *On the Nightmare*, p. 96.

through a window and sees a supposedly pure woman mating with
a beast—is one that Yeats used again in *Purgatory*, where the Oedipal implications are ineluctable.

The similarities between the corresponding situations in *Purgatory* and *The Player Queen*—the dark house, the lighted window,
the hidden observer watching an act of intercourse that horrifies
and fascinates him—are striking; and the fact that in *The Player
Queen* it is a boy who peeks through the Queen's window height-
ens the suggestion that Yeats is representing a childhood fantasy.
The visual elements in the description, a damaged old wall and
a window, are present not only in the two plays but in Yeats's first
recorded memory in the *Autobiography* (p. 3): "I remember . . .
looking out of an Irish window at a wall covered with cracked and
falling plaster, but what wall I do not remember, and being told
that some relation once lived there." A house, its walls broken and
cracked, where a relation once lived (the protagonist's mother), is
the setting for *Purgatory*. The memory recorded in the *Autobiography* would seem to be a screen memory in which the cracked
wall stands for the mother. Looking through the window at the
wall relates to a childhood fantasy or experience of covertly observing parental intercourse. What the child Yeats saw or imagined
was the primal scene. Similarly, in *The Player Queen* the Boy observes the mating of his supposedly chaste Queen and a Unicorn
(the wall is still there, not only cracked but full of holes, into which
the Boy puts his toes as he climbs). In *Purgatory* the Old Man
looks through a similar window and observes his long-dead mother
having intercourse with a "tired beast," his father. Yeats's construction of the episode in *Purgatory* suggests (though in reverse) the
way in which the gaping wall came to replace the repressed primal
scene. The Old Man and his son are both looking toward the
ruined house, but whereas the Old Man sees his parents' intercourse, the Boy sees only "a gap in the wall"—the covering memory of *Autobiography*.

In Scene I of *The Player Queen*, as Ure points out, suspense
mounts over whether the Queen does or does not couple with the

Unicorn.[25] But this suspense evaporates in Scene II when we see the nun-like Real Queen, timid and afraid of sex. Her desire to be trampled to death by the Unicorn seems a hysterical fantasy, and the crowd's belief that she couples with the Unicorn a morbid illusion.

The story of the Real Queen parallels and contrasts with the story of Septimus. Both suffer deprivations (Septimus loses his wife, the Queen her father) and consequently crave supernatural sustenance. But the Queen, unlike Septimus, cannot get this sustenance because she lacks the capacity to assume a mask, to be reborn as something not herself. The stories of Septimus and the Real Queen were initially even more closely interwoven. In early drafts of the play the inspired beggar who in the final version announces the New Dispensation, appears as the Real Queen's father returned from Purgatory. In these early versions the beggar and Septimus do not join forces. The ghost returned to haunt the living brings to mind a long poem of 1913, in which a queen's husband from a previous incarnation returns as a great white stag.[26] If we take the mad-beggar episode and the returning white-stag husband as two aspects of an encompassing fantasy from which *The Player Queen* crystallized, we have a fantasy in which the Queen's father returns as her lover. The father is doubly represented—in degraded form as the mad beggar, in exalted form as the supernatural Unicorn. In the final version of the play, both fathers (beggar and Unicorn) are linked to Septimus. Their role is apparently to sanction or reinforce Septimus's fantasies. "Ah!" says Septimus to the beggar, "you are inspired. Then we are indeed brothers" (I, ll. 380–81).

Though self-debased and degraded when we first see him, Septimus soon swings to the opposite state of exaltation through his sympathetic fusion with the Unicorn. The drunken Septimus has reached a state of helplessness that presages identification with the magnificent Unicorn, or to put it more strongly, participation in

25 Ure, *Yeats the Playwright*, pp. 137–38.
26 "The Two Kings," *Variorum Poems*, pp. 276–86.

the Unicorn's character. Participation begins when Septimus, during his defense of the Unicorn, takes on characteristics of Yeats's
white swan, symbol of poetic inspiration: "my breast-feathers thrust
out and my white wings buoyed up with divinity.... I will not
have it said that there is a smirch or a blot, upon the most milky
whiteness of an heroic brute" (I, ll. 279–81, 294–96). Septimus as
divine swan has himself become like the Unicorn he is defending.
What Yeats seems to have done here is to insert a version of an
intensely satisfying infantile fantasy of participation with an awe-
inspiring father.

Several critics have been troubled by Septimus's defending the
Unicorn's chastity when the Unicorn's most striking physical characteristic, the single horn, is phallic, and his function is to copulate.[27] Helen Vendler suggests that Septimus is simply misled by
the Unicorn's traditional purity. In this view, Septimus unwit-
tingly shares some of the crowd's values, relating the Unicorn's
worth to its chastity rather than its energy. Norman Newton argues
that because he is an idealist, Septimus assumes that beauty and
chastity go hand in hand.[28]

Septimus's defense of the Unicorn's chastity can better be understood in the light of Yeats's tendency to classify sexual experience
as either clean and exalted or dirty and disgusting. In *Purgatory*,
for example, the Old Man attempts to eradicate the dirty aspect
of his father's wedding night by killing his son, who is vile like
his grandfather and would pass pollution on. After he has killed

[27] The Unicorn does, however, have some female aspects, though Yeats emphasizes the male. For one thing, Septimus compares his wife to the Unicorn:
"Beautiful as the Unicorn, but fierce" (II, l. 499). The Unicorn's flightiness
and fierce chastity are shared by the frigid queens of the dance plays, and
Septimus's emotional defense of its purity sounds like a defense of the mother.
He stresses the Unicorn's milky color—"It has a milk-white skin and a milk-
white horn, and milk-white hooves" (I, ll. 251–53)—at a time when he is feeling in need of protection. The association with mother's milk is strengthened
by the fact that in his following speech, Septimus associates milk and helpless
infancy: "All creatures are in need of protection at some time or other. Even
my wife was once a frail child in need of milk, of smiles, of love" (I, ll. 351–53).
All this suggests that the Unicorn was a hermaphroditic image. We will see
another such image in the Herne.

[28] Vendler, *Yeats's* Vision, p. 129; Norman Newton, "Yeats as Dramatist:
The Player Queen," Essays in Criticism, 8 (July 1958): 269–84.

his son, the Old Man feels that his mother, previously sullied, is "all cold, sweet, glistening light." Such dichotomization is itself a means of coping with disgust. Yeats's early aversion to sexuality is noted in the *Autobiography*: an older boy's explanation of the mechanics of sex "made me miserable for weeks" (*Autobiography*, p. 16). To avoid being miserable, Yeats either cleans up his disgusting thoughts or externalizes and repudiates them. Septimus's Unicorn fantasy is an embodiment of clean sex: a purified father. His defense of the Unicorn's cleanness also seems to be part of a general defense of the forbidden (incestuous) fantasy at the heart of the play and of the body and sexuality. Septimus asserts that the Unicorn is "a most religious beast" who "dances in the sun." He preserves his pristine whiteness by bathing three times a day, in contrast to the dirty mob who, as Septimus points out, are washed only at birth and at death. The mob wants to lower the Unicorn to their level by dirtying him. The Unicorn's very whiteness makes him vulnerable—like the swan of Yeats's that is so white one fears "it can be murdered with a spot of ink."[29] Septimus tries to protect the Unicorn's purity: "I will not have it said that there is a smirch or a blot upon the most milky whiteness of an heroic brute."

Yeats's clean-dirty dichotomy is part of a larger tendency to divide things into contrary pairs. In the mask concept, all that is heroic in a person is condensed in his mask; traits and thoughts belonging to his ordinary, degraded self are repudiated. Similarly, in Yeats's myth of the New Dispensation, Christianity and the new religion of Oedipus represent polar opposites: one is a religion of shame and repression; the other of freedom. In one, incest is the supreme sin; in the other, a religious act. In *A Vision* Yeats describes the two religions as the two scales of a balance: "What if every two thousand and odd years something happens in the world to make one sacred, the other secular; one wise, the other foolish; one fair, the other foul; one divine, the other devilish?" (*Vision*, p. 29). It is no coincidence that while Yeats was working on *The Player Queen* he was also preparing to put on his translation of

[29] Yeats, "Coole Park and Ballylee, 1931," *Variorum Poems*, p. 491.

Oedipus Rex for the "New Year" (1910), and in this connection fighting the English censorship, which found the play immoral because Oedipus commits incest. Later he was to write that the play could be performed in Dublin because Ireland has "an old [i.e., pagan] historical religion" (*Letters*, p. 537n).

The old religion conforms to the outline of the body, but Christianity distorts and hides it (*Letters*, p. 537n). The Real Queen and Decima can be taken as symbolizing, respectively, Christianity and the old religion (or the New Dispensation, which returns to the old pattern). The Real Queen clings to her shapeless dress, which she explains is a punishment for sin. Yeats stresses, not without humor, her need to bruise the body in the name of the soul. She greatly envies her patron saint, who was thrown by a Unicorn and trampled to death by a mob. The Queen longs for similar martyrdom, even to the detail of walking before the people with bleeding feet. Obviously she suffers from an active fantasy life; martyrdom will deliver her from temptation. In a speech to the Player Queen, who has agreed to impersonate her, she admits her fear of love and its consequences (II, ll. 656–64):

I have never known love. Of all things, that is what I have had most fear of. Saint Octema shut herself up in a tower on a mountain because she was loved by a beautiful prince. . . . I am not naturally good, and they say people will do anything for love. . . . But you will escape all that and go up to God as a pure virgin.

Her desire to ride the Unicorn and be thrown to her death is a masochistic expression of her own repressed desires.

Decima, by contrast, unashamedly acknowledges her sexuality. Unshackled by inhibitions, she uses her attractiveness as a weapon. She gloats at the thought that if she refuses to play Noah's wife, Septimus will go to prison, where he would be forced to think of her "every time he felt the hardness of the stone floor, every time he heard the chains clank" (II, ll. 164–66). Nona, whose view of love is gentle and protective, exclaims that he would hate her; and Decima answers her with a comparison between Septimus's love for her and Nona's love for God: "If that Holy Image of the church where you put all those candles at Easter was pleasant and affable, why did you come home with the skin worn off your two knees?" (II, ll. 171–74). Decima knows that Septimus's love thrives on her coldness, and she will not discard her mask. The lyric "Put off that mask" is used in a sadistic context: the mask enables Decima to torture Septimus with doubt about her real feelings. In the final version of the lyric, in the *Collected Poems*, man is possessor of the mask, the creation of which, in the context of the poem, can be seen as an act of self-protection.[30] Its rationale, however, seems to be a combination of self-love and cruelty.

When Nona boasts that Septimus is her lover, Decima begins to dance among the players, now dressed as the animals on Noah's ark, looking for a beast to take as her lover. While Decima dances Septimus announces the end of the Christian Era, and calls on the Unicorn to initiate the New Dispensation. Decima's mating dance among the beast-men is a grotesque version (again the clean-dirty dichotomy) of the exalted union with the Unicorn, which I have suggested had its source in a primal scene fantasy. Septimus prevents this degraded union by announcing the Unicorn's exalted marriage. The shift from Septimus as passive spectator to Septimus as impresario of the marriage strongly suggests an attempt by Yeats to master an overwhelming experience by taking an active role in it. Septimus's urging the Unicorn to consummate his marriage corresponds to a fantasy in which the child gets his parents to copulate and participates in the act.

Yeats's interest in the relationship between Septimus and Decima apparently declined after he became preoccupied with the Unicorn fantasy. The result in the final version is that Decima shares the stage with the Unicorn and Yeats turns Septimus's interest away from Decima toward the mythical beast. So marked is this shift that it has led critics to see two plots in the final play, one concerned with Decima and her mask, the other with Septimus and the Unicorn. From our vantage point we can see that the two are connected: Yeats's absorption in his hero's degradation before a woman prompted a reaction; the Unicorn replaced an unresolvably problematic human relationship.

30 "The Mask," *Variorum Poems*, p. 263.

As Yeats's need to represent his relationship with Maud became less compelling, he deleted many of the most personal lines and episodes. Among the deleted passages we may cite Martin's attempt to rescue the Player Queen from the crowd, and a passionate speech at the end of Scene II when he tries to get her to escape with him: "Could you know how utterly I long to give you all you ask, but I know you would despise me if I gave it. I love you with every kind of love, with a love that is full of passion . . . yet I know I must seem the coldness your wild heart has need of."[31] Through the unicorn fantasy, Yeats mastered feelings of helplessness before both traumatic memories of childhood and adult fears of a potentially annihilating sexual relationship. At the same time the unicorn fantasy gratified his deepest desires, combining past incestuous wishes with present longings for Maud, and projecting them as a necessary pattern on the future.[32]

The unicorn fantasy resolves Yeats's ambivalent feelings toward Maud in yet another way. Insofar as Decima is Maud (and as we have seen, the identification is only partial), Yeats had mixed feelings about her success as Queen. To become Queen, Decima had to disavow both the part of Noah's wife and her husband Septimus. She wants to escape the humiliation of being "a stupid woman" who is beaten with a stick and forced with the other brutes onto Noah's ark. She wants to escape being a brute, i.e., a sexual creature. Spurning Septimus, she pushes him into the embraces of Nona. (Vendler points out that the two women have the same relationship as the chambermaid and her mistress in Yeats's late poem "The Three Bushes," in which a poet's chastity-obsessed lady delegates her sexual role to her maid.)[33] Yeats describes what Decima is moving away from in sexual terms. He calls her "ditch-born"; in his later poetry, as mentioned above, the "fecund ditch"

---

[31] Unpublished draft, National Library, Dublin.

[32] An episode in the spiritual marriage of 1909 may have reinforced Yeats's fantasy of bestial union. Maud wrote Yeats that he had appeared to her in the night (presumably on the astral plane), uniting with her in the shape of a great serpent. Imagined union with Decima-Maud in the shape of a unicorn would fit the pattern established here of renouncing in order to regain in animal shape. V. Moore, *Unicorn*, pp. 199–200.

[33] Vendler, *Yeats's* Vision, p. 131.

is a symbol of woman's sexuality. Decima's whole progress is from the ditch to the throne, where she puts on "golden slippers." In the dance plays Yeats would describe love as containing both "dung of swine" and "crown of gold," but here the alternatives seem mutually exclusive.

The New Dispensation to be ushered in by the Unicorn imposes a different ending on Decima's progress. Not only is the rejected poet vicariously united with his love through the Unicorn, but the disdainful lady is forced back into a sexual role. Yeats gives Decima the song of the daughter of "a mad singing harlot" to show, as Ure points out, that Decima was the harlot-Eve.[34] Until her mating dance, however, Decima is in no sense a harlot. On the contrary, she is moving away from sexuality. It is Septimus's refusal to give up Nona that leads to her taking the role of Queen and future bride of the Unicorn. Yeats thus regains control over his heroine. She gets to be Queen, yes, but the Queen becomes the harlot-Eve.

Yeats adds a further ironic reflection of his relationship with Maud by having Decima marry the Prime Minister while waiting for the Unicorn. Maud, he said, had taught him hate by giving "kisses to a clown."[35] The Prime Minister is a stupid fellow, with all the traits once associated with the doltish stage manager. He wants the play of Noah's ark performed because "when Noah beats his wife to make her go into the ark everybody understands, everybody is pleased, everybody recognizes the mulish obstinacy of their own wives, sweethearts, sisters." Even an ephemeral marriage to such a man is hardly a happy ending.

Thus seen, Yeats's construction of *The Player Queen* is somewhat like the construction of dreams. The early drafts, so full of references to Yeats's frustrated relationship with Maud—as well as to the repressive nature of contemporary politics, literature, etc.—resemble the part of the dream that reflects the experiences of the previous day. (The analogy of course is only partial—there are fantasy elements here as well.) As Freud pointed out, this ma-

34 Ure, *Yeats the Playwright*, p. 139.
35 Unpublished poem as quoted in Ellmann, *Man and Masks*, p. 177.

terial, which may represent frustrations or unpleasantness, is not by itself sufficient to construct a dream. The dream must be given shape by a wish, and this wish usually comes from the dreamer's remote past. Yeats's idea of the New Dispensation, brought about by the coupling of Queen and Unicorn, is what gives the play its ultimate shape, and, as we have seen, this somewhat incongruous solution is basically an incestuous fantasy derived from Yeats's early life.

Two Dance Plays

More than ten years elapsed between *The Player Queen* and two dance plays that also feature capricious queens: *The King of the Great Clock Tower* (1934) and *A Full Moon in March* (1935). By then Yeats was a happily married man with children, and his fever of excitement over Maud Gonne had subsided. The two dance plays seem to have little connection, as he himself noted, with his personal experience (*Letters*, p. 819). The female protagonists are archetypal figures and the plays themselves present a single, formal, ritual action: the love and sacrificial death of the poet-hero.

Yeats wrote *The King of the Great Clock Tower* at a low point of poetic inspiration, to "force myself to write lyrics" (*Letters*, p. 845). Since Lady Gregory's death in 1932 he had written almost nothing. In January 1934, after completing the play, he writes: "I made up the play that I might write lyrics out of dramatic experience, all my personal experience having in some strange way come to an end. They are good lyrics a little in my early manner" (*Letters*, p. 819). By "personal experience," he seems to mean the sort of frustrating love experience he had had in the past, for though ill, he continued to experience family love and friendship. It is this frustrated love that, as we have seen, stimulates Yeats to write and seemingly makes him feel most alive. In search of artistic stimulation and renewed vitality, Yeats returns to his early work, notably *Oisin*, and interacts with it much as he had done earlier with *Anima Mundi*.

And in fact his work on the play did make him feel intensely alive. He wrote Olivia Shakespear, when he had almost finished the play, that he was in a state of extreme "excitement," from which he found "rest" in seeing people—i.e., in the humdrum business of everyday life (*Letters*, p. 819). Yeats probably meant sexual as well as mental excitement. The play has a sexually provocative theme, and ill health was probably imposing abstinence on the ailing poet. A few months earlier, he had written about the equally exciting Crazy Jane poems: "Sexual abstinence fed their fire—I was ill and yet full of desire. They sometimes came out of the greatest mental excitement I am capable of" (*Letters*, p. 814).

When he began *The King of the Great Clock Tower*, Yeats not only felt his personal experience was at an end, but also was filled with thoughts of his own approaching death—thoughts in which his old theme of love-death might be expected to assume a new immediacy. In November 1933, in a letter to Olivia, he mentions the play for the first time. He encloses a draft of the play's opening song, which contrasts the timeless union after death with the encapsulated isolation of living lovers. In the same letter, Yeats mentions having an apparition of a child holding a playing card, a five of diamonds: "does it promise me five months or five years?" (*Letters*, p. 817). The Macbethian vision suggests an unconscious fear on Yeats's part that he was about to be superseded by his children. (*Purgatory* shows a specific aspect of his fear in the son who wonders whether he is strong enough to kill his father. But there was also the more general fact that his children's growth reminded him continually of his own aging and made it harder for him to deny his approaching death.) Two months later, in January, Yeats reports a second vision of his death, this time an arm waving goodbye (*Letters*, p. 819).

Thus the emotional background of the play includes Yeats's bad health, his thoughts of impending death, and his feeling that his personal experience was at an end. When, in defiance of all these things, he turns to his past for stimulation, what he finds are the pervasive themes of incestuous longing and love-death. He describes the two dance plays to Dorothy Wellesley as "a fragment of the past that I had to get rid of" and he writes to Edmund

Dulac that he is obsessed with blood symbolism: "I do not understand why this blood symbolism laid hold upon me but I must
work it out" (*Letters*, pp. 830, 843).

What Yeats calls blood symbolism in the plays is basically a
masochistic fantasy of dismemberment and death at the hands of
a woman. In Chapter 3 we examined Yeats's vision of the mother-
goddess and star-son and the poem on the same theme, "The Cap
and Bells." Waning potency and approaching death apparently
reawakened a deep-seated masochism Yeats had never been able
to eradicate entirely. Thirty years after "The Cap and Bells," in
"Parnell's Funeral" (1932), Yeats returns to the theme of a son's
ritual death at the hands of his mother.[36] The poem, which makes
Parnell the son and Ireland the cruel mother, specifically recalls
Yeats's early vision:

> A beautiful seated boy; a sacred bow;
> A woman, and an arrow on a string;
> A pierced boy, image of a star laid low.
> That woman, the Great Mother imaging,
> Cut out his heart.

Yeats incorporated this poem into *A Full Moon in March*, the
revised version of *Clock Tower*, in which he again takes up the
theme of sacrificed son and murderous mother. He speaks of the
play's secret meaning (as he had spoken earlier of *Oisin's*) in his
preface and explains only that it has to do with "the old ritual of
the year: the mother goddess and the slain god."[37]

Though both *A Full Moon in March* and *The King of the
Great Clock Tower* end with the hero's decapitation and union
with the Queen, there are significant differences between the two
plays. The triangle of *Clock Tower*—King, Queen, and Stroller—
is reduced to a dialogue between Queen and Swineherd in the later
play. Though Yeats has used triangular conflicts dramatically before, and will again, here he is plainly less interested in a struggle
with the paternal figure than in an essentially poisonous relationship between son and mother. Indeed, the King in *The Great*

---

36 *Variorum Poems*, pp. 541–43.
37 *Variorum Plays*, p. 1311.

Clock Tower is not much of a rival, and the Stroller's relationship to the Queen is undeveloped. Insofar as the Queen has a character in the earlier play, it is timid and masochistic. She is both tempted and terrified by the sexual act, which she speaks of —when her silence is finally broken—as an act of aggression ("He longs to kill / My body") deadly in its consequences ("O, what may come / into my womb, / What caterpillar / My beauty consume?" (ll. 111–12, 115–18). Intercourse, the growth of a child in the womb, and the creation of a poem are all seen as analogous —and destructive—events. The poet "consumes" or devours his object—daimon or mother—in order that the poem or butterfly may be born.

This view of sexuality is consistent with the evidence of oral trauma we have observed in Yeats's work (*The Countess Cathleen, The King's Threshold*) and with his many evocations of a primal scene (*Where There Is Nothing, The Unicorn from the Stars, The Player Queen*). As a result of this oral trauma and rage Yeats perceives the sexual act as aggression; his desire for his mother is experienced as a desire to beat, consume, or dismember her. This desire is projected onto the mother, who retaliates by dismembering him. In Yeats's fantasy, after he has been dismembered, his mother will love him again and he will be united with her.

The death-union theme is the same in *The King of the Great Clock Tower* and *A Full Moon in March*. In the earlier play the song of the severed head, like the original lyric in the letter to Olivia, contrasts "living wretches" (l. 134) and their insatiable desire with the pleasures of perfect union after death: "Crossed fingers there in pleasure can / Exceed the nuptial bed of man" (ll. 138–39). The implication that the Stroller, having atoned with his death for his sinful desire, will find satisfaction becomes explicit in *A Full Moon in March*, where the stage directions make it clear that the Queen's dance represents intercourse and orgasm: "She takes the head up and dances with it to drum-taps, which grow quicker and quicker. As the drum-taps approach their climax, ... her body shivers. ... The drum-taps cease. She sinks slowly down, holding the head to her breast" (following l. 179). And as

Yeats has given us to understand (ll. 116–20), she conceives of the head's blood.

Yeats had felt that the main flaw in the earlier version lay in the King: "In *The King of the Great Clock Tower* there are three characters, King, Queen and Stroller, and that is a character too many; reduced to the essentials, to Queen and Stroller, the fable should have greater intensity. I started afresh and called the new version *A Full Moon in March*."[38] With the King gone, Yeats is free to explore the tortured relationship between son and mother.[39] In doing so he gives an increased emphasis to the body and sensuality—expressed in correspondingly pungent language. This increased earthiness occurs within a framework of allusion to the story of Oedipus, whose importance in Yeats's thinking we have already discussed.

A Full Moon in March is structured around three familiar, interconnected Yeatsian fantasies: fantasies of the primal scene, of incest, and of the union of mother and child. To take the last one first, in this version the Queen explicitly calls the Swineherd's severed head "child" as she holds it against her breast. Once dead —and symbolically castrated—the Swineherd becomes the child he once was. The Queen lavishes all the love she had previously denied him on his severed head. Singing to it as "child and darling," she attributes her murderous act to her role as muse: "Wrong came not from me / But my virgin cruelty" (ll. 156–57). The Swineherd answers with a nursery rhyme, the final embodiment of Yeats's vision of star-son and murderous mother (there is a similar use of nursery rhyme in *The Herne's Egg* and in *Purgatory*):

[38] *Variorum Plays*, p. 1311. A second reason for dissatisfaction was Ezra Pound's condemnation of the prose speech of *The King of the Great Clock Tower* as "nobody's language." This, as Yeats said, reinforced "my fear that I am too old." Curtis Bradford, *Yeats at Work* (Carbondale: Southern Illinois University Press, 1964), p. 268. But it also stimulated him first to rework the play in verse and then to rewrite it completely as *A Full Moon in March*.

[39] Vendler interprets the relationship between Swineherd-Stroller and Queen in the plays as a relationship between poet and muse. Vendler, *Yeats's* Vision, p. 153. As we have seen, Yeats's muse or daimon is also the Oedipal mother. Yeats, in removing the King from the play, is denying the father's importance while taking his place. The "essentials" consist of Queen and hero.

I sing a song of Jack and Jill.
Jill had murdered Jack;
The moon shone brightly;
. . .

Jack had a hollow heart, for Jill
Had hung his heart on high;
The moon shone brightly;
Had hung his heart beyond the hill,
A-twinkle in the sky.
A full moon in March.

(ll. 166–77)

The cruelty of the Queen is essential to this version; the lover wants and expects it: "Desiring cruelty, he made you cruel" (l. 77). Throughout their wooing, the Swineherd provokes her cruelty by casting his desire for her and its consequences in the most humiliating terms: "She shall bring forth her farrow in the dung" (l. 99). He makes her dirty; she decapitates him in retaliation.

Yeats uses the story of Oedipus to reinforce his own perception of the tragic but artistically stimulating relationship between son and mother, poet and muse. The Swineherd no longer asks for just a dance and a kiss as his predecessor, the Stroller, had, but for "kingdom and lady, if I sing the best" (l. 52). Moreover, the comically particularized Stroller has become a mythic figure, a Swineherd (recalling Celtic swineherd-priests in the service of the death goddess). Like Oedipus he knows nothing about his real origin, and would not know his mother if he saw her. Oedipus was so significant for Yeats not only because he had committed the longed-for act, but also because he exemplified the self-possession and self-sufficiency Yeats wished for: "he knew nothing but his mind" (*Vision*, p. 28). Yeats had first worked on a translation of *Oedipus Rex* in 1909; it had been revised and produced several times. In the 1920's he translated *Oedipus at Colonus*, which was also produced by the Abbey Theater. The plays meant a great deal to him. He wrote of the production of *Oedipus Rex* that he sensed "the actual presence in a terrible sacrament of the god" (*Letters*, p. 720).

In mythicizing the Swineherd, Yeats links him specifically to excrement—"the dung of swine." The symbolic dirtiness of the

Swineherd and his impulses seems related to Yeats's attitude toward his own early incest fantasies. The first time the Swineherd heard the Queen's name, he says "I rolled among the dung of swine and laughed." In an early passage not included in the final version, the Swineherd adds, "O, I forgot the best of the story. When I sat there heaping the dung of swine upon my body, I foresaw everything. First you shall kneel before me. . . ."[40]

The Swineherd's vision of union seems to derive from Yeats's description of his own first orgasm in the *Memoirs* (pp. 71–72):

> I had been bathing, and lay down in the sun on the sand on the Third Rosses and covered my body with sand. Presently the weight of the sand began to affect the organ of sex, though at first I did not know what the strange, growing sensation was. It was only at the orgasm that I knew. . . . It was many days before I discovered how to renew that wonderful sensation. From then on it was a continual struggle against an experience that almost invariably left me with exhausted nerves. . . . It filled me with loathing of myself.

Not only has the sand of Yeats's memory changed to dung and the boy clean from a swim to a filthy swineherd, objectification of Yeats's "loathing," but the fantasy that may well have accompanied the original excitement is reinstated—an incestuous fantasy of the mother's submission.

The fact that the Swineherd sees the Queen as "kneeling before me," combined with the excremental imagery, suggests that the fantasy includes ideas of oral or anal contact in which the Queen is further degraded. Yeats's insistence in an early draft that the Swineherd cannot remember when he first thought about the Queen ("My memory is gone") symbolically reflects the far-away time when the thought of her was first imprinted. Furthermore, it is the ideal scene that matters, and not the real woman who embodies it. As the Swineherd says (l. 110) when the Queen refuses to drop her veil, "What do those features matter?" Yeats's fear of solitary fantasy and its consequences, noted in the previous chapter, is reflected by the Swineherd's statement, "great solitudes have driven me mad" (l. 46).

[40] Bradford, *Yeats at Work*, p. 273.

At the end of the play, the fantasy of incestuous union is joined
ingeniously by suggestions of a primal scene. After the Swineherd's death, Yeats has the Second Attendant sing as the Swineherd. The Swineherd is thus split into two: Swineherd committing
incest and Swineherd watching. The Second Attendant expresses
all the dismay of the Old Man in *Purgatory* who watches his aristocratic mother "descend" and embrace the drunken groom, his
father. Like the Old Man in what is explicitly a primal scene, the
Second Attendant is horrified by what he sees and cannot understand it:

> Why must those holy, haughty feet descend
> from emblematic niches ...
>
>   . . .
>
> My heart is broken, yet must understand.
> What do they seek for?
>
>   (ll. 180–84)

The answer offered by the First Attendant is: "desecration and the
lover's night" (l. 191). The images of filth with which Yeats describes desecration express his initial horror at the primal scene
and at sexuality. By insisting that the pure Queen descend into
the dung of passion and by identifying with the Swineherd, Yeats
turns this initial horror into pleasure. The Second Attendant accepts the answer (the need for desecration), and even requests that
it be repeated: "Delight my heart with sound; speak yet again"
(l. 192).

Though both plays end in the union of Queen and Head, there
is a marked difference in emphasis. In *The King of the Great Clock
Tower*, written in a period of low energy and preoccupation with
death, the emphasis is on satisfaction after death; heaven is described as a ruined house filled with "all the lovely things that
were." *A Full Moon in March* was written during the burst of
creative activity that followed Yeats's Steinach operation in May
1934. His intense need to deny physical decay and the approach
of death by reasserting sexual potency is reflected in the play's
emphasis on the body and sensuality. But an older man who
stresses sexuality runs the risk of appearing foolish. This accounts,

in part, for the emphasis on degradation and filth, which will become increasingly important in *The Herne's Egg*, where the ideal
of the hero's sexual vitality is itself mocked.[41]

'The Herne's Egg'

The Herne's Egg (1935) is a grotesque farce that seems to ring
a minor variation on the classical Oedipal situation of King,
Queen, and Swineherd. Congal is the presumptuous son who denies his father the Herne, steals his father's bride Attracta, and
after punishment is reconciled with the woman who now represents the loving mother. But on closer inspection the theme of
an inverted Oedipal triangle, i.e., of rivalry with the mother,
proves equally plausible as an organizing principle. Congal envies and depreciates Attracta, steals the Herne's eggs that are
in her care, and dies. The dominant fantasy here, as in *The King's
Threshold*, is of outdoing the mother, arrogating her feminine
privileges with the father, and putting her down.

These two organizing themes are joined by many others. The
various themes are poorly orchestrated. There are at least two
strikingly different points of view from which the action presses
to be seen—the heroic and the mockingly ironic. Critics are understandably preoccupied with what Yeats really meant—that is,
with whether he saw the action heroically or ironically. In the
battle between Congal and Attracta (and the Herne), for example,
did Yeats intend Congal to appear as hero or fool? Ure, who considers the play a serious attempt to portray two equally valid
viewpoints—that of a heroic man fighting destiny and that of the
god who creates destiny—finds Congal's degradation at the end
contradictory to the main tendency of the play: instead of showing two ways of looking at life, "the play begins to look like a
parable about the superiority of the mystical to the heroic life."[42]
Wilson sees the play as Yeats's affirmation of the heroic self and
rejection of Attracta's mystical denial of life. In this view, Congal
is an absolutely "self-sufficient" hero who "transcends his humili-

---

[41] For further discussion of *A Full Moon in March*, see pp. 215–17.
[42] Ure, *Yeats the Playwright*, p. 155.

ation" and "defeats the Herne [by] dying with real, if tragi-comic dignity."[43]

Whitaker agrees with Wilson that Congal has won "a subjective victory over Nobodaddy in the sky," but notes the seemingly inconsistent fact (which bothered Ure, too) that Attracta "comes off somewhat better in her madness."[44] Moore sidesteps the question of Congal's final status: "It is hard to say whether he is more fool than hero, but there is no doubt that in his own eyes he wins the battle to retain his human dignity."[45] And finally Bloom (trying to show that the Emperor has no clothes) asserts that there is no structured opposition of viewpoints, that Congal is "a travesty of the hero," Attracta a "crazed, bloody-minded ... prophetess," and the play as "bitter as it is confused and every sort of failure."[46]

There are two main factors in the play's incoherence. First, Yeats wrote it "in the happier moments of a long illness that had so separated me from life that I felt irresponsible."[47] Believing that his present life was empty, he concentrated on the fantasies that welled up from within. The fantasies amused and stimulated him, and he put them into the play relatively raw and unassimilated. This lack of synthetic energy in relation to his material permitted him to express two different points of view—the heroic and the ironic—without working for a higher synthesis that would give the reader his bearings.

The second factor in the incoherence of *The Herne's Egg* is the incoherent nature of the fantasies being expressed. These fantasies are full of sex and violence, perceived or imagined by a small child in ways that seem wild and strange to an adult. The reader experiences a confusion like that of the child. Yeats himself called the play "the strangest wildest thing I have ever written" (*Letters*, p. 845).

Since the play is so confusing, a brief summary of the plot may

[43] F. A. C. Wilson, *W. B. Yeats and Tradition* (London: Gollancz, 1961), pp. 136, 133.

[44] Whitaker, *Swan and Shadow*, p. 291.

[45] John Rees Moore, *Masks of Love and Death: Yeats as Dramatist* (Ithaca, N.Y.: Cornell University Press, 1971), p. 297.

[46] Bloom, *Yeats*, pp. 422, 424–25, 426.

[47] *Variorum Plays*, p. 1311.

be helpful. The play starts with a battle between the two kings, Congal and Aedh. They call a truce and Congal decides to steal the eggs of the mystic Herne—a proper food for heroes—to celebrate their truce. Congal encounters Attracta, who says that she is a priestess and the Herne's bride. He puts her down as a hysterical woman, joking that the embrace of seven men would cure her of her delusion. In stealing the eggs he incurs the Herne's curse: he will live and die a fool and meet his death at a fool's hands. Attracta, walking in a nuptial trance, substitutes a hen's egg for Congal's Herne's egg. Congal, thinking Aedh had made the substitution, kills him, thus partially fulfilling the Herne's curse. On finding that Attracta had given him the wrong egg, Congal and his men retaliate by raping her. Afterward, seeing Attracta evoke a manifestation of the Herne's power as thunder, Congal is persuaded of the Herne's existence, submits, and goes to his death at a fool's hands. As he is dying, Attracta gives him motherly affection. She tries to become his mother in a future life, but it is too late. He dies, and we are told that he will be reincarnated as a donkey.

Let us now examine the play in more detail. As the curtain opens, we are confronted by the ambiguous and awe-inspiring figure of the Herne, who appears "high up on backcloth," standing on a rock, "its base hidden in mist."[48] The ambiguous existence and nature of the Herne are suggested by the mist. He is a strange, hermaphroditic figure, possessor not only of the phallic beak and legs, but of the eggs (though it is his phallic attributes, like the Unicorn's, that are most important for the story). He may or may not have lost a leg. Corney, Attracta's servant, suggests that he is "Pretending that he had but the one leg / To fool us all" (Scene II, ll. 132–33). This doubt may derive from Yeats's infantile perplexity over erection and its subsidence; it also expresses his preoccupation with castration. Attracta, like the Herne, is a hermaphroditic character: she has a beaked god in her "gut" (II, l. 103). The punishment for despoiling the Herne—appropriate to

[48] Stage directions, *Variorum Plays*, p. 1012. All citations of *The Herne's Egg* are from *Variorum Plays*, pp. 1012–40.

a castration fantasy—is wittlessness, the symbolic equivalent of the punishment meted out in the dance plays: one way or another, you lose your head.

A nursery atmosphere befitting the primitive fantasies being depicted is established at the beginning of Scene II, when Corney wheels in a toy donkey, "like a child's toy, but life-size."[49] Indeed, the battle between Aedh and Congal with which the play opens is reminiscent of the battle between the prototypical siblings Tweedle Dum and Tweedle Dee. The absolute and ridiculous symmetry—they fight the same number of battles and exchange exactly the same number of similarly located blows—makes them seem almost like mechanical toys. The male characters have very little individuation and, as Ure has pointed out, seem childish. In addition to the childlike men, the toy donkey, and the play battle, there are episodes throughout the play that sound like nursery lessons in deportment. When Congal wants to take the Herne's eggs from Attracta, he is told to remember his "manners" (II, l. 18) and ask her first. Corney is also reprimanded like a child when he wants to punish Congal. Attracta reminds him that he "must obey / All big men" (II, ll. 111–12). And when Congal and his men rape Attracta, his insistence that she will be all the better for it seems to parody the remark that so often accompanies spankings, "It's all for your own good."

In the play's opening scene, Yeats presents a grotesque parody of both childish or feminine dependence and the aggressive behavior characteristic of "big men." The battle between Aedh and Congal echoes the heavenly battles described in *The Unicorn from the Stars* as "the perpetual clashing of swords," but as Bloom puts it, one would have to be "tone-deaf" to perceive them as visionary.[50] In the earlier play, the ideal of masculine aggressive activity was balanced by an opposite ideal of peaceful "drinking from the cup of life"—the infant at the breast. Yeats degrades both ideals in *The Herne's Egg* in his opening parable of two fleas whose ac-

---

[49] Stage directions, *Variorum Plays*, p. 1014. Ure pertinently notes that this childish quality seems out of keeping with the violence of the rest of the play —it is unassimilated (p. 146).

[50] Bloom, *Yeats*, p. 424.

tivity parallels that of the heroes. The fable is told by Aedh during a lull in the fighting:

> Aedh: A story is running round
>   Concerning two rich fleas.
> Congal: We hop like fleas, but war
>   Has taken all our riches.
> Aedh: Rich, and rich, so rich that they
>   Retired and bought a dog.
> Congal: Finish the tale and say
>   What kind of a dog they bought.
>   . . .
> Aedh: A fat, square, lazy dog,
>   No sort of scratching dog.
>   (I, ll. 18–31)

The theme of oral satisfaction, expressed here in terms of fleas who suck blood from a tolerant dog, is stated in human terms in Scene II, with Congal's announcement that he will steal the Herne's eggs to celebrate his truce with Aedh.

The Herne's egg, belonging as it did solely to the Herne himself and to no one else—must be taken literally in the play as forbidden food; it may also be taken metaphorically as forbidden knowledge. Wilson notes that Yeats equated the egg not only with the "boundless infinite" (or *Anima Mundi*) but with forbidden knowledge, " 'that circle pass not' so much talked of in theosophical mysticism."[51] As I pointed out earlier, one of Yeats's earliest mythic interests was the Eden legend about a young man who stole "the food of the gods" and died from eating it. In adapting the myth of forbidden food in his *Island of Statues*, Yeats puts the forbidden flower of wisdom into the hands of a female guardian. In *The Herne's Egg* the god-food again becomes concrete, but it retains its connections with forbidden wisdom. In his later work, Yeats sometimes used these ideas in a totemistic form. In "Parnell's Funeral," for example, those who ate Parnell's heart would gain Parnell's virtues. Eating sacred eggs is a variation, with mystical overtones, on the idea of eating a part or substance of the body.

Implicit in the insult offered Congal by Attracta's substitution

---

[51] Wilson, *Yeats and Tradition*, p. 114.

of a hen's egg for a Herne's egg is a contrast between the valuable
male egg of the Herne and the degraded female egg. The episode
also represents anger at the mother for providing bad or inadequate food (compare the spiritually malnourished women in *The
King's Threshold* who produce cripples).[52] One of Congal's men
explains the insult in a drunken speech:

> Herne's egg, hen's egg, great difference.
> There's insult in that difference.
> What do hens eat? Hens live upon mash,
> Upon slop, upon kitchen odds and ends.
> What do hernes eat? Hernes live on eels,
> On things that must always run about,
> Man's a high animal and runs about,
> But mash is low, O very low.
>
> (IV, ll. 30–37)

The distinction seems to reflect the theory—common in early childhood—that both men and women give birth. Yeats depicts the
male product or offspring as clean and beneficial, the female as
dirty and degraded. The filthy hen's egg had to be "spat upon by
a kitchen wench" and "wiped on her apron" (IV, l. 21). The
Herne's egg is, by implication, clean. Also implicit is the idea that
generation is achieved by eating the parent's substance. If one becomes, and in turn reproduces, what one eats, then it is obviously
important to eat the right things. The Herne's egg will be con-
ducive to heroic activity because the Herne has been eating the
phallic eels. The hens, by contrast, have been eating slop. Congal,
trying to provide the right food for himself, is forestalled by Attracta.

Congal's assumption that Aedh gave him the false egg initiates
a wild brawl in which Aedh is killed by a blow from Congal's table
leg. As Congal comments, we had "forgotten what we fought about,
/ So fought like gentlemen, but now / Knowing the truth must
fight like beasts" (IV, ll. 63–65). The painful thought is not just that

---

[52] In his memoirs John Butler Yeats says that as a child, his son Willie
typically asked "such questions as 'Is it only wicked mothers who give their
children bones to eat?'" His father comments, "What hobgoblin fancies were
going through his mind no one troubled to ask." Cited in Murphy, "Father
and Son," p. 86.

he has been tricked, but that the good food ("the one sole dish that takes [his] fancy" [II, l. 56]) is reserved for Attracta alone. Rivalry over coveted food is not necessarily limited to siblings. Melanie Klein, in her studies of young children, demonstrates convincingly that many of them imagine that the father is also a rival for the breast.[53] Yeats suggests that the quarrel between his prototypical siblings also represents a battle between father and son by alluding, as Wilson notes, to the murder of Caesar by Brutus.[54] "He was a noble character," one of Congal's men says of Aedh, "And I must weep at his funeral" (IV, ll. 49–50). The punishment for Congal's crime is, as in Shakespeare, the downfall of the hero, whose death falling on a spit echoes that of Brutus. Yeats's portrayal of Aedh as Caesar corresponds to a view of the father as an older brother or comrade that is common in late childhood. The awe-inspiring and mysterious Herne reflects a much earlier view.

When Congal learns that it was Attracta who substituted the hen's egg, he orders his men to join him in raping her. Two interwoven fantasies lie behind this act of revenge: a fantasy of revenge on the bad mother who gives the child bad food, and a fantasy of sadistic sexual possession of the mother. The rape is surrounded by extreme ambiguity. Afterward, when Attracta emerges from her trance, she insists that she was not raped, that what had occurred was the consummation of her marriage with the Herne. "I lay beside him, his pure bride" (V, l. 29). Her behavior suggests, as Ure notes, that the Herne had used the rape to effect the consummation of his marriage: "the mystery of the sacred bride-bed is that the men have acted as the surrogates of the god."[55]

One of the things Yeats seems to be describing here is a very

[53] Melanie Klein, *Psychoanalysis of Children*, p. 188.

[54] Wilson, *Yeats and Tradition*, pp. 127, 128. There is a well-known legend, the source of two plays by Alfieri (*Bruto Primo* and *Bruto Secondo*), that Brutus was Caesar's illegitimate son. Caesar was supposed to have said in Greek when Brutus stabbed him, "And you, my child." Several psychoanalytic interpretations of Shakespeare's play also see the conflict as one between father and son.

[55] Ure, *Yeats the Playwright*, p. 152. Wilson shows that Yeats was aware of the idea of a surrogate relationship with the god in both Plutarch and Indian legend. In *A Vision*, Yeats records that a god might descend to a supplicant by possessing the body of a "wandering priestess." Cited in Wilson, *Yeats and Tradition*, pp. 116–17.

young child's feeling that he is participating in an observed act. Such feelings are characteristic of the oral mode of experience— re-created so insistently in the play—in which both people and characteristics (such as male and female) tend to fuse in an undifferentiated manner. Yeats expresses this sense of participation in relation to father and son in *The Player Queen*, where Septimus becomes impresario at the Unicorn's marriage, and with greater directness in *A Full Moon in March*, where the Swineherd is split into two parts, one enacting, one observing, the sexual act. As we saw, the Swineherd's incestuous possession of the mother-queen seems to be experienced as a reenactment of the primal scene, with the hero taking the father's place. In *The Herne's Egg* Congal denies that there has been a union between the Herne and Attracta; that is, he denies the primal scene. He, Congal, is to be the one to possess Attracta. The ironic idea that the Herne was using Congal's body not only expresses the child's fantasy of participation in reverse (it is the father who participates), but further degrades Congal, who becomes only a manipulated puppet. However, at the same time as Yeats represents the tendency to fusion, he represents Congal struggling against it. Congal's most convincing heroic moment comes when, struggling to maintain his separate identity, he refuses to deny that he, and not the Herne, had possessed Attracta.

There are essentially two points of view toward Attracta expressed in the play. In the first she is obsessed, foolish, and neurotic, whereas in the second she is mysterious and powerful. Congal sees Attracta's belief in her mystic marriage as a fantasy generated by repressed sensuality: "As boys take common snow, and make / An image of god or bird or beast / To feed their sensuality" (II, ll. 65–67). In Congal's opinion Attracta's icy fantasies can only be dispelled by sexual contact: "For nothing less than seven men / Can melt that snow, but when it melts / She may, being free from all obsession, / Live as every woman should" (IV, ll. 116–19). Yeats here belittles Attracta and ironically represents his own early body-denying self. Wilson points out that Attracta is derived from Seraphita, the heroine of Balzac's Swedenborgian novel, whose disembodied purity Yeats rejects.[56] Yeats's ironic self-representation is thus linked to a literary model representing views he had turned away from.

Attracta's orientation toward death also links her to such earlier Yeatsian figures as the narrator in "Rosa Alchemica" and the Real Queen. She describes her marriage in a way that underlines her death wish:

> That I may lie in a blazing bed
> And a bird take my maidenhead,
> To the unbegotten I return,
> All a womb and a funeral urn.
> (II, ll. 96–99)

Yeat's (i.e., Congal's) view of Attracta as deluded and neurotic conflicts with his view of her—corresponding to a child's earliest perception of his mother—as mysterious and powerful. This alternative view is conveyed in several different ways. First, the movement of the plot counteracts Congal's depreciation of Attracta and suggests Yeats's uncertainty about Congal's championship of healthy impulse. The Herne, after all, appears to be right, and "unhealthy fantasy" ultimately wins. Second, in her speech Attracta exudes power and confidence. Unlike the pathetic Real Queen, whose talk about a mystic ride was plainly masochistic fantasy, Attracta speaks in a high style, filled with images of masculine power that cannot fail to influence the reader. She prays, for instance, that "all foliage [i.e., her body] gone" she "may shoot into my joy" (II, ll. 187–88), and declares that after her marriage she lay with the Herne's thunderbolts in her hand (II, ll. 60–61). Her phallic imagery, which suggests that in consummation she shares the phallic power of the Herne, might be seen as the deluded expression of repressed sexuality; but when her invocation of the Herne in the final scene is answered by thunder, the reader, like Congal himself, begins to respect her power.

Attracta is not only obscurely powerful, but uncanny. Her nuptial trance, in which she moves "like a doll upon a wire" (II, l. 198), is the most striking manifestation of her uncanniness. Her jerking

<hr>

[56] Wilson, *Yeats and Tradition*, p. 104.

movements convey the impression that she is a degraded puppet-child manipulated by a greater power. Attracta would be classed by Yeats as an objective personality who is seeking to lose herself in a greater whole. Onto this personality type, described in *A Vision*, Yeats seems to project the passivity and helplessness he felt as a child. At the extreme of objectivity, the being is described as either completely plastic—a lump of dough—or rigid and manipulated by someone else. Yeats used puppets symbolically to depict sibling rage at the arrival of a new baby in his poem "The Dolls." In the poem "The Double Vision of Michael Robartes," Yeats describes the unfortunate spirits at the objective dark of the moon as dependent puppets who are connected with a human child by the "I's" initial expression of frustration at his lack of freedom:

> When had I my own will?
> O not since life began.
> Constrained, arraigned, baffled, bent and unbent
> By those wire-jointed jaws and limbs of wood,
> Themselves obedient.

Attracta's puppet-like, jerking movements when called by the god to consummate her marriage suggest those of the spirits at the dark of the moon, but in the clearly sexual context of the play, where the movements are observed and wondered at by the village children, they also suggest a child's perception of the primal scene as a series of incomprehensible and uncanny movements. The extreme artifice of the play, often commented upon, the stylized battles, Attracta's movements, Congal's falling beside the spit—all these may be efforts to distance the traumatic scene by abstraction. The stage directions stipulate that the fighters in the opening scene should not actually hit each other; similarly, Congal falls alongside the spit without touching it.

In Yeats's representation of Congal's death, two different fantasies merge. The first fantasy concerns Congal's punishment, symbolically suited to his crime. He was going to eat the forbidden eggs of the Herne; now he himself becomes like a spitted chicken ready for eating. (This is a much less dignified version of a similar fantasy in *The Shadowy Waters*, where Forgael is to be "the sacri-

ficial flesh.") The fool who is to kill Congal comes armed with
kitchen implements: a roasting spit, a cauldron, and a cauldron
lid. Whereas in the earlier play *On Baile's Strand* the chicken
killed by the Fool is a symbolic equivalent of Cuchulain's son, in
The Herne's Egg Congal himself becomes like the chicken he de-
spises, ready for the pot. The spit on which Congal is symbolically
impaled recalls the Herne's beak, which Corney earlier begged
Attracta to bring out of her "gut" and use to impale Congal and
his men "like eels" (II, ll. 103–5). The punishment represents a
sadistic consummation of the inverse Oedipal relationship (that
is, union with the father), seen in terms of being pierced and eaten.

The second prominent fantasy involved in the ending is the familiar love-death theme of the dance plays. Aggression against the
mother is followed by punishment and final reconciliation. Attracta's final tenderness toward Congal echoes the tenderness of
the Queen to the severed head. The hero dead or on the point of
death is no longer a sexual threat, but a child. Near death, Congal
accepts a dependent role: Attracta now appears supernaturally
powerful. "Even the thunder obeys you," he says, and asks for her
protection after death, when he will again be as helpless as an
infant. She answers, "I will protect you," and asserts her willing-
ness to be his mother in a future life.

A major difficulty with the play—reflected, as we have seen, in
the variety of critical interpretations—is the uncertain point of
view, which reflects both Yeats's uncertainty about his heroic mask
and the incoherent nature of the fantasies he is presenting. Critics
like Wilson, who fail to make proper allowance for Yeats's irony,
naturally overestimate the heroic aspects. At the other extreme,
Bloom's extreme sensitivity to the play's irony leads him to see
Congal as merely "a travesty of the hero" (as exemplified by Cuchulain).[57] In most of Yeats's work, fantasies are submitted to an
organizing principle that allows character and meaning to emerge.
In *The Herne's Egg* there are no characters in the ordinary sense,
but rather collections of often contradictory fantasies and memories subsumed under various names. The dramatic meaning of the

[57] Bloom, *Yeats*, p. 422.

character's speech and action shifts as different fantasies come to the fore. My discussion of the play has been essentially descriptive and possibly reductive because no appreciation of the play in its own terms is possible.

Certain biographical facts may cast light on the reasons for the play's incoherence. As we noted earlier, when he began working on *The Herne's Egg*, Yeats felt that nothing was happening in his life. He writes during his convalescence, while working on the scenario, that although he is full of creative impulse, "there is nothing to record—always the same bright white walls and blue sea" (*Letters*, p. 422). At the time of the dance plays, Yeats turned back to his early literary work for stimulation. Now he seems to be allowing himself to regress, to return to his infantile past, perhaps because his illness made him feel passive and reminded him of childhood deprivations and humiliations. His doctors had restricted his diet. Shri Purohit Swami, who was working with Yeats during his convalescence, applauded the doctors' restrictions on meat, telling Yeats, "Give an ageing man food and he turns it into poison" (*Letters*, p. 847).

Yeats's ill health made him subject, like the child, to endless restrictions, and painfully dependent on others. He writes in December 1935 that he is struggling to "keep Shri Swami from treating me as an invalid; if I would let him I should be helped up and down stairs" (*Letters*, p. 844). In April 1936 he complains to Olivia that Mrs. Yeats "means to look after me for the rest of my life—'You must never go away without Anne or me'—and that will not suit me at all. . . . O my dear, as age increases my chains, my need for freedom grows" (*Letters*, p. 852). And finally, in a letter to Dorothy Wellesley, he denounces the pervasive passivity in a novel he had just read: "Fundamentally I hate the book, the hero is passive & the assumption throughout is that everybody is passive. . . . Some few of us . . . have in the very core of our being the certainty that man's soul is active" (*Wellesley Letters*, p. 56). However much he hated passivity, he was not in a position to feel like an active hero, worried as he was about becoming "a useless hulk for friends and relatives to haul about and stumble over" (*Wellesley Letters*,

p. 50). Whereas previously he had achieved mastery through dreams of heroism, he now turned, in this case with less success, to irony and self-mockery.

Feeling that his life was offering him no new material, he not only turned back to his childhood, but, as Wilson shows, drew on literary sources ranging from Indian philosophy to Celtic mythology to Balzac.[58] A few points might be added here about the influence of Dorothy Wellesley. Yeats's budding relationship with Lady Gerald Wellesley seems to have been in part a re-evocation of his relationship with Lady Gregory. Lady Gregory, as we have seen, served as a mother to Yeats in numerous ways, notably in helping him to use ordinary speech. In November 1935, Yeats writes Dorothy Wellesley that the "swift rhythm" of her poem "Fire" helped him decide on the rhythm for *The Herne's Egg*: "I have a three-act tragi-comedy in my head to write in Majorca, not in blank verse but in short line[s] like 'Fire' " (*Wellesley Letters*, p. 40). In December Yeats writes that he is trying to "emulate" Dorothy's "natural style" in *The Herne's Egg*, and goes on to compare her to Lady Gregory: "With you it is not a question of the speech of the common people—as with Synge and Lady Gregory—but the common speech of the people." The following May, planning to visit her after his convalescence, he writes, "I long for quiet, long ago I used to find it at Coole." And his next letter develops the implicit comparison between the two women. "I long for your intellect & sanity. Hitherto I have never found these anywhere but at Coole" (*Wellesley Letters*, pp. 45, 62, 63). The rhythm of "Fire" was probably so stimulating to Yeats precisely because he associated Lady Gerald with Lady Gregory and his really fruitful relationship with her.

Dorothy Wellesley's poetry had a philosophic cast, as Yeats notes in his introduction to her work, and he probably felt she would approve of his new play's "philosophic depth" (*Wellesley Letters*, p. 40). However, as Wilson shows, the argument owes little to her.[59] Yeats himself asserts that he was influenced by Shri Purohit Swami: "the play is his philosophy in a fable, or mine confirmed by him"

[58] Wilson, *Yeats and Tradition*, pp. 95–136, esp. pp. 95–108.
[59] *Ibid.*, p. 95.

(*Wellesley Letters*, p. 42). Possibly, as Wilson suggests, Yeats intended to portray the Indian concept of the Divinity of the Self in his hero Congal,[60] but his mood of self-doubt certainly deflected any such aim. More important perhaps than Yeats's philosophic pretensions here is the fact that certain cosmic images, with which Yeats was familiar—such as the bisexual Brahma laying the golden world egg—reinforced Yeats's personal fantasies. Perhaps reassured by the thought that he was writing philosophy, he could let the fantasies surface with only a modicum of restraint, producing as he said, "The strangest wildest thing I have ever written."

'Purgatory'

In *Purgatory* (1938) Yeats portrays the themes of love-hate for the mother and rivalry with the father in unequivocal, not to say sordid, terms. There is no ambiguity about the central character or his actions; he is a despairing, dirty old man. There is no hint at future gratification of the protagonist's passion for his mother or even a reconciliation between them as there was in *The Herne's Egg*. Instead, the Old Man is forced to watch the traumatic primal scene and must concede his own impotence to stop it. Finally, in grief and rage, he kills his son.

Yeats is returning, in *Purgatory*, to the theme of one of his early plays, *On Baile's Strand*—the murder of a son by his father. The two plays can profitably be compared. *On Baile's Strand* is one of Yeats's finest plays, written during the hopeful period when he was trying to create a heroic mask and come to terms with himself and his body. *Purgatory* is a play from a bitter period in Yeats's old age, a period when he seems to feel the futility of any mask. The murder of a son has correspondingly different meanings in the two plays. Let us turn first to *Purgatory*.

The plot of this short play is simple. An Old Man and his son arrive at a ruined house. The Old Man reminisces to the Boy about his past: his aristocratic mother, who died giving birth to the Old Man, and the drunken groom who married her and brought ruin on her and her house. Once father, mother, and house have been described, the Old Man reveals that his father had burned the

60 Ibid., p. 113.

house down, and that he, the Old Man, had "killed him in the burning house." As he reflects on his past, he sees the house lit up and his mother's ghost appear framed in the window. She is waiting for his father; it is the anniversary of her wedding night, the night the Old Man was conceived. As he watches his mother and father have intercourse, the Old Man grows frenzied and kills the Boy, hoping thus to stop his mother's reenactment of the scene. Shortly afterward, however, he hears the returning hoofbeats of his father's horse. The scene is about to begin again.

The mechanism that makes the action of *Purgatory* possible is what Yeats calls the Dreaming Back. When the Old Man shows the house to the Boy, he tells his son that there is somebody in it. The Boy thinks the Old Man is crazy, but his father persists and explains that souls in Purgatory return to their habitations:

> Re-live
> Their transgressions, and that not once
> But many times; they know at last
> The consequence of those transgressions
> Whether upon others or upon themselves;
> Upon others, others may bring help,
> For when the consequence is at an end
> The dream must end; if upon themselves,
> There is no help but in themselves
> And in the mercy of God.
>   (ll. 33–42)

Yeats describes the Dreaming Back in detail in *A Vision*, as we shall see in Chapter 5. To summarize briefly here, after the soul has grown used to death, it enters a second state called Meditation, or Dreaming Back, in which it attempts to rid itself of all sexual obsession through long and painful dreams of the past. This is the stage pictured in *Purgatory*. Dreaming Back includes the Return, which Yeats calls the "true second state," in which the Spirit must relive events in the order they occurred because the abstract mind must (*Vision*, p. 226)

trace every passionate event to its cause until all are related and understood, turned into knowledge, made a part of itself. All that keeps the *Spirit* from its freedom may be compared to a knot that has to be untied or to an oscillation or a violence that must end in a return to equilibrium.

In Dreaming Back, the Spirit is imprisoned by events; in the Return it turns them into knowledge and then falls again into the Dreaming Back. The more complete the Dreaming Back, the more complete the Return and the more successful the next incarnation, when the Spirit may explore not only the causes of an event but also its consequences. And because these are likely to be numerous, the process can continue for centuries. In the concept of the Dreaming Back and the Return, Yeats transposes to the afterlife the process by which he attempts to master the obsessive ruminations that plague him.

The mother in *Purgatory*, then, is reliving her wedding night, an event of utmost intensity and consequence. Out of a considerable body of abstraction Yeats takes just what is necessary for his play: the idea that souls must rework their past lives until their feelings, particularly sexual feelings, are understood, and thus no longer induce excitement or pain. The Old Man's obsession with the mother's act joins her own obsession with it, and it is anguishing to them both. The son is mistaken, however, in thinking that he can end his mother's reenactment of the pleasurable yet painful deed by eliminating its ultimate consequence, his son. She herself must purge her emotions.

Let us reexamine the plot of *Purgatory* in the light of these concepts. *Purgatory* begins with a description of Dreaming Back, followed by the Old Man's reminiscences of his father, his mother, and the house. The Old Man is identified with the Great House through an aristocratic Anglo-Irish mother. Yeats's lines describing the house recall earlier poems written to extol the virtues of the Great Houses, "Ancestral Houses" and "Upon a House Shaken by the Land Agitation":

> Great people lived and died in this house;
> Magistrates, colonels, members of Parliament,
> Captains and Governors, and long ago
> Men that had fought at Aughrim and the Boyne.
> Some that had gone on Government work
> To London or to India came home to die,
> Or came from London every spring
> To look at the may-blossom in the park.
>
> (ll. 61–68)

We have mentioned Yeats's nostalgia for Coole and Lady Gregory. Now, in *Purgatory*, he movingly fuses his longing for the maternal Lady Gregory with his obsessive desire for his idealized natural mother.

Set in a fable of incestuous passion and death, the concrete language and specific references to aristocratic values take on an evocative richness, which recalls and blends with the House of Ireland in *The Green Helmet*, the Heavenly house, repository of all the lovely things that were, in *The King of the Great Clock Tower*, and the dwelling of the queen who shuts the door in the face of the poet-lover in "The Cap and Bells." In these earlier works the house functioned as a symbolic representation of the mother; here Yeats deliberately uses the house this way—to powerful effect. The destruction of the house and the mother's ruin stem from her act of intercourse.

The felt destructiveness of the primal scene is convincingly tied to a set of social and historical circumstances that make it possible for the reader to react with the intended horror. The Old Man's father is lower class, "a groom in a training stable," who "squandered everything she had." The groom, moreover, is a braggart and a drunkard—but obviously sexually attractive. The last element is the one Yeats stressed in the Old Man's reminiscences. The Old Man says twice of his mother that "she looked at him and married him," thus emphasizing not only the physical basis of the relationship, but his own wonder that it occurred. The base groom's seduction of the fine lady and his destruction of the house, its threshold "gone to patch a pig-sty," is Yeats's undisguised representation of the primal scene and his emotional reaction to it. It is this scene and Yeats's original disgust that he is reacting to when he has the Swineherd-son, the hero of *A Full Moon in March*, dethrone the Queen and threaten that he will make her "bring forth her farrow in the dung."

Having described his ancestry and ancestral home, the Old Man makes two revelations that lead into the action of the play. The first is that the Old Man's father burned the house down while drunk, and the second is that the Old Man killed his father with

the "knife that cuts my dinner now." This grotesque detail—the
final permutation of the oral motif—suggests a token feast in which
a sacrificial victim representing the father is killed and eaten. The
Old Man is not ashamed of his deed, but rather filled with hatred
of his father and jealous compassion for his mother. His thoughts
are of the wedding night when he was begotten, and he cannot
understand how his wonderful mother could have consented to
sleep with his loutish father. Even now, as an aged man, he cannot
bear the thought. "Do not let him touch you!" he cries to his
mother's ghost (l. 140). The situation, like many others in Yeats's
plays, is sado-masochistic. Mother and son are tortured together,
he by observing the scene, she by her posthumous knowledge—
which accompanies her pleasure in the act—that she is begetting
her husband's murderer. The son, watching and ruminating, begins talking to himself: his father is a "tired beast" (l. 181). The
line "Then the bride-sleep fell upon Adam" (l. 183) comes to his
mind—an ironic comparison, as Moore notes, of his own begetting
to the creation.[61]

The Old Man's watching is interrupted by the Boy's attempt to
steal from him. Roused to anger, the Old Man grapples with the
Boy and his money is scattered. He briefly resumes his obsessive
watching, then turns and kills the Boy, reasoning that he will keep
him from passing pollution on. (The fear of pollution was, as we
have seen, the subject of Yeats's own Swiftian ruminations.) He
also forestalls his own murder at the hands of his son, who openly
contemplates the deed, and who, as Yeats points out, is sixteen,
the same age the Old Man was when he killed his father—and the
same age as Yeats's own son, Michael, when Yeats was writing the
play.[62] We have seen in Yeats's letters hints that he feels threatened

[61] J. R. Moore, *Masks of Love and Death*, p. 314. This line is quoted repeatedly by the Prime Minister in *The Player Queen* when he thinks about
Decima's wickedness and the woes brought into the world by Eve's sin.

[62] Michael Yeats was born in August 1921, and thus was still sixteen in March
1938 when his father began writing *Purgatory* (*Letters*, p. 907n). Hone points
out resemblances to *Purgatory* in a ghost story told by Yeats around 1913.
If Hone's recounting is accurate, the story shows Yeats's longstanding preoccupation with the murderous Oedipal jealousy and hereditary taint of *Purgatory*.
The ghost story is as follows: A man who, until his wife became pregnant,

by his children (*Letters*, pp. 817, 819). Seeing them mature seems to have made it more difficult for him to deny the approach of his own death. Here he reverses the natural order; it is the son who dies.

The significance of the conflict for Yeats goes beyond the familial. The new Irish Constitution was also sixteen years old in 1938. Appropriately, the Boy in *Purgatory* has the qualities of ignorance and greed that Yeats associated with democracy. The Old Man, because he is partly the child of his aristocratic mother, received a good classical education. The Boy has only "the education that befits / A bastard that a pedlar got / Upon a tinker's daughter in a ditch" (ll. 88–90). The movement of generations is downward, which accords with Yeats's notion that the world was going through an "objective" cycle, a cycle that would shortly come to a violent end.

After the orgiastic murder, the Old Man lapses into a childish rhyme:

> 'Hush-a-bye baby, thy father's a knight,
> Thy mother a lady, lovely and bright.'
> (ll. 195–96)

Though sung to his son, it refers also to himself. By killing his son, the Old Man feels, he has demolished the horrible past and restored his mother to her first condition as a lady, lovely and bright. He is also free to imagine an ideal father, a knight. However, his dream lasts only a moment because he remembers that the rhyme is not true; it is only something he has read. The following lines make it clear that the nursery rhyme lady is his mother the way he wants her to be, pure and cold. "Study that tree," he says to the dead Boy. "It stands there like a purified soul, / All

---

"had been tender and trusting, became sullen and suspicious, often giving himself up to lonely bouts of drinking." When a son was born to the couple the man rushed, drunk, into his wife's room, "wrested the baby from her breast," and dashed its brains out. The despairing mother jumped to her death. Her ghost continued to haunt the spot and reenact her suicidal plunge for generations, even after the family castle was destroyed by fire. She appeared finally to one of the last members of the family, who, watching her plummet to her death, feels that "he had watched this melancholy scene innumerable times before," and realized that his blood and that of all his descendants was tainted by an inexpiable crime. Hone, *W. B. Yeats*, pp. 302–3.

cold, sweet, glistening light" (ll. 199–201). Fifty years before, the tree had had "Green leaves, ripe leaves, leaves thick as butter, / Fat, greasy life" (ll. 22–23). The crime of the mother was a sensual love for one beneath her: "She should have known he was not her kind" (l. 174). The play's final irony, however, is that despite the Old Man's deed his mother remains in the dark and must continue to dream through her fateful coupling with his father. The pattern continues, and all the Old Man can do is pray: "O God, / ... Appease / The misery of the living and the remorse of the dead" (ll. 220–23).

The Old Man's talks with the Boy reveal that he lives in the past, brooding on his mother's marriage and her ruin. Seeing his parents relive their wedding night, he feels a helplessness to change things and a Hamlet-like self-contempt because of his helplessness: "Go fetch Tertullian; he and I / Will ravel all that problem out / Whilst those two lie upon the mattress / Begetting me" (ll. 154–57). He stops brooding abruptly when his son tries to rob him. He is stunned when he sees that his son regards him as a crazed old man, too obsessed by dreams to protect his property. "Come back! Come back! / And so you thought to slip away, / My bag of money between your fingers, / And that I could not talk and see!" (ll. 157–60). They struggle briefly. Then the Boy begins to share his father's vision. He looks into the lighted window and, appalled, sees his grandfather's ghost. Knowing the ghosts will see nothing, the Old Man stabs the Boy to death.

The Old Man's abrupt switch from helpless contemplation of his parents to brutal action against his son recalls the shift from passivity to activity made by Septimus in *The Player Queen* through his participation in the nature of the Unicorn. Both shifts can be understood as expressing a fantasy in which the child attempts to master a traumatic experience by becoming an active participant. Moreover, since Yeats suggests in his evocation of the primal scene that he experienced it as a destructive attack on the mother by identifying with the active father-figure, he avoided the danger of feeling like the victimized mother. In *Purgatory* the Old Man victimizes the Boy as the father victimized the mother. The Boy is

not only physically assaulted but mentally overpowered by the
Old Man's vision. The murder is accounted for in the play as self-
defense or ritual exorcism; only by murdering the Boy can the
Old Man eradicate the evil. His conviction that the exorcism will
work derives from the underlying fantasy that violent participation will make the appalling event cease to haunt him. But the
attempt to secure control by decisive action fails. Like an infant
screaming beside the bed of self-absorbed parents, the Old Man
is ignored by the ghosts. He notes the impenetrability of the bar-
rier when he comments that the ghosts "know nothing, being nothing" (l. 190).

'On Baile's Strand'

Moving back from the hopeless and degraded world of *Purgatory* to the heroic mood of Yeats's early play *On Baile's Strand*
(1903–6) makes one overwhelmingly aware of important differences between Yeats's early and late relationship to his mask and
to the theme of fathers and sons. The murder of a son in *On Baile's
Strand* has a markedly different meaning than it has in *Purgatory*.
Despite ambivalent elements in Cuchulain's feeling toward his
son, Yeats seems primarily to be conveying a fantasy of heroic
closeness brought to a bad end by external forces. The play begins
with low farce. A Fool and a Blind Man are partners in theft. The
Fool steals a chicken and the Blind Man prepares to cook it so
that they can eat it together. The Blind Man says he has heard
that the warrior queen Aoife has sent her son to kill Cuchulain.
The action shifts to the throne room. Cuchulain, whose father is
Mannanan, god of the sea, is pressured by the High King Conchubar to give up his wild ways and take an oath of allegiance.
At length, Cuchulain submits and takes the oath; immediately
afterward a strange Young Man (Cuchulain's son by Aoife, unknown to his father) arrives, and refusing to identify himself chal-
lenges Cuchulain. Cuchulain, reminded by the Young Man's features of his beloved Aoife, pledges friendship, but persuaded by
the High King that he has been bewitched—that the Young Man

is an enemy—he fights with him and kills him. On finding out from the Fool that he has killed his son, he goes mad and rushes off with his sword to fight the waves. The play ends as the Fool, who has been tricked of his chicken by the Blind Man, nonetheless admits his dependence on him and, still directed by him, takes advantage of the distraction to steal bread from the ovens. We shall see the relevance of this subplot in a moment.

The basic situation is, as Ellmann points out, an opposition between Cuchulain, "impulsively loving and hating," and Conchubar, who tames him and forces him to submit to apparent reason.[63] Conchubar functions in the play as a father figure—probably derived from Yeats's memories of late childhood—who asks the child to renounce instinctual satisfactions and fantasies of heroism and be reasonable. In the first episode—during the dialogue between Cuchulain and Conchubar—Cuchulain resists control. "I'll not be bound. / I'll dance or hunt, or quarrel or make love, / Wherever and whenever I've a mind to" (ll. 210–12). Cuchulain looks back with longing to the time when he loved the fierce Queen Aoife, so unlike the tame sweethearts of other men.

During the conversation, it is revealed that Cuchulain desires a son, not an ordinary child but some supernatural hero, created in his own image, whose mother fittingly would be Aoife. Immediately after Cuchulain, worn down by Conchubar, takes the oath, a stranger who perfectly fits his ideal of son and companion arrives. Yeats here develops a fantasy of wonderful closeness between heroic figures in a mythical golden age. Cuchulain says: "You will stop with us, / And we will hunt the deer and the wild bulls" (ll. 511–12). In heroic fashion, Cuchulain gives gifts to the Young Man and receives the promise that "We'll stand by one another from this out" (l. 587). Yeats contrasts Cuchulain's spontaneous and primarily loving feelings toward his son with the distrust Conchubar arouses, a distrust that drives him to the tragic duel. In creating an opposition between impulse and reason in which reason is the villain, Yeats seems to be externalizing a tendency to

63 Ellmann, *Man and Masks*, p. 166.

self-distrust and rumination so that he may free himself of it and act in self-confidence and pride.[64]

In the first of the two published versions of the play (1903), the conflict between Cuchulain and Conchubar is not fully developed. Cuchulain's shift from love to distrust can be attributed to his own ambivalence rather than external pressure. Though a chorus of Kings cries witchcraft, Cuchulain seems free not to listen to them; as Bushrui says, "Witchcraft is not a convincing explanation: there should be some more effective cause of Cuchulain's abrupt submission."[65] In the new version of 1906, Yeats effectively externalizes the conflict. He makes reasonable Conchubar morally responsible for the murder of Cuchulain's son. Yeats now adds the details pointing to Cuchulain's desire for a son, and elaborates the fantasy in which father and son are heroic companions, both driven by love for Aoife the fierce warrior mother.

Yeats's opposition between impulse and reason tends to divert attention from the sado-masochistic aspects of his fantasy of a heroic family. In this golden age, probably based on early childhood memories in which parents and son are totally and passionately involved in one another, the family members (Mannanan, Cuchulain, Aoife, and the boy) both hate and love one another. Between fathers and sons, fighting seems a precondition of affection. Cuchulain would not have loved his son if the Young Man had not been willing to fight him as Cuchulain in his youth had offered to fight his own father. (Mannanan, having risen from the sea to confront Cuchulain, revealed his identity in time to avert tragedy, leaving as a gift a cloak that Cuchulain in turn gives his son before the fatal battle.) Love between heroic man and woman is also tied to hatred. It is "a kiss / In the mid-battle, and a difficult truce / . . . A brief forgiveness between opposites / That have been hatreds" (ll. 332–38). Love, so inextricably tied to hatred, reaches a fitting climax in the love-death of Cuchulain's son. The poisonous relationship between Aoife and Cuchulain has a direct influence on

[64] As we saw in Chapter 3, Yeats's development of the spontaneous mask in the early 1900's was part of a struggle to defend against obsessive thinking and regain confidence in his emotions and impulses.

[65] Bushrui, *Yeats's Verse-Plays*, p. 63.

the tragedy: it is Aoife who sent the Young Man to kill his father. But Aoife is also indirectly responsible for the slaying. Yeats implies that her rejection of Cuchulain caused him to fear and distrust love. Yeats emphasizes that Cuchulain has something aloof and proud about him "as if out of sheer strength of heart or from accident he had put affection away" (*Letters*, p. 425).

In his description of Aoife, Yeats combines elements relating to his mother's felt coldness with elements arising from his frustrated passion for Maud Gonne. (Bushrui points out that Aoife becomes more obviously linked to Maud—and a much bitterer portrait—in the revised version written after Maud's marriage.)[66] Aoife first seduces with her beauty, then spurns with her sword: She "breaks away when you have thought her won" (l. 198, early version). Yeats eroticizes the early painful experiences of coldness and inconsistency, making them something valuable. Cuchulain defines his pleasure in terms of an insatiable hunger. "For I'd be fed and hungry at one time." The farcical subplot reinforces the suggestion here that the picture of Cuchulain's starved love derives from Yeats's regressive cannabalistic fantasies. As the father figure deprives Cuchulain of his beloved son, so the Blind Man deprives the Fool of the chicken he wants to eat. The parallel is ironic. It depreciates the noble action of the hero by suggesting his similarity to the Fool who is in effect a hungry child, deprived of what he wants.[67]

Yeats's scheme of conflict between three generations in *On Baile's Strand* enables him to move freely between the roles of father and son, seeing himself now as Cuchulain the son, now as Cuchulain the father. In addition to moving between generations, Yeats moves between views of the family derived from different epochs of childhood. The heroic family of Mannanan, Cuchulain, and Aoife, the romantic family of a young child's imaginings, is contrasted with the more staid family of Conchubar, his tame wife,

---

[66] *Ibid.*, pp. 66–68.

[67] Yeats's father seems to have sensed something of the underlying fantasy. He disliked the hero's coming on in good spirits after the killing, he said, because it "rather suggests that the father killed the son as you would a chicken." Quoted in *ibid.*, p. 47.

and their pale son, the prosaic and restrictive family perceived by an older child.

In both *On Baile's Strand* and *Purgatory*, the hero is Janus-faced, looking both toward his father and toward his son. *On Baile's Strand* is the first major work in which Yeats attempts to master conflict with his father by identifying with him. To make this identification easier, the father is split into two personae: Mannanan, the "good," heroic father, and Conchubar, the "bad," restrictive one.

The fantasy of heroic closeness between Cuchulain and his son —interrupted by the "bad" father Conchubar—is transformed in *Purgatory* into a grim portrayal of estrangement and hatred. The Old Man is cut off both from his father's airy ghost and from his own coarse son. He does succeed, as John Moore observes, in imposing his horrible vision of reality on the Boy before he kills him —hoping by murder to destroy that reality.[68] But the fantasy of active mastery in *Purgatory* is engulfed in a sustained tone of helpless defeat that contrasts markedly with the heroic tone of *On Baile's Strand*. The Old Man's attempt to exorcise his past fails pitifully; the failure would seem to reflect Yeats's strong if not constant feeling that what remains at the end of his life is a horrible obsession he cannot break free of.

[68] J. R. Moore, *Masks of Love and Death*, p. 312.

FIVE

Toward the Holy City: 'A Vision' and Related Poems

A DETAILED EXPLICATION of Yeats's *A Vision* would demand much more space than can be devoted to it here, but one can hardly discuss Yeats's later poetry and ignore *A Vision*. We have seen Yeats use certain ideas from the book as the framework for *Purgatory*. He draws on other ideas from *A Vision* continually in his late poetry. Many of these ideas are not new, but a systematized reworking of material already familiar to us. Because of *A Vision*'s obscurity and occult paraphernalia, however, it is worthwhile making some of the connections explicit.[1]

In the Introduction to *A Vision*, Yeats explains that the book originated with his wife's automatic writing, which began four days after their marriage in October 1917—an acknowledgment that assigns responsibility for any disturbing fantasies or wishes, any obscurities or irrational arguments in his book, to the supernatural world. *A Vision* thus becomes an apocryphal scripture. Though Yeats sometimes seems surprised or apologetic, he obviously exults in the irrationality of his source. After conceding, for example, that his most valued readers will be "repelled by what must seem an arbitrary, harsh, difficult symbolism," he concludes defiantly: such symbolism "has almost always accompanied expression that unites the sleeping and waking mind" (*Vision*, p. 25).

One apparent effect of Mrs. Yeats's coauthorship was to buttress Yeats's confidence in his argument and his determination to impose it on his terms on the reader. Yeats had noted long before in

---

[1] Since the differences between the earlier and later versions of *A Vision* are not relevant to my argument, except where otherwise indicated I have cited throughout this chapter the more easily accessible version of 1937.

connection with Paul Ruttledge's arrogance in *The Unicorn from the Stars* that people objected to having opinions rammed down their throats.[2] In that case he had revised, cloaking the hero's hostility in humility and making aggression, in the form of supernatural commands, come from outside him. Here, Yeats takes a posture similar to his hero's (everything comes from the spirits), but clearly enjoys forcing the reader to take it in. Vendler, describing the effect of *A Vision* on the reader, uses an illuminating metaphor: "Parts of *A Vision* deserve gravity, but others must be taken with a grain of salt, and not even the most admiring critic can swallow *A Vision* whole."[3]

The indigestibility of *A Vision* may reflect a transformation from passive acceptance of psychological blows to active efforts to master them. We know that Yeats had trouble learning and incorporating academic material as a child. He may also have suffered from an unassimilable early trauma—perhaps the primal scene discussed in Chapter 4. The mating of beast and woman which in *A Vision* results in the new era and the new God seems to be yet another representation of the primal scene, now projected and exalted as an apocalyptic moment in the historical process.

Both the learning difficulty and the earlier trauma presumably left Yeats overwhelmed by sensations he could not deal with. In reproducing his confusion rhetorically in the textual obscurity of *A Vision*, Yeats becomes active rather than passive and inflicts a confusion—similar to the ones he suffered as a child—on the reader, who will "crack his wits / Day after day, yet never find the meaning."[4] Yeats assumes the role of teacher, and it is his reader who, as Bloom puts it, "having learned one barbaric terminology . . . is reluctant to learn another."[5] The idea of impelling his readers to "find the meaning" in his work occurs decades earlier in a letter to Mary Cronan. Yeats, who hated examinations, describing them as "parching" the thirsty minds of his schoolmates

2 *Variorum Plays*, p. 1166.
3 Vendler, *Yeats's* Vision, p. vii.
4 Yeats, "The Phases of the Moon," ll. 134–35, *Variorum Poems*, p. 377.
5 Bloom, *Yeats*, p. 263.

(*Autobiography*, p. 91), imagines his poetry as the subject of future examinations: "my peculiaritys ... will never be done justice to until they have become classics and are set for examinations."[6] John Butler Yeats gives a striking example of an even earlier instance in which Yeats mastered an apparent learning disability and triumphantly reversed roles with his supposed teacher. In his unpublished memoirs the elder Yeats relates how, after thinking he had failed to teach his son to read, he found him one day with a chemistry primer that he himself had discarded as too difficult:

I found Willie reading it. I said to him, "It is nonsense your trying to read that for you can't read the words." However, at his entreaty I questioned him, and we very quickly changed parts. I became his pupil, intelligent as I could manage to be, and he explained the book which he could not read, that is, read properly. And I asked myself, "Is he a ne'er do well or a genius?"[7]

Indeed, Yeats himself hints that aspects of unconscious reliving and correcting of early learning experiences were involved in *A Vision*. Through Mrs. Yeats, he says in the Introduction, the spirits encouraged him to read history and biography. And this time he was an apt pupil: "I read with an excitement I had not known since I was a boy" (*Vision*, p. 12). He depicts learning as a type of reciprocal feeding. The spirits give Yeats abstract ideas and he gives them back concrete examples. "And if my mind returned too soon to their unmixed abstraction they would say, 'We are starved' " (*Vision*, p. 12). As teacher and nurturer, Mrs. Yeats was following in the footsteps of Lady Gregory. Not surprisingly, Yeats begins his Introduction with a passage implicitly comparing his two teachers and congratulating himself on the progress he had

[6] *Letters*, p. 30. In his article "Yeats and the Professors" (*Ariel*, 3 [July 1972]: 5–30), Maurice Elliott discusses Yeats's ambivalence toward scholarship and professors. The pattern of role reversal helps explain some of the forms this ambivalence took. Yeats's painful early schooling was partially responsible for his intense efforts at self-education, as well as his sometimes ungenerous need to put down men like Professor Dowden and his wish to force people to take in his ideas. Thus in spite of his avowed dislike of academic institutions, he could contemplate becoming a professor, "a personage," as he said when he received his honorary degree from Trinity (Elliott, p. 23).

[7] Murphy, "Father and Son," pp. 87–88.

made with his new one. "The other day Lady Gregory said to me: 'You are a much better educated man than you were ten years ago and much more powerful in argument.' And I put *The Tower* and *The Winding Stair* into evidence to show that my poetry has gained in self-possession and power. I owe this change to an incredible experience." (He then describes his wife's automatic writing [*Vision*, p. 8].)

When asked whether he believed in the reality of his system, Yeats answered that he regarded it as "a stylistic arrangement of experience, comparable to the cubes in the drawing of Wyndam Lewis and the ovoids in the sculpture of Brancusi," which made it possible to hold "in a single thought, reality and justice"—that is, necessity and wish or what is versus what ought to be (*Vision*, p. 25). This description evokes Yeats's view of Dante, who in his poetry, Yeats felt, restored in a superior form an object denied him by reality. Derided and frustrated in love, Dante in his poems "found the unpersuadable justice, he found / The most exalted lady loved by a man."[8] The chief injustice imposed by reality seems to be the frustrated desire for an ideal image. *A Vision* accordingly both describes obsessive passion and promises satisfaction of incestuous impulses in another incarnation.

In the explanatory letter to Ezra Pound that Yeats uses to help introduce his book, he is quite specific. *A Vision*, he says, will proclaim Oedipus the "new divinity." As in *The Player Queen*, the gratification of impulse is contrasted to Christian abstinence. Christ, having suffered crucifixion, ascended into the "abstract sky." "Oedipus lay upon the earth... until amidst the sound of thunder earth opened riven by love, and he sank down soul and body into the earth" (*Vision*, p. 27). In deifying Oedipus, Yeats exalts his own incestuous desires and attempts to justify his right to enjoy his impulsive life as a whole.

Oedipus also represents Yeats's belief in the omnipotence of his thoughts. A man who "knew nothing but his mind," Oedipus yet could change kingdoms "according to his blessing and his cursing"

8 Yeats, "Ego Dominus Tuus," ll. 36–37, *Variorum Poems*, p. 369.

(*Vision*, p. 28). As we shall see, the theme of the poet's self-sufficiency is central to *A Vision*.

"The Great Wheel"

The first and longest of *A Vision*'s five books presents Yeats's
principal symbol, the Great Wheel. Book II describes the four
principles important in life after death. Book III, "The Soul in
Judgment," describes the stages of life after death. Books IV and
V deal with Yeats's philosophy of history based on the cyclical
movement of the Great Wheel. The two main concepts of *A Vision*,
the Great Wheel and life after death, are interesting not only as
a representation of aspects of the creative process, but also as a
form of autobiography—a systematized presentation both of Yeats's
development and of his psychic tendencies.

Yeats uses the Great Wheel both to organize his recollections
about his own development and to deal with his wish for self-sufficiency and his fears of dependence and death. History and individual life are seen as moving around the 28 phases of the Wheel
toward the perfect self-definition and self-sufficiency of phase 15
or toward absorption into something external, Nature or God.
The Wheel is divided into halves: a subjective or "good" half and
an objective or "bad" half. (As we shall see, there is an exception
to this in the beginning of the objective first quarter.) The phases
from 8 to 22 are those of what Yeats calls the subjective man, the
artist who actively creates his own reality; the phases from 22 to 8
are those of objective or uncreative man, passive and imposed upon
by external reality.

The subjective half of the Wheel being primarily that of the
artist, Yeats's description of individual phases in that half reads
like a catalogue of poets: Dante, Blake, Keats, Goethe. Yeats's description of the few poets he places in objective phases—Whitman,
for example (at phase 6) and George Herbert (at phase 25)—makes
clear by contrast what he valued in his subjective poets. Whitman
is a cataloguer for whom "experience is all-absorbing" (*Vision*, p.
114). At the other end of the objective half, Herbert is an accepter

of "organized belief: the convictions of Christendom" (*Vision*, p. 173). Yeats seems interested in the objective phases, particularly phases 1–8, mainly as a quarry for masks and images. He describes phase 3, for example, as follows (*Vision*, pp. 108–9):

Seen by lyrical poets, of whom so many have belonged to the fantastic Phase 17, the man of this phase becomes an Image where simplicity and intensity are united, he seems to move among yellowing corn or under overhanging grapes. He gave to Landor his shepherds and hamadryads, to Morris his *Water of the Wondrous Isles*, to Shelley his wandering lovers and sages, and to Theocritus all his flocks and pastures.

Yeats places himself at the "fantastic Phase 17," slightly beyond the ideal state of self-sufficiency and harmony. He sees himself (like Dante) approaching self-sufficiency through poetic re-creation of the lost object. He also sees himself as more capable of sustaining contact with reality in his maturity than he was as a young man in flight from experience and his body. This increased ability to assimilate experience derives from the mask that made spontaneous emotions and experiences accessible to him.

More specifically, the Wheel organizes Yeats's recollections of the past and his fears for the future as an old man. The individual life is one of the many cyclical movements represented by the Wheel. The semicircle from phase 1 to phase 14 corresponds to childhood and adolescence. The natural man of the earliest phases who lives in harmony with his source, maternal nature, is also the young child not fully differentiated from his mother. Such harmony precludes mask-wearing, which is not possible, Yeats tells us, until phase 8, with its budding sense of personality. The mask of this second quarter is described as "revelation" because through it a man achieves knowledge of himself as a distinct entity. The third quarter, phases 15–21, represents symbolically Yeats's poetic maturity; to these phases he assigns many of the world's greatest poets. The fourth quarter represents what Yeats most feared about old age: the helplessness and dependency of second childhood.

In three poems contemporaneous with *A Vision* (which Yeats called "Texts for Exposition"), "The Phases of the Moon" (1918), "The Double Vision of Michael Robartes" (1919), and "Michael

Robartes and the Dancer" (1919),[9] as well as in the related earlier poem "Ego Dominus Tuus" (1915), Yeats indicates the relation of the Wheel to his view of his own life and the construction of his mask. These poems and the essay *Per Amica Silentia Lunae* (1918) take up the thoughts about masks that Yeats had first dramatized in *The Player Queen* and would subsequently systematize in *A Vision*.

In "The Phases of the Moon," which Yeats incorporates into *A Vision*, Aherne and Robartes come to Yeats's tower (his home after his marriage) and find him engaged in contemplation. Yeats, Robartes says, has found "after the manner of his kind, / Mere images" (ll. 12–13) and lives in the tower because of its symbolic value. Here, withdrawn from the world, he is toiling after the truth he will never find. As Bloom points out, Yeats's irony here is double-edged, directed not only against poets in general but specifically against the occultist Robartes, whose "true song" of the moon's phases also contains a "mere" image, the Great Wheel.[10]

Yeats's description of the early phases in "The Phases of the Moon" departs from the general negative value he attaches to the objective side of the Wheel. In the main body of *A Vision* he makes a clear distinction between the earliest phases (1–4), which come before what he refers to as the Fall or "separation from innocence," and the subsequent phases of the first quarter. The phases after the "separation from innocence"—or differentiation from the mother or maternal nature—represent the beginnings of individuality: artificial individuality (phase 6), assertion of individuality (phase 7), and war between the individual and the race (phase 8). In this system, Yeats, being a poet of phase 17, would find his mask or contrary in these early phases of guiltless activity. The bard, creating from joy in his own body and in the world, served as such a mask.

The phases of the second quarter (8–15) are a symbolic representation of the adolescence of both man and race. Robartes describes the individual as following "whatever whim's most difficult / Among whims not impossible" (ll. 40–41). This, as Yeats tells us elsewhere, refers to the construction of a mask. According to Yeats's system, the mask for a man of the second quarter would come from the opposite phases of self-negation near the dark of the moon (phases 23–28). In terms of individual development, this would mean that the adolescent masters his sexual appetites by dramatizing himself as one who spurns such desires—a program with obvious relevance to Yeats's stated aim as a young man, to master desire for women and live an ascetic life on an island.

Yeats moves from dramatizing himself as an ascetic to dramatizing himself as a hero:

> Athene takes Achilles by the hair,
> Hector is in the dust, Nietzsche is born,
> Because the hero's crescent is the twelfth.
>
> (ll. 45–47)

The hero, here, is both a historic figure (Achilles or Hector) who could be used as a mask in the way Yeats used Cuchulain, and a type of contemporary psychological hero (Nietzsche). In *A Vision*, Yeats describes the hero primarily in the psychological sense, giving Nietzsche as an example; the hero, he says, is "the man who overcomes himself, and so no longer needs . . . the submission of others. . . . The sanity of the being is no longer from its relation to facts, but from its approximation to its own unity" (*Vision*, p. 127). The hero of phase 12 seems to approximate Yeats's ideal of the artist-god, which may be why Yeats named him the "Forerunner," the forerunner, that is, of the true God, Oedipus. The hero masters himself through his mask, which Yeats defines as being like the style he sought for himself—"emotionally cold" and "marble pure" (*Vision*, p. 128). The man of phase 12, before he achieves his mask, is "fragmentary" and "violent," qualities that recall the sporadic violence of Nietzschean works like *The Unicorn from the Stars*.

In the next two phases (13–14) Yeats describes states of "self-hatred," connecting them with physical impotence: before the full moon, Robartes says, man grows "helpless as a worm" (l. 49). These states, which found expression in early works like "Rosa Alchemica," are linked in *A Vision* with the intense but frustrated desire Yeats considered characteristic of certain Romantic poets, notably Keats, presumably cited because he was ill and thwarted in his desire for Fanny Brawn.

At the full moon, Yeats presents a temporary solution; now, as Robartes says, "All thought becomes an image and the soul / Becomes a body" (ll. 58–59). Yeats expands this statement in *A Vision*, explaining that "Now contemplation and desire, united into one, inhabit a world where every beloved image has bodily form, and every bodily form is loved" (*Vision*, p. 136). This is, as Vendler observes, analogous to the poetic act, a materialization of the idea in appropriate form.[11] In representing his ideal state (phase 15), Yeats is faced with the solipsist's dilemma. If the man of phase 15 attains the desired object, i.e., merges with it, then it is destroyed as a separate entity. If, on the other hand, the object remains outside him, he risks losing it. Yeats solves the dilemma by keeping the object separate but immobile; it cannot disappear and leave him alone. It thus functions somewhat as the transitional object does, being separate—and so a companion—but permanently there. In Robartes' words:

> For separate, perfect, and immovable
> Images can break the solitude
> Of lovely, satisfied, indifferent eyes.
> (ll. 81–83)

The beloved woman, mother or sweetheart, becomes a poetic image no longer able to frustrate the poet. In *A Vision* Yeats distinguishes between the Romantic poets who came before phase 15 and are tortured by their love for an image, and the more self-sufficient poets who came after phase 15 and whose chief love is for their masks—that is, for the creation of their own personality.

Yeats implies that only men know the self-sufficiency of phase 15. The climax of woman's development is not self-sufficiency, but beauty ("her masterpiece that shall be at the full moon") (*Vision*, p. 132), which is derived from suffering in the present or in previous incarnations. As Aherne tells Robartes:

[11] Vendler, *Yeats's* Vision, pp. 14–15.

> ... Those that we have loved got their long fingers
> From death, and wounds, or on Sinai's top,
> Or from some bloody whip in their own hands.
> They ran from cradle to cradle till at last
> Their beauty dropped out of the loneliness
> Of body and soul.
>
> (ll. 66–71)

The beautiful woman is represented as a person in only two phases (14 and 16), immediately before and after the crucial phase 15, the phase of absolute beauty. Even in phases 14 and 16 the woman's chief role is to cultivate herself as a beautiful object for the poet to appropriate as his image. As Bloom perceptively remarks, Yeats uses the Wheel to distinguish between the two main types of women in his life. His description of the beautiful but gentle women of phase 14, "touching in their beauty" (*Vision*, p. 132; whose beauty "dropped out of the loneliness / Of Body and Soul"), recalls Olivia Shakespear. This type of woman, whom Bloom describes as "Yeats's actual Muses, with whom he has been to bed,"[12] is contrasted to the aggressively beautiful women of phase 16, in particular Maud Gonne: "They walk like queens, and seem to carry upon their backs a quiver of arrows, but they are gentle only to those whom they have chosen or subdued" (*Vision*, p. 139). The distinction between the two types of women is the same as the distinction we discussed in connection with *The Shadowy Waters* between victim and tyrant, devoured and devourer. While Olivia and the women of phase 14 are victims, Maud Gonne comes "in the first phase of those who do rather than suffer violence."[13]

In the third quarter, and increasingly in the fourth, as sung by Robartes, the man seeks service, not self-expression. Soon he must flee his mask. The saint, for instance, must shake off a mask from the phases of sensuality. In this flight the body becomes deformed "because there is no deformity / But saves us from a dream" (ll. 101–2). Bodily deformity here clearly symbolizes an inner deformity. Robartes speaks of the creatures at the dark of the moon

---

[12] Bloom, *Yeats*, p. 253.
[13] *Ibid*, p. 252.

with disgust: "deformed beyond deformity" (l. 111), they cry like bats, no longer conscious enough of themselves to triumph in their absolute obedience.

Yeats does not particularize any of the phases between phase 15 and phase 22 in "The Phases of the Moon." Yet this "servile crescent" is the birthplace of some of the world's greatest poets, including Yeats himself. For a closer look at the poet of the third quarter we must return to "Ego Dominus Tuus." This poem forms the initial section of Yeats's *Per Amica Silentia Lunae* and, as Bloom notes, is similarly concerned with mastery and how the poet achieves it.[14] The poem consists of a dialogue between Ille, presumably Yeats himself, in search of images, and Hic, objective man, critical of the poet's deluded search for "magical shapes" (l. 7).

Hic shares the modern writer's desire to "find myself and not an image" (l. 10). According to *A Vision*, personality or true selfhood is attainable only through mask and image. In our century, which belongs to the fourth quarter of the Great Wheel, true selfhood is increasingly difficult to attain. By the beginning of true objectivity—phase 22, the phase of Flaubert and Darwin—personality is barely possible. Man, instead of seeking his complementary mask, "needs nothing but what [he] may call 'reality,' 'truth,' 'God's will.'" In art, the beginning of objectivity manifests itself as the impartiality of the realist, "the mirror dawdling down a road" (*Vision*, pp. 159, 160). The mirroring realist or introspective modern is not self-sufficient, but dependent on fact or existing reality; he does not create but merely records. In "Ego Dominus Tuus" Yeats consequently attacks the modern writer, who, hoping to find himself, loses the power to create boldly. Ille laments:

> We have lit upon the gentle, sensitive mind
> And lost the old nonchalance of the hand;
> Whether we have chosen chisel, pen or brush,
> We are but critics, or but half create,
> Timid, entangled, empty and abashed
> Lacking the countenance of our friends.
> (ll. 12–17)

[14] *Ibid.*, p. 197.

Hic ripostes by citing Dante, "the chief imagination of Christendom" (l. 18), as someone who found himself so utterly

> That he has made that hollow face of his
> More plain to mind's the eye than any face
> But that of Christ.
>
> (ll. 20–22)

Ille, giving Yeats's view, assures Hic that what he thought was Dante's true face was really the image of his anti-self. Personal frustrations were the force behind Dante's creation of mask and image. The mask's worn cheeks were hollowed by desire for "the apple on the bough / Most out of reach" (ll. 24–25). And the divine image of Beatrice is a superior compensation for what had been lost in experience:

> Derided and deriding, driven out
> To climb that stair and eat that bitter bread,
> He found the unpersuadable justice, he found
> The most exalted lady loved by a man.
>
> (ll. 34–37)

Passionate emotion is of particular importance to the poets of phase 17, Dante and Yeats among them. The mask of phase 17, which he calls the "mask of simplicity" (*Vision*, p. 141), must be emotional to balance the increasing intellectuality and abstraction of the third quarter. This mask is drawn from the first quarter, that of childhood. Yeats's formula for escaping barren intellectuality is a schematized version of his own method of fighting ruminations and abstract thought. Incorrect use of the intellect at phase 17, represented by Hic in "Ego Dominus Tuus," is what Yeats calls in *A Vision* (p. 140) "enforced self-realization" (Hic's desire to find himself), which replaces an effort to find the right emotional mask. At this phase the will is breaking down, and only the mask can hold the personality together.

Hic, not at all convinced of the poet's need for opposing mask and compensating image, mentions the work of Keats as an example of poetry written out of love for the world, rather than the loss of it. But Ille explains that Keats's art is in fact compensation:

> I see a schoolboy when I think of him,
> With face and nose pressed to a sweet-shop window,
> For certainly he sank into his grave
> His senses and his heart unsatisfied,
> And made—being poor, ailing and ignorant,
> Shut out from all the luxury of the world,
> The coarse-bred son of a livery-stable keeper—
> Luxuriant song.
>
> (ll. 55–62)

The description of a hungry boy outside the sweet-shop window relates to Yeats's own feelings of boyhood deprivation, seen retrospectively as a stimulus to art. The lines also recall Yeats's description of Aleel, in *The Countess Cathleen*, as like a "fly upon a window-pane in the winter"—shut out from warmth and love. Keats as Yeats sees him resembles the early Yeats of the lush, Italianate *Oisin*, which Yeats later connected explicitly with his own frustrated sexual hunger: "I that set him on to ride, / I, starved for the bosom of his faery bride."[15]

Dante, by contrast, Yeats associates with aspects of his own later style and his conception of himself as a mature poet. Dante excelled in replacing the lost object with something better. Beatrice is not just a lovely woman, nymph, or other luxurious echo of reality; she is inherently more valuable. And Dante's mask, chiseled from "the hardest stone" (l. 32), like Yeats's rocky face and golden bird, suggests an invulnerability and permanence, a transmutation of passion, that is lacking in Keats's "luxuriant song."

"Ego Dominus Tuus" ends with the poet's reiterated assertion that he must seek an image to complete him:

> I call to the mysterious one who yet
> Shall walk the wet sands by the edge of the stream
> And look most like me, being indeed my double,
> And prove of all imaginable things
> The most unlike, being my anti-self.
>
> (ll. 70–74)

"The Double Vision of Michael Robartes" describes with considerable power the two absolute states of the Great Wheel—phase

15 Yeats, "The Circus Animals' Desertion," ll. 15–16, *Variorum Poems*, p. 629.

1 and phase 15. Robartes' first vision, of the "cold spirits" of phase 1, is a vision of extreme helplessness, in which the being is manipulated like a puppet by superior puppets:

> When had I my own will?
> O not since life began.
>
> Constrained, arraigned, baffled, bent and unbent
> By these wire-jointed jaws and limbs of wood.
>
> (ll. 7–10)

I suggested earlier that this passage represented the frightening dependency of the infant. Similarly in "The Dolls" (1914), the child's impotent rage at the birth of a sibling is expressed by the dolls: "The man and the woman bring / Hither, to our disgrace, / A noisy and filthy thing."[16]

Robartes' experience also recalls psychotic or drug-induced states of mind. Timothy Leary describes in terms strikingly like Yeats's an LSD-induced experience of the disintegration of the self. As Leary explains, either you accept the fragmentation of form into waves as a feeling of ecstatic harmony with all beings (this roughly corresponds with the view of Yeats's saints, who seek union with God), or you fight it: "You are a helpless marionette, a plastic doll in a plastic world.... Others ... are seen as wooden ... cold ... grotesque." "The terror comes with the discovery of transience. ... You feel ultimately tricked."[17] Later Leary explains that the experiencing of the self and others as dead comes from the fight of the ego to reestablish control.

Whether or not Yeats's terrifying vision of the puppets reflects an actual memory, it certainly reflects a fear of the altered ego state he portrays. Indeed, not only does Yeats recoil in terror from helplessness, he seems to find intolerable the idea that reality itself cannot be controlled, whether by the child faced with the birth of a sibling or by the old man facing death. For Yeats the strong poetic personality is the one who creates his own reality, who depends only on his own mind. Yeats tries to walk a tightrope be-

---

16 *Variorum Poems*, p. 319 (ll. 10–12).
17 Timothy Leary, Ralph Metzner, and Richard Alpert, *The Psychedelic Experience* (New Hyde Park, N.Y.: University Books, 1964), p. 66.

tween external reality and the imagination. The real world cannot be dispensed with entirely, because it provides the poet with material, but he must avoid succumbing to it. At the same time, admitting the importance of external reality leads to a diminished sense of self-importance and an acknowledgment of helplessness and dependence.

The vision of phase 15 described in the second section of the poem is Yeats's contrasting vision of the ideal state. The images of Sphinx and Buddha, central to this section of the poem, are difficult; they become clearer when we turn to *A Vision*. There, Yeats tells us that they are the guardians of phase 15—the Sphinx looking backward to earlier phases, the Buddha looking forward to the dissolving personality. Whereas the Sphinx finds its pleasure within itself, "with introspective knowledge of the mind's self-begotten unity," the Buddha's thoughts are directed outward to the external world, to "love and its lure." Yeats says in his description of these guardians that he "should have put Christ instead of Buddha" in the poem (*Vision*, p. 207): this would have made the contrast clearer. The opposition between Sphinx and Buddha can be seen as a contrast between mental self-sufficiency and the dependence on an external object characteristic of someone who is in love. Like the subjective poet-god Oedipus, the Sphinx knows only his own mind. In his ambiguous sexuality, the Sphinx recalls the Herne and the Unicorn: the Sphinx has "woman breast and lion paw" (l. 18). The subjective poet, having everything, including the female, within his own mind, has no need to love anything else. Christ, by contrast, exists because of people's need for him. By offering men love he binds them to him, makes them dependent on him. Later, in his play *The Resurrection*, Yeats speaks of Christ's disciples as dogs without a master, contrasting them with the water birds (subjective men) who need neither Christ's love nor his sacrifice.[18]

Yeats's description of the Sphinx in "The Double Vision of Michael Robartes" suggests both pride in the imagination and pride in masculinity. The Sphinx gazes upon all things "In tri-

18 *Variorum Plays*, p. 906.

umph of intellect / With motionless head erect" (ll. 31–32). (As we have seen, triumphant was a crucial word in *The King's Threshold*, where it was associated with both poetry and masculinity.) In contrast the Buddha is untriumphant and without peace, "for those that love are sad" (l. 36). The Buddha's feminine sadness reflects Yeats's feeling that to need someone is dangerous, that it makes you passive and unhappy like a woman—his depressed mother, for instance. Several contrasts are operating here simultaneously: between self-sufficiency and dependency, between poet and lover, between Christian and secular man, and between the "triumphant," imaginatively active male and the passive, despondent female.

Balanced between Sphinx and Buddha, between imagination and reality, spins the dancing girl, the perfect artifact. Together the three form an archetypal family, parents and child. As Bloom notes, this aspect of the symbolism is clearer in the Shelleyan analogue to the image: Prometheus, Asia, and mythic infants in Act IV of *Prometheus Unbound*.[19] Sphinx and Buddha are as indifferent to the girl dancing between them as the controlling puppets, also parent figures, of phase 1, who "do not even feel, so abstract are they / ... Triumph that we obey" (ll. 14–16).

> O little did they care who danced between,
> And little she by whom her dance was seen.
> (ll. 37–38)

The spinning girl, like the puppets, suggests feelings of depersonalization. The dancing girl differs from the puppet-children in one important way, however: they are constrained and dependent, she is free and self-sufficient. The frustration and dependency embodied in the puppets' jerking movements are counterbalanced and symbolically mastered by the girl's spinning, that is, by the poetic act. The girl has achieved independence; she does not care who watches her. Suspended, as if in a trance, she enjoys a perfect body and perfect mental equilibrium:

19 Bloom, *Yeats*, pp. 207–8.

So she had outdanced thought,
Body perfection brought,

For what but eye and ear silence the mind
With the minute particulars of mankind?

Mind moved yet seemed to stop
As 'twere a spinning-top.

(ll. 39–44)[20]

In the concluding section of the poem, Yeats links the spinning dancer—symbolic of both the artifact and the poet's whirling mind—with the poetic image that arises from *Anima Mundi*. He is attempting to represent both the moment when conscious or abstract thought is replaced by unconscious thought—symbolized by the body of the whirling dancer—and the image the unconscious then creates.[21] Robartes identified the dancer with "That girl my unremembering nights hold fast" (l. 50), as well as with daydreams that vanish "if I should rub an eye" (l. 52). "Homer's paragon" (l. 56) is both Maud Gonne and the incestuous image or Over Shadower that haunts the poet. Robartes' reaction to his dream image's cold yet maddening beauty is, as Bloom points out, a double one.[22] First, he abases himself both before the image and more generally, one feels, before objective reality. At last he triumphs— as do Sphinx and girl—by arranging it all "in a song."

Life After Death

In Book III of *A Vision*, "A Soul in Judgment," Yeats's own obsession with incest comes to represent every soul's experience after death, when Yeats maintains it is bound by its strongest passion. Life after death allows the spirit to work free of its obsession, which Yeats describes as "a knot that has to be untied" (p. 226).

[20] As Dr. Estelle Rogers of San Francisco has pointed out to me, Yeats's image resembles the electromagnet, with negative and positive poles of force that set the rotor spinning between them.

[21] Geza Roheim discusses whirling motion as characteristic of the moment of falling asleep and of the primary process. *Gates of the Dream* (New York: International Universities Press, 1952), p. 291.

[22] Bloom, *Yeats*, p. 209.

Yeats's purgatorial process is comparable in important ways to the reexperiencing of past events and relationships in psychoanalysis. In both cases remembering or reliving past events serves the ultimate purpose of arriving at self-knowledge and freedom from compulsion.[23] In Yeats's system, the spirit is rewarded for its work by a body transfigured to match its insights, and a new chance to live: "The more complete the *Dreaming Back* the more complete the *Return* and the more happy or fortunate the next incarnation" (*Vision*, p. 227).

Though the purgation is painful, the idea of reincarnation is a denial of death's finality. Yeats once wrote that life would be without meaning if we did not think we could continue our work in a future life (*Letters*, p. 165). Within the purgatorial process, certain stages, such as the Beatitude, represent gratification of wishes, notably the wish for self-sufficiency. But as we shall see, the most striking example of wish fulfillment is in the concept of reincarnation, which permits satisfaction of incestuous desire.

Vendler suggests that Yeats intended life after death as a parable of the "state of artistic creation."[24] The ordering of chaotic sense impressions and experiences and the distancing of emotion that characterize the spirit after death also characterize the poet when he creates. Vendler's brilliantly presented notion of a correspondence between life after death and the creative process provides an appealing way of looking at Book III as an organized whole; but, as Bloom has noted, the analogy is only partial, and certain things it omits require a different sort of explanation.[25]

During life after death there are states like the Phantasmagoria and the Shiftings whose connection with the creative process is at best, as Vendler admits, "cloudy."[26] Bloom even suggests that certain of the states are parodies of the creative process or antithetical to it.[27] We can deepen our understanding of these obscure states

---

[23] See, for example, Freud's *A General Introduction to Psychoanalysis* (New York: Pocket Books, 1952), p. 451.

[24] Vendler, *Yeats's* Vision, p. 50.

[25] Bloom, p. 185.

[26] Vendler, p. 78.

[27] Bloom, pp. 270–71.

by considering their function as wish fulfillments or as techniques for mastering unpleasant mental states (ruminations, guilt feelings, fantasies) by representing and systematizing them. The style of "The Soul in Judgment" is notably obscure. Vendler warns us against seeking "to impose an artificial clarity on this section [dealing with the Beatitude] because one of the impressions the book exists to convey is the sense of mystery attendant on the workings of the imagination; on the other hand, Yeats was not above making deliberate gestures of mystification."[28] With this cogent warning in mind, let us turn to Yeats's description of life after death. It is composed of six states:

    1. Vision of the Blood Kindred
    2. Meditation
      A. Dreaming Back
      B. Return
      C. Phantasmagoria
    3. Shiftings
    4. Beatitude
    5. Purification
    6. Foreknowledge

Yeats presents the six states as a necessary progression, leading to understanding and freedom; but as Bloom points out, it is difficult to see in what sense they are necessary.[29] Why, for instance, in the Return, should the spirit be compelled to a tracing of causes, a "pernicious casuistry," as a condition of freedom? It would appear that whereas Yeats took the idea of a purgatorial process from tradition, his version of it was uniquely tailored to his own mind. The spirit must engage in "pernicious casuistry" essentially because Yeats was tormented by obsessive ruminations. Representing such ruminations as a necessary part of the purgatorial process he borrowed from tradition justified the ruminations and probably made Yeats feel less alone.

Among the six states, particularly the early ones, there seems to be a perceptible movement from outer to inner experience. In the Vision of the Blood Kindred, the first state after death, the soul,

28 Vendler, p. 75.
29 Bloom, p. 270.

adjusting to its new condition, sees all those people who were bound to it by sense and instinct. In the tripartite second state, Meditation, the spirit aims to shed its "passionate body" and see and understand its celestial body or ideal form. The spirit is hindered in this aim by its attachments to the real world, especially sexual passion. If passion has been particularly strong, the spirit, like the ghost of the mother in *Purgatory*, must struggle through long and painful dreams of the past. In the Dreaming Back, the first stage of Meditation, it relives the events that moved it most in the order of their "intensity or luminosity, the more intense first, and the painful are commonly the more intense, and repeat themselves again and again" (*Vision*, p. 226). Yeats is representing not only his own obsessive incestuous passion here, but also his compulsion, like the Ancient Mariner's, to tell his tale of obsession over and over again. Moreover, Yeats attributes this sort of obsession to a Dreaming Back spirit who enters the mind in dreams or appears as a ghostly vision. In *Purgatory* the spirit is that of the mother; elsewhere Yeats represents the mother symbolically as a sweetheart from a past life.

The Return, the second part of Meditation, is the most obviously therapeutic. In the Return the spirit begins to understand its obsessions and to work free of their painful "knot." Freud describes an analogous stage in the working out of "transference" in psychoanalysis. At first the patient, responding to the analyst as though he were the patient's father, mother, or sweetheart, reenacts aspects of these original relationships. Once the patient's emotions gain concrete form through this transference, he and the analyst attempt to analyze their meaning. "The transference is overcome by showing the patient that he is reproducing something that happened to him long ago. In this way we require him to transform his repetition into recollection," and eventually into insight.[30] Yeats provides a guide through the past in the form of "teaching spirits," analogous to the psychoanalyst, who conduct the spirit through its past acts and help it to understand them.

30 Freud, *General Introduction*, p. 451.

But knowledge of the actual past is not enough. In the third part of Meditation, the Phantasmagoria, fantasies are freely acted out and accompanied by punishment that materializes to meet the particular person's sense of guilt. In this phase, the dead must exhaust emotion by reliving not what actually happened, but what they hoped or feared might happen, completing "not only life but imagination" (*Vision*, p. 230). The full expression of morbid fantasy has a prophylactic function here, as it does in Yeats's late dance plays—plays which involve incestuous fantasies, and which, in Yeats's words, represented a "fragment of the past that I had to get rid of" (*Letters*, p. 843). The symbolic expression of fantasy, whether in art or in life after death, vitiates its power to obsess.

In representing the guilty conscience in Phantasmagoria, Yeats distances and attempts to exorcise his own feelings of guilt. Guilt here is proportionate to inner scruples rather than to any external reality or code: punishment is equal to the spirit's feeling of what it deserves. Yeats gives an example to illustrate the reality of the self-created punishment to the sufferer (*Vision*, p. 231):

I think of a girl in a Japanese play whose ghost tells a priest of a slight sin, if indeed it was sin, which seems great because of her exaggerated conscience. She is surrounded by flames, and though the priest explains that if she but ceased to believe in those flames they would cease to exist, believe she must, and the play ends in an elaborate dance, the dance of her agony.

By stressing the subjectivity of guilt, Yeats symbolically cuts a link with the outside world. The spirits in Phantasmagoria—like the girl in the play—insist on taking their sense of guilt from no one but themselves. Vendler suggests, correctly I think, that the girl's exaggerated conscience, which gives rise to the images of flame, resembles the sensibility of the poet in demanding visible manifestation.[31] Moreover, Yeats glories in this sensibility even when its imaginings seem inappropriate (as they do in the girl's case) to others. It is what he feels, imagines, or dreams that is real. The representation of punishment in Yeats's work (e.g., "The

31 Vendler, p. 79.

Cap and Bells," *A Full Moon in March*) can be highly eroticized: punishment is gratification. An example of eroticized punishment that is relevant to Phantasmagoria may be found in Yeats's poem "The Cold Heaven" (1912), in which the living poet's experience foreshadows his experience after death. Here punishment becomes a kind of love-death. The cold and uncaring heaven of the poem expresses the feelings of abandonment that Yeats experienced both with Maud, the sweetheart of the poem, and earlier with his mother. This feeling of coldness was, as we have seen, related to the cold emotion—"as though ice burned and was but the more ice" (l. 2) that Yeats wanted in his style. The sky, as the poet stares at it, not only freezes but burns, expressing simultaneously arousal and frustrated desire. As the poet looks up at this image of his past emotions, he remembers his "love crossed long ago" (l. 6). His memories make him take "all the blame" for love's failure "out of all sense and reason" (l. 7).

As with the girl consumed by flames in *A Vision*, the poet's sense of guilt creates an image. But the image in the poem is highly erotic; it clearly represents both punishment and the longed-for consummation. The hitherto cold and uncaring sky assaults the poet: "I cried and trembled and rocked to and fro, / Riddled with light" (l. 8). A similar phrase, "nodding to and fro," occurs in Yeats's early poem "The Two Titans," which involves a conflict between a young man and the frustrating maternal sea. In *Oisin* the demon-father rocks back and forth crooning to himself in his wasteland. In both cases the rocking movement occurs in a context that suggests a frustrated craving for life-giving moisture and fertility coupled with self-gratification. The movement is perhaps ultimately derived from the desperate head-banging or rocking motion of infants longing for maternal comfort.[32] "The Cold Heaven" ends with a comparison of the poet's experience with

32 The poet's father describes his son as going into a trance-like state while composing a poem: "swaying his head from side to side wherever you met him, in the house or in the street, he looked at you with unseeing eyes" (Murphy, "Father and Son," p. 92). In this case, head-rocking is associated with the gratification of composing poetry, the kind of gratification most appropriate to Yeats's ideal of the self-sufficient poet who nourishes himself on his own words.

that of the dead—presumably in Phantasmagoria—where his spirit will be "sent / Out naked on the roads ... and stricken / By the injustice of the skies for punishment" (ll. 10–12).

In the Shiftings or third state of life after death, a man's nature is reversed. "In so far as the man did good without knowing evil, or evil without knowing good, his nature is reversed until the knowledge is obtained" (*Vision*, p. 231). Yeats stresses the spirit's independence from the outside world, this time from its moral judgments—thus continuing the resistance (manifest in *The Player Queen*) to often harsh traditional values that heightened his sense of guilt. This third state continues Yeats's attempts to reverse traditional values of good and evil. The spirit needs the Shiftings, Yeats explains, because it is still unsatisfied: "The emotional and moral life is but a whole according to the code accepted during life." As Yeats presents this state, however, it is mechanical, as Bloom notes, and not very interesting.[33]

The fourth state, the Beatitude or Marriage, is a respite, albeit temporary, after the pain of purgation, a kind of reward after punishment, a moment of equilibrium in which contraries "vanish into the whole" (*Vision*, p. 232). This state is like phase 15 of Yeats's Wheel, analogous to the moment of creation when all is harmonious and unified. Though Yeats says very little about the Beatitude in *A Vision*, in his *Autobiography* it appears as a return to childlike innocence.[34] In his poem "Shepherd and Goatherd" (1918), written after the death of Lady Gregory's son Robert, Robert's reexperiencing of his life after his death culminates in a return to his mother. This poem is particularly interesting in view of Yeats's filial relationship to the dead man's mother. Though Yeats wrote the poem to commemorate Robert, he devotes equal space to praise of Lady Gregory. The thought Yeats hopes will make her grief "less bitter" (l. 87) is not the traditional one, that her son is in heaven, but that as one of the dreaming dead he is returning to her side. In Yeats's poem, Robert Gregory's happiness consists in unpacking the "loaded pern" (l. 97) of all he had

33 Bloom, *Yeats*, p. 271.
34 Vendler, pp. 82–83.

thought or done, and the climax is not union with God but a blissful return to infancy:

> Knowledge he shall unwind
> Through victories of the mind,
> Till, clambering at the cradle-side,
> He dreams himself his mother's pride,
> All knowledge lost in trance
> Of sweeter ignorance.
>
> (ll. 107–12)

One might expect the Beatitude to be Yeats's concluding state, but it is followed by a fifth state of final Purification. Perhaps the idea of a "marriage" of conflicting elements that vanish into a whole aroused his fears of being swallowed up, and compelled him to go on to portray another state of separateness. The emphasis in Purification is on the spirit's self-sufficiency; it depends on nothing but itself, and this self is not in static harmony but in active self-definition. "It becomes self-shaping, self-moving, plastic to itself" (*Vision*, p. 233). Yeats links the spirit's self-shaping with artistic creation: the spirit molds itself after an ideal form, like those copied, Yeats suggests, in works of art. "The *Spirit's* aim . . . appears before it as a form of perfection, for during the *Purification* those forms copied in the Arts and Sciences are present as the *Celestial Body*" (Vision, p. 234). If the spirit is a unique one (like Yeats's), it may wait centuries before finding an ideal place for its reincarnation. Reincarnation is in any case preceded by the sixth state, Foreknowledge, in which the spirit reviews and accepts its future life as just.

One purpose of the time between lives is to allow the spirit to work free of its obsessive passions. This purgatorial process is undercut by Yeats's suggestion that in successive incarnations a man lives through all possible combinations of family relationships (*Vision*, p. 237):

We all to some extent meet again and again the same people and certainly in some cases form a kind of family of two or three or more persons who come together life after life until all passionate relations are exhausted, the child of one life the husband, wife, brother or sister of the next.

Yeats thus explains and gratifies incestuous wishes while escaping responsibility for them, substituting the concept of past life for the fantasies of childhood. The impotence of men like Forgael in *The Shadowy Waters* who are obsessed with an ideal can now be explained with reference to a past life. In the same way the poetic image, along with the dream images from which it may be derived, reflects an actual past relationship, not the individual ego.

Yeats uses his theory of life after death and reincarnation to explain the symbolic distortions observable in dreams (*Vision*, p. 229):

Much of a dream's confusion comes from the fact that the image belongs to some unknown person [i.e., to a dreaming-back spirit], whereas emotion, names, language, belong to us alone.... So long as I dream in words I know that my father, let us say, was tall and bearded. If, on the other hand, I dream in images and examine the dream immediately upon waking I may discover him there represented by a stool or the eyepiece of a telescope, but never in his natural shape, for we cast off the concrete memory ... but not the abstract memory when we sleep.

In an elaborate note to his poem "Image from a Past Life" (1920), Yeats mentions the possibility that dream images are "personal":

Were these images, however, from the buried memory? had they floated up from the subconscious? had I seen them perhaps a long time ago and forgotten having done so? Even if that were so, the exclusion of the conscious memory was a new, perhaps important truth.[35]

Having suggested a psychological interpretation, as usual he retracts his suggestion. His dream images and half-waking visions are not personal because the elaborate landscapes he sees do not remind him of anything he saw as a child. If they do not come from childhood, he reasons, they must come either from *Anima Mundi* or from a "previous existence." Speaking through the persona Robartes, Yeats presents in his note what for him is the crucial explanation of dreams: the dream image or ideal form from which the poetic image is often derived and which dictates a man's choice of sweetheart can ultimately be traced back to a woman

---

35 *Variorum Poems*, p. 822.

loved in a past life. Yeats "quotes" from a letter Robartes wrote
Aherne:

"No lover, no husband has ever met in dreams the true image of wife or
mistress. [What he meets] are the forms of those whom he has loved in
some past earthly life, . . . and through them . . . the dead at whiles out-
face a living rival." They are [Yeats explains] the forms of Over Shadow-
ers . . . but it is only in sleep that we can see these forms of those who as
spirits may influence all our waking thought. Souls that are once linked
by emotion never cease till the last drop of that emotion is exhausted . . .
to affect one another. . . . Those whose past passions are unatoned seldom
love living man or woman but only those loved long ago, of whom the
living man or woman is but a brief symbol.[36]

Yeats explains, still citing Robartes, how the choice of sweetheart
and the poetic image derive from unconscious memory of the original love.

The form . . . enters the living memory; the subconscious will . . . selects
among pictures, or other ideal representations, some form that resembles
what was once the physical body of the Over Shadower, and this ideal
form becomes to the living man an obsession, continually perplexing and
frustrating natural instinct.[37]

Yeats tells a story related by Robartes about Kusta-Ben-Luki to
show how the Over Shadower works. During sleep, Kusta-Ben-
Luki saw a woman's face. He then found in a Persian painting a
face resembling his dream woman, and considered it a woman he
had loved in a previous life. Presently he met and loved a beautiful woman whose face also resembled that of his dream. Having
decided that the painting bore the closer resemblance to the dream,
he made a trip to purchase it, and found, on his return, that his
mistress had left him in a fit of jealousy.[38]

[36] In his youth, Yeats spoke of Laura Armstrong and Maud Gonne as merely
symbols of something else.

[37] Yeats had, it seems, read Freud by this time, for he comments on Robartes'
explanation of dreams: "I thought it contradicted by my experience and by
all that I have read, not however a very great amount, in books of psychology
and of psycho-analysis." However, the extent to which Yeats's own theories, particularly those concerning the obsessing or incestuous image that appears in
dreams, were derived from Freud or were a reaction to him is unclear. We do
know that in a debate with the psychologist Flournoy, Yeats weighed "the theory
of subconscious telepathic action against the spirit theories," and decided for
the spirits. V. Moore, *Unicorn*, p. 228.

[38] *Variorum Poems*, p. 821.

"An Image from a Past Life," the poem to which this long note is appended, is itself a study of the rivalry between living sweetheart and image. As in "The Cold Heaven," Yeats describes a scene —this time of starlight on dark water—which, experienced together with a scream "from terrified, invisible beast or bird" (l. 6), makes the man suddenly remember something: an "image of poignant recollection" (l. 7). Though the man is deeply stirred, the woman standing beside him responds to the scream as to "an image of my heart that is smitten through" (l. 8). The visual scene now becomes identified with a sweetheart from a past life who materializes above the water. The "starry eddies of her hair" (l. 27) seem to grow from the starlit river. Her paleness links her to the women of Yeats's early verse, making her an image in another sense: the image of beauty he had created as a young man. The poem's final scene represents the triumph of the image over the living woman.

In "Towards Break of Day" (another poem of 1920), dream images of ideal loves appear to both man and wife. The man sees the waterfall his "childhood counted dear" (l. 7; see my discussion in Chapter 1 of the Knight of the Waterfall); the wife, the male "stag of Arthur" (l. 23). (Yeats had used the stag earlier, in "The Two Kings," to represent a woman's husband in a past life.) Of the two images, Yeats is far more interested in the waterfall. On waking, the dreaming husband realizes that even had he touched the desired waterfall, "my finger could but have touched / Cold stone and water" (ll. 13–14). He would have touched only the actual, physical waterfall, not its symbolic equivalent, and with physical contact the symbol's emotional power would have dissolved.

The cold waterfall, like the ghost who rises from starlit water, is the daimonic muse of *A Vision*—the idealized incestuous object, perpetual antagonist to normal, fulfilled love. Entering a man's mind through dreams or visions, she tries to seduce him and keep him from sexual union with another woman. Though opposed to satisfied love, the daimon joins forces with a similarly untouchable sweetheart. Maud Gonne is linked in "The Cold Heaven" to a coldness which, like that of the waterfall, arouses and frustrates the lover. And as we have noted (in our discussion of Dante, Beatrice, and the creative process in Chapter 3), it is through this combination of arousal and rejection that, in Yeats's view, the creative mechanism is set in motion and the poet delivered to his destiny by his daimon.

"Supernatural Songs"

The "Texts for Exposition" illustrate Yeats's feelings about essential aspects of his childhood, adolescence, and maturity. None of these poems deal in depth with the fourth quarter of the Great Wheel, or Yeats's feelings about his approaching old age and death. For a sense of what this final quarter meant to Yeats we must look elsewhere. The twelve late poems in the collection "Supernatural Songs" are particularly illuminating in this respect because their chief persona, the monk Ribh, belies our expectations of the objective final phase.

The "Supernatural Songs" present two ways of dealing with age and death. The predominant way is Ribh's defiant insistence on sexuality as the central fact of both natural and divine experience. (All but one of these poems were written in the summer of 1934 after Yeats's Steinach operation, and stem from the same need to deny the loss of potency.) But the way of renunciation is also present, in "Meru," the final Supernatural Song.

In a general way, the final quarter represents feared changes associated with aging and death: diminished sexual vitality, increased intellectuality, dependence on others, and finally renunciation and complete passivity. Jacques in Shakespeare's *As You Like It* says that in old age a man is "sans teeth, sans eyes, sans taste, sans everything." As he has done often before, Yeats turns a dread necessity into choice, thus lessening its horror: he describes a saint who would, if possible, "not even touch or taste or see" (*Vision*, p. 181). The saint deals with death by means of a voluntary repudiation of the senses.

Yeats's projection of himself as the hermit Ribh is a striking (and perhaps deliberate) contrast to the picture of saintly self-abnegation described in *A Vision*. In "Ribh at the Tomb of Baile and Aillinn," the first of the Supernatural Songs, Ribh stands in "the pitch-dark night" (l. 1), emblem of the cycle's end. As Yeats tells us elsewhere, the eagle who looks into the sun symbolizes solar or objective man. Ribh's "aquiline" eyes, like the saint's, have been sharpened to vision by "water, herb and solitary prayer" (l. 23). Were Ribh a proper saint, such discipline might lead to a vision of God. Instead, Ribh's darkness is illuminated by the intercourse of angels:

> ... when such bodies join
> There is no touching here, nor touching there,
> Nor straining joy, but whole is joined to whole;
> For the intercourse of angels is a light
> Where for its moment both seem lost, consumed.
> (ll. 12–16)

Ribh's participation in the lovers' sexual vitality counters the unpleasant facts of age—e.g., the "voice that ninety years have cracked" (l. 5).

The union of the angelic lovers in the poem, like the Unicorn's projected marriage in *The Player Queen*, is both good and clean: the lovers are "purified by tragedy" (l. 21), their intercourse is a light (l. 15). Yeats not only reverses early feelings of disgust here, but hints at the relation of those feelings to his reading difficulty later in childhood. In the poem Ribh is a looker; his aquiline eyes suggest that he can even look into the sun. Not only can he contemplate without dismay the sexual act, he can even read his holy book by its light. Yeats is implicitly referring to *A Vision*, his own holy book. Like *A Vision* and the earlier *Player Queen*, "Ribh at the Tomb of Baile and Aillinn" reverses traditional values. Ribh, a servant not of the established church but of its native Irish predecessor, has a vision that, in its sexuality and poetry, is specifically antithetical to established Christianity as Yeats perceived it. The orthodox Christian Dante placed the unfortunate lovers Paolo and Francesca in Hell. Not only does Yeats place his lovers in heaven, but their embrace may itself be seen as heaven.

In the next Supernatural Song, "Ribh Denounces Patrick," Yeats again attempts to transform the abstract and energy-denying pattern of Christianity into his own opposing myth. Ribh's denunciation of the "abstract Greek absurdity," i.e. the masculine trinity (l. 1), reflects Yeats's longstanding struggle to come to terms with his physical and emotional life, a struggle that took on new urgency with advancing age. Ribh announces at the outset of the poem that the true base of both religious myth and art is not the absurd masculine trinity, but the family triangle of father, mother, and child. The real divine is the natural: the family unit with its patterns of love and hate.

In the second stanza Ribh becomes still more explicit, asserting that the Godhead, like man, discharges sexual energy in intercourse:

Natural and supernatural with the self-same ring are wed.
As man, as beast, as an ephemeral fly begets, Godhead begets Godhead,
For things below are copies, the Great Smaragdine Tablet said.

(ll. 4–6)

("Self-same ring" puns on the double meaning of ring: wedding ring and female genitals.)

As in the preceding poem, the orgasmic moment is seen as a "conflagration" in which individual differences are consumed, a loss of self that both attracted and frightened Yeats. Here Ribh seems to be in love with the natural world, in which the "conflagration of . . . passion" is "damped" by the individual body or mind (l. 8). The moment of fusion of separate selves is replaced by the new creature, the child.

Ribh's vision of an unending succession of births reminds us of Yeats's preoccupation at this time with thoughts of his children succeeding him. In such a frame of mind, he presumably found little solace in the prospect of an endless succession of natural children. In the final stanza, he hints at a more satisfactory solution: Men, if they loved enough, could "beget or bear themselves" (l. 12). The ideal of male-female intercourse is replaced by the ideal of a self-loving, self-propagating God. The ecstatic moment remains, but both the possibility of fusion and the endless succession of progeny are superseded. The image is related to that of the perfectly self-sufficient being of phase 15, as well as to the God of the 13th Cone.

The quest for passionate self-sufficiency continues in the following poem, "Ribh in Ecstasy." Indeed, self-sufficiency is the central fact of the experience described in the poem: "My soul had found / All happiness in its own cause or ground" (ll. 39–40). This happiness is based on participation in the Godhead's "sexual spasm" (l. 5). The clear connection between a deliberately obscure style—the poem begins, "What matter that you [the reader] understood no word!"—with a theme of participation in God the Father's sexual act lends weight to our speculation that in Yeats obscurity is a defensive response to confusing early impressions of sexual activity, notably parental intercourse. In "Ribh in Ecstasy" Yeats not only turns passivity into activity by confusing the reader, but represents himself as an active participant in the sexual act rather than a passive bystander.

In this moment he obtains the long-sought feeling of self-sufficiency and no longer needs to communicate with anyone—including his readers. The only reason he writes down his experience is, presumably, that it did not last: "My soul forgot / Those amorous cries . . . / And must the common round of day resume" (ll. 6–8).

"Ribh Considers Christian Love Insufficient," the fifth Supernatural Song, attacks the problem of the aging Yeats's growing feelings of rage and hatred. Bloom says the poem "may be counted as one of Yeats's apologias for his own hatreds."[39] Ellmann says the poem's source was one of Mrs. Yeats's spirit "communicators."

He said "hate God," we must hate all ideas concerning God that we possess, that if we did not absorption in God would be impossible . . . always he repeated "hatred, hatred" or "hatred of God" . . . said, "I think about hatred." That seems to me the growing hatred among men [which] has long been a problem with me.[40]

Once again, supernatural communications justify Yeats's feelings—in this case, hatred. The poem begins with Ribh's rejection of Christian love, which continues the rejection of orthodox Christian values maintained throughout "Supernatural Songs":

> Why should I seek for love or study it?
> It is of God and passes human wit.
> (ll. 1–2)

39 Bloom, *Yeats*, p. 412.
40 *Ibid.*, p. 411.

In asserting that he prefers hatred to love because it is "a passion in my own control" (l. 4), Ribh is attempting to deny hatred's power over him. Hatred becomes even tamer in the next lines— a housewife's broom:

> A sort of besom that can clear the soul
> Of everything that is not mind or sense.
> (ll. 5–6)

Approaching hatred from another direction in the second stanza, Ribh admits it is a force he does not understand. Asking, "Why do I hate man, woman or event?" (l. 7), he explains hatred as a "light" sent by his jealous soul. Like a jealous god, the soul seeks to annul the claims of everything, relationships or events, that is not itself. Rationally, it is difficult, as Bloom notes, to see how specific hatreds can free the soul from "terror and deception."[41] But the assertion makes sense when the preeminent value is self-sufficiency. Hatred becomes a defense against the "terror and deception" brought about by dependence on the outside world.

The desire for an independent self is linked, in the next stanza, to a desire for forgiveness and closeness to God. Yeats seems to be struggling with feelings of guilt over his hatred and his wish for independence. The poem denies the need to feel guilty: hatred, like sexuality in "Ribh at the Tomb," is good. Far from being chastised for hating, the soul will be rewarded by acceptance as God's bride.

As I read the poem, there is a tension built up in the first two stanzas. Yeats's defense of hatred puts the reader on his guard. It seems too obviously, as Bloom says, an apologia for Yeats's own hatreds. It is therefore with considerable relief that one sees Yeats move in the third stanza toward a more abstract and logically meaningful hatred of dogma and outworn concepts that keep the soul from direct experience of God:

> Thought is a garment and the soul's a bride
> That cannot in that trash and tinsel hide:
> Hatred of God may bring the soul to God.
> (ll. 16–18)

41 *Ibid.*, p. 412.

The relevation that God will accept the soul as bride despite, or rather because of, its hatred has great emotional appeal, not only because of the originality of the conceit, but because of the preceding anxiety-arousing expression of hatred and self-sufficiency, which the reader experiences as resolved by forgiveness. It is interesting in this connection that Bradford, perhaps expressing his own relief, sees more humility in the soul than Yeats actually expresses. She "creeps to God . . . in the nakedness of bridal surrender."[42]

The tone in which the bridal metaphor is continued:

> What can she take until her Master give!
> Where can she look until He make the show!
> What can she know until He bid her know!
> (ll. 21–23)

suggests that Yeats was tempted to end on a note of self-abnegation. But the last line reverses this: "How can she live till in her blood He live!" (l. 24). The realization of God in her blood is not the self-abnegating absorption in God that the spirit communicator speaks of and that Yeats speaks of in *A Vision*, but rather the experience of an inflowing force akin to imagination, which Yeats often described as flowing into the mind from outside. God has not absorbed the soul, but the soul God.

"What Magic Drum?" returns to the opposition of the natural family to the abstract trinity. Yeats's family in the seventh Supernatural Song is the familiar mythic one of beast-father, mother, and child. Yeats celebrates the visit of the beast-father to his offspring, the father's experience of "Primordial Motherhood," and his licking of his child into shape. The poem is characterized by an ambiguous blurring both of sexes and of subject and object. It is unclear from the opening lines whether there is an actual mother present (as Bloom suggests),[43] or whether the father, alone with the child, experiences the feeling of "Primordial Motherhood" when the child drinks "joy as it were milk upon his breast" (l. 3).

42 Bradford, *Yeats at Work*, p. 139.
43 Bloom, p. 415.

Through the evocation of a mood, Yeats seems to be trying to capture a magic moment in which intense sexual desire, held in check, produces an almost mystical experience of motherhood:

> He holds him from desire, all but stops his breathing lest
> Primordial Motherhood forsake his limbs, the child no longer rest,
> Drinking joy as it were milk upon his breast.
>
> (ll. 1–3)

In later years, in discussing the Crazy Jane poems, for example, Yeats explicitly connected sexual desire with his own creativity as well as with spiritual insight. Yeats sexualizes the description of the father licking his child and blurs father, child, and possibly mother together, giving them all a serpentine or phallic quality. As in the first stanza, generalized sexual excitement seems part of the experience: "Down limb and breast or down that glimmering belly move his mouth and sinewy tongue" (l. 5). Licking the child into shape is usually the mother's job; it is also analogous to the first shapings of a poem—a moment of incipience. The magic drumbeats that herald the licking derive from the sensation of pulsating blood, from the drumbeats that accompany manifestations of the godhead in Hindu philosophy, and from the rhythmic tune that Yeats spoke of hearing in one's mind while composing a poem.[44]

The next poem, "Whence Had They Come?" relates our sensations of eternity, and presumably other transcendent feelings, to sexual passion:

> Eternity is passion, girl or boy
> Cry at the onset of their sexual joy
> "For ever and for ever."
>
> (ll. 1–3)

The poem describes three kinds of passion and the ideas or phenomena they generate: the sexual love of the adolescent, the passion of the mature poet, and the zealous passion of the religious fanatic. There is a progress in the poem, corresponding to the progress from youth to age on the Wheel, from more open forms

---

[44] Yeats, *Essays and Introductions*, "Speaking to the Psalter," p. 15.

of sexuality to its complete disguise or repression. Sexual love between adolescents gives rise to the idea, still highly erotic, of eternal love. Passion in the poet—the "passion-driven exultant man"
(l. 5)—expresses itself in poetry that deals with sexuality in a more
general way. Like Ribh in ecstasy, this poet sings "sentences that
he has never thought" (l. 6), i.e., he gives voice to forbidden
thoughts.

In the Flagellant, finally, sexual passion is repressed entirely
and provokes a cruel attack on the offending part: "The Flagellant lashes those submissive loins" (l. 7). The Flagellant's actions,
like those of lovers and poet, come from cyclic movement—the
rise and fall of sexuality. Continuing the whip metaphor, Yeats
extends the Flagellant's actions into history in the form of a
question:

> Whence had they come,
> The hand and lash that beat down frigid Rome?
> (ll. 9–10)

Christianity's triumph over Rome becomes a sadistic sexual assault,
the implication being that violence will rouse Rome once again
and initiate a new cycle. This implication is continued by the final
sexual metaphor:

> What sacred drama through her body heaved
> When world-transforming Charlemagne was conceived?
> (ll. 11–12)

The conception of Charlemagne—who would impose Christianity
by violence—is represented as an orgasmic moment[45] that will
awaken Rome to the experience of Christianity. A violent act initiates a masochistic era.

"Meru," the powerful sonnet with which the sequence closes, is
the only poem in it that may antedate Yeats's Steinach operation.[46]
If so, this would help account for the poem's austere, renunciatory

---

[45] This moment is implicitly parallel to Leda's shudder at the conception of
Helen's mother, the initiation of a subjective era, in Yeats's poem "Leda and
the Swan" (1923).

[46] A. Norman Jeffares, *A Commentary on the Collected Poems of W. B. Yeats*
(Stanford, Calif.: Stanford University Press, 1968), p. 433.

tone, which contrasts markedly with Ribh's defiant sexuality and presents an alternative to Ribh's way of facing old age, a voluntary renunciation of the world and body: "Egypt and Greece, good-bye, and good-bye, Rome!" (l. 8).

As we mentioned in connection with *The Herne's Egg*, Yeats's concept of the mask began to fail him in old age. His carefully constructed technique for dealing with reality seemed at times to be breaking down. In "Meru" this breakdown, broadened into the breakdown of all "illusion," is presented as a courageous quest for reality. Once again passivity is turned to activity:

> Civilization is hooped together, brought
> Under a rule, under the semblance of peace
> By manifold illusion; but man's life is thought,
> And he, despite his terror, cannot cease
> Ravening through century after century,
> Ravening, raging and uprooting that he may come
> Into the desolation of reality.
>
> (ll. 1–7)

In *A Vision* Yeats disparages the objective man's thirst for reality, preferring the poet's covering illusions. Here, there is clearly a different tone, a suggestion of heroism in man's "ravening" mind.

Yeats takes a similar view of the ravening mind of his God-hero Oedipus. Oedipus's probing revealed the passionate substructure of civilization—man's desire to kill his father and lie with his mother. Despite the horror of the revelation, Oedipus did not renounce his senses, and at his death descended into the bowels of loving mother earth. The objective hermits of "Meru" go much further than Oedipus or subjective man. They also strip away the passions and numb the senses. They are left with a world of ice. Yeats's wintry imagery well expresses the look and feel of things without either illusion or its passionate source:

> Hermits upon Mount Meru or Everest,
> Caverned in night under the drifted snow,
> Or where that snow and winter's dreadful blast
> Beat down upon their naked bodies, know
> That day brings round the night, that before dawn
> His glory and his monuments are gone.
>
> (ll. 9–14)

The inspiration for the sestet seems to have been Shri Purohit Swami's book (for which Yeats wrote the introduction) describing an Indian mystic's search for God on Mount Meru.[47] Like the hermits of Yeats's poem, the Swami endures the torments of ice and snow. (The climax of the experience the Swami describes is the descent of God, who tenderly covers the mystic's body with kisses and holds him like "the Divine Mother.")[48] Possibly Yeats experienced the punishing cold as itself an erotic experience ("winter's dreadful blast" on "naked bodies") akin to the eroticized cold light in "The Cold Heaven." Certainly he suggests that the hermit's suffering is only a prelude—if not to direct gratification, at least to a new birth. They are "caverned in night" as if in a womb, awaiting the dawn that will presumably bring new imaginings.

47 *Ibid.*, pp. 433–34.
48 Yeats, *Essays and Introductions*, pp. 478–79.

SIX

The Transfigured Body

THE THREE GREAT POEMS of Yeats's maturity to be discussed in this chapter—"A Dialogue of Self and Soul," "Sailing to Byzantium," and "Byzantium"—all deal with threats to integrity, with fears of bodily injury, fusion, and destruction, imagined in relation both to sexuality and to death. With extraordinary economy, Yeats represents his obsessive Oedipal wishes and fears along with later fears and fantasies of death. In "A Dialogue," the sexual theme is presented separately. In "Sailing to Byzantium," by contrast, the themes of sexuality and death are merged in the concealed figure of the cruel Oedipal mother.

In studying these poems we will examine Yeats's characteristic ways of representing woman—both directly as a real but mythicized figure, and more abstractly, by symbolic body parts. As often before, in these poems Yeats presents woman as both good and evil, as both nurturer and devourer. We will see Yeats using the female body as a general symbol of what threatened him, whether in sexuality or in death, as well as the prototype of life after death, i.e., *Anima Mundi*. The male body in these poems is also the Self of the protagonist, and it is symbolized in a way designed to counteract the threat posed by female sexuality or by death. Finally, we will examine Yeats's brilliant defensive use of fetish-like objects —the sword and the golden bird.

"A Dialogue of Self and Soul"

"A Dialogue of Self and Soul" was written in 1927, shortly after Yeats's "first severe illness since childhood."[1] He wrote Olivia

---

[1] Bloom, *Yeats*, p. 373.

Shakespear in September that he had "suddenly awakened out of despondency" after praying and receiving a comforting dream-vision of "a 'key' and . . . a long white walled road" (*Letters*, p. 728). Several weeks later he wrote Olivia again, describing "A Dialogue," which, he says, "is a choice of rebirth rather than deliverance from birth."[2] In the poem, a strong sense of self stands in opposition to threats of dissolution posed both by death and by aspects of life. The Soul of the poem—in general, objective man—represents Yeats's fears, probably intensified by his illness, of loss of identity and passivity. Soul addresses Self:

> Fix every wandering thought upon
> That quarter where all thought is done:
> Who can distinguish darkness from the soul?
>
> (ll. 6–8)

Self, ignoring Soul's question, broods on his ancestral sword. The sword, like Oisin's earlier word sword, is a talismanic object, which here serves as a defense against fears of nothingness and loss of individuality—the "darkness" mentioned by Soul.

In *Oisin*, the sword's significance was almost lost in Yeats's description of Oisin's battle with the demon. In "Dialogue" the sword is pure emblem, and the reader's attention is focused upon it. That the sword's unique and precious qualities have been preserved is emphasized by Yeats's repeated use of the word "still":

> The consecrated blade upon my knees
> Is Sato's ancient blade, still as it was,
> Still razor-keen, still like a looking-glass
> Unspotted by the centuries.
>
> (ll. 9–12)

The blade, an image of concentrated force, is a symbol of the masculine self at its most coherent: the essence of sexual and artistic potency. In "Parting," the male protagonist, originally a swordsman, is threatened by the woman's "dark declivities."[3] In "A Dialogue" the sword's implicit enemy is the "most fecund ditch of all"

---

[2] It is tempting to connect the key and long road with the theme of rebirth elaborated in the poem. See *Letters*, p. 729.

[3] "Chosen" and "Parting," two paired poems of 1926, are in many ways, notably the use of female imagery, a trial run for "A Dialogue."

(l. 61), which can soil or blunt it, but in Part I of the poem Yeats is presenting a nonthreatening ideal relationship. The sword is protected from harm—it is "unspotted" by time or blood—by an embroidered sheath. The embroidered silk that protects the sword was torn from a "court-lady's dress," as was, in fact, the embroidered sheath covering the Japanese sword Yeats had been given by Junzō Sato.[4] Yeats may also intend an allusion here to Lady Gregory or to Mrs. Yeats, whose beauty he had described in "The Gift of Harun Al Rashid" (1922) as an embroidered banner.

In the last of his three speeches, Soul counters Self's defensive emblems by evoking a heaven that overwhelms the individual man:

> Such fullness in that quarter overflows
> And falls into the basin of the mind
> That man is stricken deaf and dumb and blind.
>
> (ll. 33–35)

The fountain image in Yeats's work typically has positive associations with spiritual nourishment and the good, nurturing mother. These associations may make the reader temporarily suspend judgment on Soul's ideal state, but Yeats's emphasis here is unmistakably on the price man pays for fusion: "man is stricken deaf and dumb and blind." Soul's heaven represents on one level the loss of identity Yeats feared. It is not the artistic heaven of phase 15, where distinctness of Self and loved object are retained, but rather the heaven of the saint, where the "body is completely absorbed in its supernatural environment" (*Vision*, p. 183), and bodily senses are deprived of their function.

Part II of the poem consists of a monologue by Self, which ends with a moment of acceptance or blessedness. Though the sword and its sheath no longer function explicitly as defensive emblems, their presence is implicit—"these I set / For emblems of the day against the tower / Emblematical of the night" (ll. 28–30)—and the right to use them is again asserted (ll. 31–32). The sword's remembered qualities of definiteness, purity, and strength are brought to mind continually by the enumeration in Part II of the characteristics

---

[4] Shotaro Oshima, *W. B. Yeats and Japan* ([Kanda, Japan]: Hokuseido Press, [1965]), pp. 64, 122.

of the untransformed life. The sword's razor-keen edge, for example, contrasts with the clumsy battering of Part II's fighting men, and its reflecting surface, which "like a looking-glass" allows a clear perception of self, with their blindness, brought about by total immersion in experience.

In Part II of "A Dialogue of Self and Soul" Yeats turns away from the feared loss of Self in death and the afterlife to an exploration of his past life, which, it soon becomes apparent, threatened a similar loss or confusion of identity. And though Self is describing untransformed life, he may be thought of as doing so with the protective sword across his knees. Like Virgil's golden bough, it aids the poet in his descent into the underworld of his fears and impulses.

In Part II, life is seen as humiliating or painful in all its phases:

> that toil of growing up;
> The ignominy of boyhood; the distress
> Of boyhood changing into man;
> The unfinished man and his pain
> Brought face to face with his own clumsiness;
>
> The finished man among his enemies.
> (ll. 44–49)

Even when the man is "finished," and there is a similarity between this state and that of the artifact, he is subject to disfigurement and defilement:

> How in the name of Heaven can he escape
> That defiling and disfigured shape
> The mirror of malicious eyes
> Casts upon his eyes until at last
> He thinks that shape must be his shape?
> (ll. 50–54)

The passage suggests Yeats's extreme vulnerability.[5] In addition to its general reference to enemies, the "mirror of malicious eyes" in

---

[5] In the first draft of his autobiography, he describes this vulnerability to hostility: "I found myself unpopular, and suffered, discovering that if men speak much ill of you it makes at moments a part of the image of yourself—that is your only support against the world—and that you see yourself too as if with hostile eyes." *Memoirs*, p. 84.

which he sees himself altered may refer particularly to George Moore's portrait of him in *Hail and Farewell*. Yeats's caricature of Moore in his *Autobiography* was in part a retaliation, in part an attempt to correct the distorted image of himself. As Yeats said, "I did hate leaving the last word to George Moore" (*Letters*, p. 733). In any case the enemy's distortions of Self are opposed by the reflection of the poet's essence in the mirror blade of the sword.

Man, in the opening lines of the poem's second section, is seen as a blind beggar drinking from a dirty ditch: "A living man is blind and drinks his drop" (l. 41). But, Yeats asks, with a kind of gay stoicism, "What matter if the ditches are impure?" (l. 42). It clearly did matter, at least to Yeats, who was so concerned with good nourishment, but here the lines convey a feeling of mastery. Somehow Self has prevailed over the dirty and inadequate portion as it has over the other threats Yeats depicts. The imaginative reliving of his past life—like an anxiety dream about an examination that a student has already passed—serves as reassurance and defense against future dangers.

Life, first defined in terms of orality, is now defined in terms of sexuality. Yeats goes on to express disgust at thoughts of birth and the female genitals. Again, disgust and fear are balanced by stoical acceptance:

> I am content to live it all again
> And yet again, if it be life to pitch
> Into the frog-spawn of a blind man's ditch.
>
> (ll. 57–59)

In *The Island of Statues* the Enchantress changed into a frog after her death; in *Oisin*, where Yeats used a winding stair to represent the inside of the female body, the stair was covered with green slime. Similarly, "frog-spawn" is meant to express the repellent aspects of female anatomy. The verse continues:

> A blind man battering blind men;
> Or into that most fecund ditch of all,
> The folly that man does
> Or must suffer, if he woos
> A proud woman not kindred of his soul.
>
> (ll. 60–64)

Surely the fecund ditch is akin to the woman's "dark declivities" in "Parting."[6] The contrast in the above passage, derived from Blake, is between sexual passion and spiritual harmony. Impulse leaves one vulnerable ("a blind man battering blind men"); sexual passion is particularly dangerous because the man may be lost entirely in the "labyrinth of another's being."[7]

For the rest of the poem, Self continues to invoke acceptance and forgiveness of the darkest sides of human existence as a means of fending off threats to his integrity. (In the last stanza, Self announces his intention to comprehend "Every event in action or in thought"—in the first printing of the poem the intention was to "Count every sin of action or of thought"—and "forgive myself the lot" [ll. 66–67].) Although the sins to be forgiven are not specified beyond the general "crime of death and birth" (l. 24), the hostility Self sees directed against him by enemies and by woman appears to be in part a projection of his own hostile impulses. Once Self has forgiven his own sins, his perception of the external world accordingly changes. He no longer sees it as disgusting or threatening, but as blessed.

A link between Yeats's last stanza and Coleridge's *Ancient Mariner* lends support to the idea that Yeats was coping with more specifically hostile impulses than is indicated by the vague reference to "events." Coleridge expresses a similar succession of emotions: disgust arising from guilt, followed by an impulsive rush of love and a rewarding sweet flow. Coleridge's Mariner, becalmed on the dead and rotting sea after his terrible crime, looks down into the depths. There he sees "a thousand, thousand slimy things," and is filled with despair. Watching the snakes cavort in the ship's shadow, he suddenly sees their beauty:

> A spring of love gushed from my heart,
> And I blessed them unaware.[8]

---

[6] John Holloway strangely insists that any associations with "fecund" besides squalor and worthlessness are irrelevant. See his essay "Style and World in 'The Tower,'" in Denis Donoghue and J. R. Mulryne, eds. *An Honoured Guest: New Essays on W. B. Yeats* (London: Arnold, 1965), p. 63.

[7] Yeats, "The Tower," l. 112; *Variorum Poems*, p. 413.

[8] Ernest Hartley Coleridge, ed., *The Complete Poetical Works of Samuel Taylor Coleridge*, vol. 1 (Oxford: Clarendon Press, 1957), p. 198.

The echo in Yeats's concluding lines is striking:

> When such as I cast out remorse
> So great a sweetness flows into the breast
> We must laugh and we must sing,
> We are blest by everything,
> Everything we look upon is blest.
>
> (ll. 68–72)

In Coleridge's poem, the Mariner is rewarded for his loving impulse: rain pours down "by grace of the Holy Mother," and he drinks to satiation (in his sleep). In Yeats the sweet flow is less obviously linked to milk, but it gains emotional impact from the association nonetheless. The sweet flow is opposed to other liquid images in the poem, the drop of dirty ditch water, insufficient and impure, and the overwhelming heavenly flow.

Self is more active and self-sufficient than the Mariner. His loving impulse is directed toward himself, and the sweet flow coming into his breast suggests that he sees himself as both mother and child. In this respect, the poem as a whole shows Yeats—as often before—attempting to turn passive suffering into active mastery. Self's assumption of responsibility for coming to terms with his "sins" is contrasted to the passivity of Soul, whose thought that "only the dead can be forgiven" (l. 39) increases his dependency on an external power and makes his tongue "a stone" (l. 40). The contrast between Self and Soul here is Yeats's familiar one between the active artistic personality and the passive religious one. The laughter and song that follow a series of threats to Self's integrity is the artist's joyful triumph over death and disintegration. In an essay on Synge, Yeats says that the artist's joy is one with sanctity, and describes it as a powerful and noble energy that mocks at death and oblivion. The passage, which reads almost like a commentary on parts of "A Dialogue," similarly connects creative joy and a moment of "sympathy":

There is in the creative joy an acceptance of what life brings ... or a hatred of death for what it takes away, which arouses within us, through some sympathy perhaps with all other men, an energy so noble, so powerful, that we laugh aloud and mock, in the terror or the sweetness of our exaltation, at death and oblivion.[9]

[9] Cited in Jeffares, *Commentary*, p. 324.

In his poem, Yeats has moved in a circle from contemplation of the artifact, to contemplation of life (the raw material for the artifact), to representation of the moment of inspiration that transforms the raw and painful material into a work of art. "A Dialogue of Self and Soul" can itself be seen as the result of this blessed moment of inspiration—an artifact that like the sword reflects a strong self, and signifies Yeats's triumph over the threats he so movingly depicts.

"Sailing to Byzantium"

"Sailing to Byzantium" has traditionally been read as an affirmation of the spirit over the life of the body. Elder Olson, long one of the most influential exponents of this view, sees the old man of the poem as freed by age from sensual passion and thus able "to rejoice in the liberation of the soul."[10] In contrast, Simon Lesser has recently observed that far from being an affirmation of spirit, the poem is a "cry of agony."[11] The old man is tormented by sexual desire and envy of the young; in Lesser's view it is the tension between desire and his aging body that sets the old man moving toward Byzantium, rather than an appreciation of the superior value of spirit. Lesser suggests that Olson's blindness to the old man's tortured sexuality is symptomatic of a general tendency among critics to concentrate so exclusively on a poem's intellectual framework and formal structure that they lose sight of its emotional content. He finds it impossible to justify emotionally Olson's conclusion that the old man's transformation into a golden bird represents a triumph, that the bird somehow becomes a haven for the old man's free and happy soul. To Lesser, the golden bird is merely an automaton, "a bitter, tinselly travesty of what the 'I' of the poem values . . . and would want of an afterlife."

Olson's very avoidance of the emotional issues, however, leaves him in a better position than Lesser to react appropriately to the symbol of the golden bird. The bird functions as a defense against anxieties unconsciously raised by the poem—not just the fear of

---

10 As cited by Simon Lesser in his article, "*Sailing to Byzantium*: Another Voyage, Another Reading," *College English*, 28 (1967): 293.
11 *Ibid.*

aging and thwarted sexuality noted by Lesser, but the overarching fear of a loss of integrity. The old man's anguish at being excluded from the pleasures of the young is so great not only because of sexual frustration, but because Yeats associates loss of potency with other terrifying threats to his integrity—passivity, castration, and disintegration. An old man is but "a tattered coat upon a stick." Olson's unconscious reaction both to these threats and to the bird's defensive role can be sensed in his description of the golden bird. Within the bird, the old man's soul is "free to act in its own supremacy and in full cognizance of its own excellence, incorruptible and secure" from all the ills of the flesh; his soul, that is, is active rather than passive, narcissistically gratified rather than depressed by impotence, and secure against disintegration. As Norman Holland puts it, a work of art is "a complex dialectic of impulse and defense."[12]

To appreciate the full complexity of the bird's defensive function, it is necessary to distinguish in the poem two competing but coalescing themes. The old man's frustrated sexual desire is the visible strand in what we shall see is a submerged theme or fantasy of union with the mother. Merging this fantasy with the theme of aging and death was possible for Yeats because of his masochistic attitude toward both. As we have seen, in the works by Yeats that embody incestuous fantasies, the hero is often symbolically castrated or mutilated by the mother figure before he can be loved. In "Sailing to Byzantium" Yeats endows the aging process itself with the threatening qualities of a cruel mother. Now it is age that sexually frustrates the old man and threatens him with disintegration and loss of self. In the Ribh poems Yeats fought similar fears of disintegration by stressing sexual vitality and thus intactness. This particular defensive maneuver was made easier by Yeats's Steinach operation, which increased his sense of sexual vitality. "Sailing" was written before that operation, after a spate of illnesses that undoubtedly intensified the 61-year-old Yeats's fear of death; in "Sailing" Yeats turns to another instrument of psychic defense, the talismanic object.

[12] *Psychoanalysis and Shakespeare* (New York: McGraw-Hill, 1964), p. 53.

In studying the golden bird, one is struck by its resemblance to a transitional object or to a fetish (fetish is used here in the sense of a symbolic object with phallic significance that offers protection against fears of castration). Like both the transitional object and the fetish, the bird is used to maintain psychic balance and a sense of self. Like the transitional object it is something onto which the self is projected, something partly self and partly other; Olson's feeling that the bird is an "insouled monument" expresses this double quality. The bird is also basically a "good object," one that reassures its owner and banishes feelings of sadness and inadequacy. The bird's phallic significance and its role as a defense against fears and fantasies of castration emerge clearly when the bird is compared to objects in other works that more obviously represent the phallus.

To illustrate this let us return briefly to two works already discussed, "The Cap and Bells" and *A Full Moon in March*. Both embody Yeats's fantasies of submitting to a cruel mother who cuts him up and then lavishes her love on a dismembered part. In "Cap and Bells" the beautiful imagery fails to disguise a fantasy of self-castration, though with the recent exception of Bloom, critics have tended to ignore the poem's destructiveness and the irony with which Yeats presented it as "the way to win a woman." The implication is that the only way a woman wants him is dismembered. This fantasy of "the way to win a woman" becomes more explicit in Yeats's late dance play *A Full Moon in March*, where Yeats makes it clear in his stage directions that the dismembered part, the head, represents not only the poet's talent but his phallus.

In "Sailing to Byzantium" the old man, like the Jester and the Swineherd, is tortured by sexuality, "sick with desire." Though there is no incestuous love object present and though age has taken over the mother's role of devourer or castrater, there is evidence in the drafts and early fragments that a fantasy of union with the mother was originally an element of the poem. In an almost illegible prose fragment, Yeats writes of those "that I loved in my first youth" (Maud and mother), saying that having taken off his clothes for many loves, he will now take off his body "That they [his first

loves] might be enfolded in that for which they had longed."[13]
The imagery suggests a fantasy of pre-Oedipal fusion with the
mother. (The psychoanalytic reading of the poem that, perceiving
this one element, reads the poem as a voyage back to the mother
ignores not only other unconscious elements, but also the poem's
literal meaning and effect.)[14]

As we know, however, fantasies of fusion aroused corresponding
fears, and often led Yeats to present a countering image of distinctness and integrity. Early drafts of the poem present an image of
an infant playing or "asleep upon his mother's knees."[15] The image
reinforces the "I" 's sense of loneliness and exclusion from pleasure. Yeats's revisions suppress this picture, as the imagery becomes
more virile and austere. Other explicitly Christian images were
also suppressed and, in the case of the first stanza, replaced by explicitly Irish ones. The reappearance of imagery from the early
pagan work *Oisin* suggests that Yeats was summoning up old fantasies of incestuous desire and punishment in order to rework
them, transforming an earlier masochistic defeat into triumph.
The imagery in which the "I" in "Sailing" expresses his wish to
die recalls similar imagery in *Oisin* that represents fantasies of being battered, smashed, or castrated.

The central images of "Cap and Bells," *A Full Moon in March,*
and "Sailing to Byzantium" are all objects representing both the
phallus and some aspect of poetry: talent or artifact. The difference between them can be seen not only in connection with Yeats's
relationship to his fantasies of self-destruction or castration, but
in terms of readers' reactions. The three works can be compared
from the point of view of how easy they are to take. In "The Cap
and Bells" the Jester disintegrates, but Yeats succeeds in making his
disintegration palatable (to most readers) by using beautiful imagery. He attains further distance by maintaining that the poem
came to him in a dream. He says he has never understood it, and

---

[13] Jon Stallworthy, *Between the Lines: Yeats's Poetry in the Making* (New
York: Oxford University Press, 1963), p. 89.
[14] Ruth H. Sullivan, "Backwards to Byzantium," *Literature and Psychology,*
17 (1967): 13–18.
[15] Stallworthy, p. 91.

disclaims responsibility for it: "The authors are in Eternity."[16] In *A Full Moon in March*, the shocking content is increased to the point where most readers feel some discomfort. Here Yeats uses several means to provide distance. The sexual union of Queen and Head is portrayed in pantomime with dance and music. He insists that the blood covering the Queen's hands and dress "must not be too realistic—red gloves, red cloth maybe; some kind of harmony or pattern should suggest blood."[17] In addition to abstract patterns in an situation where the content would be shocking, Yeats uses theosophical and alchemical symbols, so that the play can be read as an allegory. Several critics who like the play read it in this fashion, which enables them to accept the events without horror. In general, those who like the play see the union of Queen and Head as something else or, like Bradford, stress its generality:

Yeats has consciously raised his subject to the level of myth. . . . Stendhal's protagonists are "personalities," and because they are we look into the psychological depths which Stendhal has imagined for them to discover reasons for what they do. Yeats's protagonists are "characters" from whom personality has been carefully abstracted. . . . When protagonists become timeless "characters," . . . materials can be used . . . which produce a highly morbid impression when used in connection with "personalities."[18]

Apparently Yeats's distancing devices do not work for all readers; at least one perceptive critic, Harold Bloom, is repelled by the "masochistic death" of the hero, though admitting that the theme has "a kind of nasty power."[19]

The bird in "Sailing to Byzantium" has an opposite effect; it is neither pathetic like the cap and bells nor grotesque like the head, but beautiful. Moreover, it is not just a part of the mangled poet but is the whole poet transformed into a valuable, lasting object. The fact that the bird cannot be identified as a dismembered part is in itself a distancing device. The bird's beauty and permanence, suggesting as they do that something valuable will survive, help the reader master his own fears of old age and death.

16 Yeats, *Variorum Poems*, p. 808.
17 Bradford, *Yeats at Work*, p. 286.
18 *Ibid.*, p. 292.
19 Bloom, *Yeats*, p. 341.

Yeats's early poetry shows the development of specific means of dealing with fear through the representation of an object symbolizing art. Some of these objects seem to defend against specific fears of castration and death, while others are reassuring in a more general way. They protect the poet against unpleasant states of mind —feelings of abandonment and rejection. In one of Yeats's earliest poems, "The Song of the Happy Shepherd" (1885), the Shepherd invokes such an object for comfort in a way reminiscent of the child's use of a transitional object.[20] The poem presents a withdrawal from the world of "Grey Truth" (l. 4) and "dusty deeds" (l. 22) to the world of imaginative self-sufficiency, where "words alone are certain good" (l. 43). The dissatisfied and restless Shepherd, one of "the sick children of the world" (l. 6), is told to seek out "Some twisted, echo-harbouring shell" (l. 36) whose "lips" will be his "comforters":

> Rewording in melodious guile
> Thy fretful words a little while.
>   (ll. 39–40)

The shell is like a mother crooning to her infant, calming his fretful mood, but it is also like an extended part of its owner, repeating his words within a hard protective covering. In this sense, the shell is a prototype of the golden bird.

We have observed similar images serving a similar function throughout Yeats's work. Oisin's Druid word sword, for example, symbolized both verbal power and phallic power, and it had an aggressive as well as a protective function: Oisin used it to fight the demon (his father). The urgency of Yeats's need for a symbolic object like sword or bird to ward off fears of dissolution is borne out by such images as that of the old man in "Sailing": a "tattered coat upon a stick." The tattered coat is literally the old man's flesh, and in a late draft, Yeats is obviously thinking of this flesh

---

[20] Though the transitional object is usually something soft, Phyllis Greenacre notes that some children, usually boys, choose a hard object instead. Such a choice suggests "elements arising from early phallic associations . . . associated with a visible erection." This would accord with the fact that the twisted horn (analogous to the twisted shell) has definitely phallic connotations in Yeats's later work. "The Fetish and the Transitional Object," *The Psychoanalytic Study of the Child,* 24 (1969): pp. 144–64.

as being torn away piecemeal by time: "For every morsel torn out of the dress."[21] The use of the word "morsel" recalls the drafts of *The Shadowy Waters*, which show the hero struggling with nightmare creatures who want to tear him to pieces and devour him. It would seem that physical aging had the same meaning for Yeats as being devoured or castrated: it became a fear he dealt with by means of a defensive object. In *Oisin*, Yeats represented his sexual organs in uncastratable form as Oisin's word sword and the magic scepter wielded by Aengus, god of love and poetry. In both of these images, poetic power is linked to sexual power, and the imperishable attribute is separated from the poet and placed in an object.

Another example of attributes separated from their owner and made immortal occurs in "Among School Children," a poem which like "Sailing to Byzantium" has a tattered protagonist. Toward the end of "Among School Children" Yeats ironically describes three great thinkers whose genius was unable to keep them from aging. One of these, Pythagoras, has golden thighs, an attribute which suggests that his sexuality at least was impervious to decay. In "Sailing to Byzantium," which was finished shortly after "Among School Children," Yeats solves the problem of the poet's remaining vulnerable while his attribute is immortalized by a transformation of the whole self into the object. In "Among School Children," more things are lost than are retained: Pythagoras's golden thighs symbolize a retention of potency, but the rest of Pythagoras disintegrates, and the narrator loses his "pretty plumage." In "Sailing" nothing at all has been renounced; everything is still there.

As the works we have discussed suggest, Yeats was always obsessed with death. We have seen him dealing with it in two important ways: denial and gaiety. Denial is expressed in the conviction that the essence of a man does not die, but is preserved in his work. Yeats transformed his sense of pain and loss at Synge's approaching death into a concern that Synge might not be able to finish his last play. When Synge managed to complete his

21 Stallworthy, *Between the Lines*, p. 108.

Deirdre, Yeats said that half the pain of loss was gone.[22] Yeats reacted in a similar way to his own illness and approaching death. When he began to spit blood, he defied his doctor's orders to rest and worked with renewed vigor on *A Vision*. His most painful thought was that he might not be able to finish (*Letters*, p. 733). Gaiety, as opposed to denial, involves a reversal of affect—a reaction of gaiety in place of the terror one might expect—which is beautifully described in the essay on Synge quoted earlier and in a letter Yeats wrote to Olivia Shakespear during a serious illness: "How strange is the subconscious gaiety that leaps up before danger or difficulty. I have not had a moment of depression—that gaiety is outside one's control" (*Letters*, p. 733).

In "Sailing to Byzantium" Yeats, in order to banish sadness, makes use of both a good object that banishes bad objects—the precious golden bird—and a good feeling (this includes denial, the thought that man survives in his work, but also contains many other elements), gaiety, that banishes bad feelings. In "Sailing" it is his gaiety that keeps the old man from being merely tatters. Though the contrast is intended to be one of bodily tatters versus the singing soul, the ultimate emotional message is that if the old man sings loudly enough, he will not disintegrate physically.

The reader will recall a similar "gay" reaction to death, expressed in similar imagery, in *Oisin*; the extent to which Yeats transcends his masochism in "Sailing" is underscored if we compare the resolutions of the two poems. When St. Patrick taunts Oisin with death and damnation, Oisin responds with defiant song:

> ... I go to the Fenians, O cleric, to chaunt
> The war-songs that roused them of old; they will rise ...
> Innumerable, singing, exultant.
>
> (III, 201–3)

Patrick reacts with increased severity to Oisin's defiance: "kneel and wear out the flags and pray for your soul that is lost" (III, 215). Overwhelmed by Patrick's threats, Oisin loses his gaiety, and it becomes clear that the gaiety is defending against a feeling of disintegration. Like the tattered protagonist of "Among School Chil-

---

[22] Unpublished letter to Mabel Dickinson, May 1908.

dren" Oisin is broken with age, a "show unto children" (III, 218). In an image that suggests the tattered coat of "Sailing," he feels "All emptied . . . as a beggar's cloak in the rain" (III, 219). The poem ends with this complete deflation of the hero. It is significant that in the drafts of "Sailing," the "I" takes a penitential position similar to the one St. Patrick urges upon Oisin. The "I" prays for death from the God who threatened Oisin, and wonders if "God's love will refuse"

> When prostrate on the marble step I fall
> And cry aloud. . . .[23]

Yeats deleted these masochistic lines—and all other Christian references—for images of his own synthesis. Throughout his work Yeats saw the Christian God as playing a punitive part in the struggle between impulsive forces (e.g., Oisin) and repression (e.g., St. Patrick), and in "Sailing to Byzantium" Yeats wanted to portray transformation, not simply destruction. In *Oisin* the hero, deformed by age and blindness, "lies on the anvil of the world" (II, 203–4). The smith who strikes the sinner is of course God. In "Sailing to Byzantium" the act of hammering becomes part of the process of making an artifact. Yeats identifies both with the artificer who destroys in order to create and with the material that is transformed. In his youth he wrote: "My life has been in my poems. To make them I have broken my life in a mortar" (*Letters*, p. 84). The destructive god who batters Oisin with age becomes a Grecian goldsmith who gives the "I" a permanent, invulnerable form.

As we have seen, one of Yeats's main concerns in "Sailing to Byzantium" is the translation of the body into an invulnerable form. F. A. C. Wilson, like Olson preoccupied by the soul-body dichotomy in the poem, calls the golden bird "the soul's image,"[24] but it is certainly the body's image as well. In the drafts, thoughts of the body clearly predominate over thoughts of the spirit. Byzantium is a place where the body is immortalized in art. The art that Yeats chooses for his Holy City is one that specifically celebrates the human body, the sculpture of Phidias. Compare two parallel

---

23 Stallworthy, p. 98.
24 F. A. C. Wilson, *Yeats's Iconography* (London: Gollancz, 1960), p. 285.

passages, the first from *Oisin* and the second from the drafts of
"Sailing":

> a countless flight
> Of moonlit steps glimmered; and right and left
> Dark statues glimmered over the pale tide
> Upon dark thrones.
>
> (ll. 34–37)
>
> Statues of Phidias
>   . . .
> Mirrored in water
>   . . .
> Statues of bronze over a marble stair.[25]

The first passage has a disembodied quality characterized by the
vague, glimmering moonlight. Forty years later, Yeats brings out
the potential hardness and precise outlines of the statues. Classical sculpture was well adapted to becoming one of Yeats's hard,
valuable, essentially phallic, symbolic objects that glorify the body
and magically preserve it from destruction.

The golden bird is perhaps the finest example of the Yeatsian
symbol whose phallic nature and talismanic qualities make it comparable in function to the fetish and the transitional object. Another group of images and symbols, less detachable from their
context but identifiable nonetheless, are basically womb symbols,
which come to represent a place of safety or source of sustenance
that often includes a talismanic object. In *Oisin*, the reader will
recall, Yeats uses a stair over which moisture continually flows,
and a dome to represent the interior of the female body. The
domed cavern's similarity to a womb is increased by Oisin's exit
through a tiny door next to a stream. Both stair and dome reappear in the early drafts of "Sailing to Byzantium," but they have
lost their natural qualities and are specifically connected with art.
The sea-slime of *Oisin*'s stair has been transformed into cold marble, and the rocky dome filled with shadowy faces into the mosaic-
filled dome of St. Sophia. This change represents a process of
repudiation, a "cleaning up" of bodily images to remove what is
ephemeral, disgusting, or dangerous.

[25] Stallworthy, p. 95.

Though the "I" longs to see the dome of St. Sopl
drafts, explicit mention of the dome has disappeared fr
draft. Its vestigial presence is definitely felt, however.
described descending a gold mosaic wall in a spiral mov
Yeats, in previous works, has associated with a dome. Giorgio
Melchiori has pointed out the descent of similar gyrating figures
from a dome in "Rosa Alchemica,"[26] but there is an earlier and
equally significant allusion to the dome in *Oisin*, where the gyrating motion is represented by the hero's circling the floor before
he exits. The dome in *Oisin* is even filled with shadowy faces (similar to the blurred figures of the later "Rosa Alchemica") "loaded
with the memory of days / Buried and mighty." The concept of a
dome filled with memories is an obvious prototype of Yeats's concept of the Great Memory, *Anima Mundi*, and is echoed in the
drafts of "Sailing to Byzantium" by the dome of St. Sophia, which,
as Yeats delightedly remarks elsewhere, was called the "Holy Wisdom" (*Vision*, p. 280).

In the revisions of "Sailing" the dome's benign wisdom is embodied by the sages. This final version differs in an important way
from earlier versions, in which the sages were saints and Yeats
prayed to them to make him like themselves:

> Consume this heart & make it what you were
> Rigid, abstracted, and fanatical.[27]

The saints were never important to Yeats in a Christian sense as
certain critics seem to think. They were important because of their
toughness and indestructibility. In this respect, they resemble other
hard defensive objects and Yeats is drawn to them. He repudiates
and replaces them, however, because of other, less pleasant associations. Like politicians and critics, the saints, in Yeats's view, are
castrated by envy and fanaticism and are hostile to both creativity
and sexuality. To become like them is to suffer castration.

In revision, Yeats turns the saints into the less threatening sages.
Oisin's experience within the domed cavern of the Isle of Fears

[26] Giorgio Melchiori, *The Whole Mystery of Art* (London: Routledge, 1960),
pp. 221–23.
[27] Stallworthy, p. 100.

illuminates the sages' function. It is within the cavern, the reader will recall, that Oisin receives the gift of the word sword, with which to fight the demon. Yeats always thought of *Anima Mundi* both as a repository of poetic images and as the place to go for "answers" when in difficulty. In "Sailing," the sages assume the dome's function as a repository of wisdom, and thus become helpful rather than castrating. The sages in Yeats's final version will not deprive the "I" of anything: they will be his "singing-masters."

"Byzantium"

The great dome of the Holy Wisdom that appears so tantalizingly in the drafts of "Sailing to Byzantium" reemerges as a central image in "Byzantium." The images of anvil (smithy), bird, and pavement also reappear, and as in the earlier poem are associated in the drafts with masochistic fears of battering, castration, and death. This is the case not only with images carried over from the earlier poem, but also with images that make their first appearance in "Byzantium." On the whole the drafts of "Byzantium" show frightening or masochistic imagery gradually giving way to the more affirmative imagery of the finished poem.

The serene and disdainful dome in the first stanza of "Byzantium" does nothing to impose its silence on the human turmoil around it; human sounds and sights simply move gradually away, leaving it the center of the scene. It is not threatening in any way, and most readers immediately feel not only its beauty, but its attractiveness. Thus Stallworthy describes the coolness of the dome as "welcome relief after . . . fevered squalor."[28] The drafts, however, show that Yeats thought of the contrast between absolute stillness or death and human activity in terms of a violent assault of one on the other that was anything but pleasant "death like sleep beats down the harlot's song / And the great cathedral gong."[29] The harlot's song represents not only sexuality but poetry as praise of sensual life; "death like sleep" is the common enemy of both sex and song. The images of assault are like the "fullness" in "A

28 *Ibid.*, p. 118.
29 *Ibid.*, p. 117.

Dialogue of Self and Soul," which, overflowing, strikes the man "deaf and dumb and blind." Yeats crossed out his first attempt at depicting the arrival of death and immediately afterward tried a new version: "And silence falls on the cathedral gong / And the drunken harlot's song." Although the sense of assault is diminished by the new formulation, still present is the idea of sound being snuffed out or muffled. In the final version, the images of fighting, sexuality, and song simply recede from the scene, and the reader is able to concentrate on the shining dome undistracted.

The process involved is similar to the one observable in the drafts of "Sailing to Byzantium," where fear is transformed into joy. By removing any suggestion of violent assault on life, Yeats allows the reader to respond to the dome's many positive associations. In *Oisin*, written at the beginning of Yeats's career, the hero is symbolically born when he leaves the domed cavern to do battle. In "Byzantium" Yeats depicts the journey's end: images of fighting and sexuality recede as the "I" prepares to reenter the matrix.

As in "Sailing" Yeats is thinking of the golden bird as the protagonist's final shape. Bird and dome are hardened forms of male and female bodies or of the organs of generation, male and female versions of perfection; yet they are not presented in any meaningful relation, unless one thinks of the bird as being enclosed in the dome of the sky. Perhaps it is the absence of any such relation that accounts for the peculiar joylessness of the imagery—as contrasted, say, with the sphere that holds the fused lovers in "Chosen," or with the egg in "Among School Children." The separation of dome and bird can be explained as part of a defense, obvious throughout the poem, against fears of being overwhelmed or absorbed. The isolated golden bird (or purified soul) retains its separate identity; there is no danger of fusion with the divine. Moreover, the overwhelmingness of death is lessened by the bird's capacity to choose between rebirth and death. He can "like the cocks of Hades crow" (signaling rebirth), or, "embittered" by frustrated love, he can choose to remain below (and scorn mere life). The golden bough introduced in the third stanza is an additional protective device. Like the bough that brought Aeneas safely from Hades, Yeats's golden bough signifies that the poet will be able to rise from the underworld if he wishes.

The bird-soul's choice rests on some sort of inner questioning, and self-judgment is one of the poem's main themes. The cool beauty of "Byzantium"'s most impressive image, the dome, suggests judgment rather than love. The emotional tone of the lines "A starlit or a moonlit dome disdains / All that man is" (ll. 6–7) resembles the icy "injustice" of the skies in "The Cold Heaven," which punishes the frightened soul after death. The disdainful dome brings us back to a key fact of Yeats's childhood, his mother's "cold emotion." Susan Yeats's disgust at reminders of the facts of life—people kissing at railway stations or wearing bathing costumes—is perfectly expressed by the dome's disdain for "The fury and the mire of human veins" (l. 8). Moreover, in the objectivity with which Yeats presents the afterlife, the relative lack of sentiment, he comes close to embodying his mother's coldness in his style. The golden bird is not only immortal, but cold. There is a certain horror in the identification of the bird's coldness with the mother's because it implies that to be like the mother one must be dead. This is a variation of the pattern of the dance plays and "Cap and Bells": before the Jester or poet is allowed to enter the sacred place—palace or woman's body—he must submit to castration and death.

The development of the mummy image in the drafts shows Yeats fighting his own deep-seated fear of what death entails. In the initial versions there is a suggestion, later dropped, of a body forcibly contained by mummy bands:

> Limbs that have been bound in mummy cloth
> May be more content with a winding path.[30]

The "winding path" is the convoluted route to self-purification described in *A Vision*. The lines imply that no one who was not so bound and constrained by death would embark on the difficult road to self-knowledge and liberation laid out in *A Vision*: given a free choice, we would all be content with unknowing, impure

---

30 *Ibid.*, p. 120.

life. The echo here of Blake's lines on "Infant Sorrow" suggests that one of the things Yeats feared in old age was a return of the constraints and helplessness experienced in infancy:

> Struggling in my father's hands
> Striving against swaddling bands
> Bound and weary I thought best
> To sulk upon my mother's breast.[31]

Yeats immediately begins to turn the masochistic imagery of the draft into something more positive; one can almost see him constructing a defense against the frightfulness of the dry, breathless thing that confronts him: "What if the bodies dry the mouths lack breath / That summons or beckons me."[32] In the drafts Yeats thus appears to be arguing with himself. The initial "What if" indicates an attempt to fight down his feelings of fear and disgust. His next lines insist that he accepts what initially repelled him: "I adore that mystery / Called death in life." (Compare the exclamation of the Chorus in *At the Hawk's Well* when faced with Fand's deathless body—"the horror of unmoistened eyes"—a reaction that does not move beyond fear.)[33] In the final version of "Byzantium" there is no longer any trace of inner argument:

> For Hades' bobbin bound in mummy-cloth
> May unwind the winding path;
> A mouth that has no moisture and no breath
> Breathless mouths may summon;
> I hail the superhuman;
> I call it death-in-life and life-in-death.
>
> (ll. 11–16)

The last two lines quoted above derive, as Stallworthy notes, from Coleridge's

> The Night-mare Life-in-Death was she,
> Who thicks man's blood with cold.[34]

The nightmare figure of the spirit woman dooms the Ancient Mariner to eternal repetition of his guilt, an existence devoid of

31 Blake, *Complete Writings* (London: Oxford, 1966), p. 217.
32 Stallworthy, *Between the Lines*, p. 120.
33 Early version cited by Bradford, p. 202.
34 Stallworthy, p. 121.

the human pleasures enjoyed by the bridegroom. This echo of Coleridge points up Yeats's interest in original sin as a theme of poetry and his belief that after death the soul relives its past. Dreaming Back, in which, as we have already noted, the soul, like the Mariner, reviews its passionate experience, is so similar to the process of creating poetry as Yeats understood it, i.e., the evocation of past events in order to master them, that Yeats can use poetry and Dreaming Back as reciprocal symbols. Regarding the afterlife as an extension of poetic activity undoubtedly makes death easier to accept. Such a view even allows the hope that the poet-soul may remain the center of consciousness, for it is the poet-soul who must "unwind the winding path" of its own experience. In the drafts, however, there is an evident tension between the passive experience of death—the spirit is made rigid, deprived of juice and breath, and forcibly bound—and an attempt to meet death actively by relating it to mastery of self and experience.

The tension between active and passive experience is evident in the syntax of "Byzantium" 's second stanza. In the drafts it is clearly the mummy who is summoning the "I" to adore the mystery. But in the final version, subject and object are deliberately confused:

> A mouth that has no moisture and no breath
> Breathless mouths may summon.
>
> (ll. 13–14)

"Breathless" may refer to others, long dead, that the mummy is calling up in its reenactment of the past, or to newly dead spirits, or to Yeats specifically. The last is most likely, but Yeats has deliberately made it unclear who is summoning whom.

Not only is confusion about subject and object introduced in revision, but the lines become more abstract and the reader's attention is drawn away from the content to the symmetrical form of the statement. This obscure passage is followed by the very definite "I hail the superhuman," which manages to suggest that if the "I" has not summoned the image, at least he is somehow in control of the situation. This feeling is strengthened by the "I" 's attempt to master the image by naming it: "I call it death-in-life and life-in-death." (Here again Yeats introduces a distractingly symmetrical pattern, equating two things that in this case are opposites.) In his late work Yeats often engaged in a ritual "calling up" and taking possession of images, people, and places. (John Holloway has a very suggestive essay on this aspect of Yeats's style in *An Honoured Guest*.)[35]

The image of the golden bird, introduced in the next stanza, continues the work of assimilating the idea of death to the process of creation. There is a momentary glimpse, in the drafts, of a supreme craftsman who created the golden bird: "What great artificer / What mind decreed or hammer shaped the metal."[36] Yeats drops this line, which draws attention toward a god and away from the self-purified soul. Until the fifth and final stanza, self-purification is the poem's central theme. The mummy unwinds his own path from death back to the womb, and the purifying flames described in the fourth stanza arise from a spirit's own sense of guilt. The changes Yeats made in the bird/petal/bough imagery at the end of the third stanza seem subtly to increase the bird's affirmative independence. According to Stallworthy, the bird first sings "Set hidden by golden leaf"; then he is singing "out of a golden bough," still as though he is hidden in a cave of leaves. The feeling of a voice hidden or protected by an enclosing form increases in the next version, in which the bird perches "under a golden or a silver petal."[37] In "Cap and Bells," the Queen takes up the dead Jester's cap and bells and covers them with her hair while she sings a love song. The petal of "Byzantium," which hides the male form of the bird, seems to be a hardened form of the Queen's "flower-like hair." But in the final version, the female petal is present only as an object of scorn, and the golden bird has emerged from hiding to be firmly "Planted on the star-lit golden bough" (l. 19).

The protection sought under the petal was associated with masochistic fantasies of death and castration, but the bough functions

35 "Style and World," p. 105.
36 Stallworthy, pp. 121–22.
37 *Ibid.*

as a magically powerful extension of self, a talisman assuring the poet that he can descend into the underworld (whether of sex or death) and return unharmed. The composite image of bird and bough seems masculine by contrast with the bird/petal image, which hinted at a type of male-female relationship. Except for the last stanza (which introduces new themes), the male and female symbols, bird and dome, are kept isolated from each other and from their surroundings. But they are symbolically united by the hardness and perfection of their forms, and more important, by their shared scorn of "Common bird or petal / And all complexities of mire or blood" (ll. 23–24).

One of the things Yeats seems to be representing here—which goes beyond the bounds of a sexual relationship—is an identification with his mother, particularly with her coldness. This coldness appeared so unrelenting or inhuman to him that he felt he could approximate it only by being dead. Connected with scorn of the merely human is the poet's obsession with self-judgment (a component of his superego) which includes his mother's judgments. Though coldness and rigorous self-judgment structure much of the poem, ordinarily Yeats felt it was impossible to be the way his mother wanted him to be. This feeling gave rise to the moving "Among School Children." In the manuscript book containing the "topic" and early drafts of the poem, he worries that he never fulfilled his parents' expectations of him.[38] In the finished poem this worry is expressed in the suggestion that any mother would necessarily be disappointed by the discrepancy between what she hoped her son would be and what he actually was sixty years later. Unhappiness at his presumed failure to fulfill his mother's expectations leads to Yeats's great plea for tolerance at the end of "Among School Children," where he imagines an ideal state in which the body—and, we might add, the human being as he actually is—is not "bruised to pleasure soul," i.e., the unattainable ideal. In "Byzantium," where Yeats faces the inevitable loss of the body as he knows it, he may find consolation in the thought that at least he is approaching that image or essence of himself, devoid of "mire

[38] Bradford, *Yeats at Work*, p. 9.

or blood," that his mother believed in. The dome may disdain man, but it does not disdain the golden bird.

This is not the only aspect, though it is perhaps the deepest, of the unconscious feelings beneath the poem's surface. In general Yeats tries to turn the process of judgment, first experienced as something external and destructive that causes him shame and guilt, into something positive and self-motivated. The dead "may unwind the winding path," that is, relive and seek to understand their past experience. They may also come to admit and understand their unconscious wishes. The fire-dance of the fourth stanza symbolizes the stage of the afterlife that Yeats called Phantasmagoria. As we saw in our discussion of *A Vision*, this stage includes both fulfillment of harmful or sexually forbidden wishes and punishment for them.

In the difficult last stanza of "Byzantium" Yeats both continues his effort to master the fear of death by portraying it as an extension of the creative process and, at the same time, turns away from death altogether—toward fantasies of sexual and pre-sexual union with the mother. If the poem proceeded chronologically, the last stanza, which describes the arrival of spirits to be purged, would precede the fourth stanza, which shows them dancing in the purgatorial flames. The poem's logic, however, does not lie in chronology.

Until the last stanza, positive and negative moods alternate: the serene dome of the first stanza is followed by the mummy, its horror muted but still there; the third stanza is taken up with the triumphant appearance of the golden bird; the fourth stanza again presents a frightening or at best neutral image of the painful process of purgation. The masochistic ideas as well as Yeats's defenses against them reach a climax in the last stanza, in which they form part of a broader tension between life and death. This tension is expressed in part by the stanza's structure; the central section (ll. 2–7), dealing with purification, is framed by first and last lines containing vigorous images of life. The logic of the poem is such that we would expect it to end, like "Sailing," with a purified image. Instead, it moves outward toward life, leaving us with an unresolved tension between life and death:

> Astraddle on the dolphin's mire and blood,
> Spirit after spirit! The smithies break the flood,
> The golden smithies of the Emperor!
> Marbles of the dancing floor
> Break bitter furies of complexity,
> Those images that yet
> Fresh images beget,
> That dolphin-torn, that gong-tormented sea.
>
> (ll. 33–40)

The chief interaction in the central portion of the stanza is between smithies, marbles, and the flood of spirits. The sentence structure reflects Yeats's struggle to view spiritual self-purification actively rather than passively. In "Byzantium" there is no Grecian goldsmith with whom Yeats can unambiguously identify, for though the smithies are technically active—they "break the flood" —they seem curiously passive in contrast to the torrential influx of "spirit after spirit." Yeats's struggle against masochism is apparent in his portrayal of the newly dead. They are not, like the mummy, bound and dry, but in exuberant rhythmical motion, a state Yeats considered characteristic not only of life, but of great art. The syntax of lines 33–34 makes the spirits indistinguishable from the sea of life on which they surge forth. Moreover, their movement toward the city is active to the point of assault. The smithies are forced into the position of a defensive bulwark against what one critic calls the "prurient torrent of life."[39] To the extent that the spirits are attackers, not victims, Yeats has succeeded in warding off passivity.

In an earlier draft that is less abstract and more suggestive of human behavior, the sexual connotations of "breaking" are clearer. "The dolphin tortured flood" dashes itself against the smithies and "breaks into spray."[40] Self-immolation by falling against a sharp, hard object is reminiscent not only of the form of suicide practiced by the Romans, but also of sexual penetration. John Donne uses similar imagery in his sonnet "Batter My Heart," in which he asks God to "burn, blow and make me new," and then to "ravish me." Donne's sonnet suggests what Freud later demon-

---

39 F. A. C. Wilson, *Yeats and Tradition*, p. 243.
40 Stallworthy, p. 126.

strated, that the fantasy of being beaten stems from a desire to be possessed sexually.[41]

As in "Sailing to Byzantium," Yeats increases his feelings of active mastery by identifying purgation and death not only with sexual activity, but with the workings of his mind. The marbles of the dancing floor were originally described as "lettered marble" and "enchanted marble,"[42] and were thus related to Oisin's word sword, the instrument of poetic power. In reading the poem one can see the marble floor that breaks "bitter furies of complexity" as a brutal yet creative instrument actively wielded by the poet. With this image Yeats masters what is essentially a rape fantasy. Similar fantasies of rape are evident throughout Yeats's work. *The Herne's Egg* and "Leda and the Swan" are perhaps the most striking examples. In the late poem "Crazy Jane Talks with the Bishop," violation appears to be a precondition of unity; as Crazy Jane says, with a double pun: "nothing can be sole or whole / That has not been rent."[43]

Yeats tries throughout "Byzantium" to come to terms with the idea of death by perceiving it as actively as possible. With the image of dolphins carrying the dead to paradise, Yeats extends his effort to make death acceptable by invoking earlier images of a place of joy to which the hero is carried. In Yeats's early work, Oisin is caried away on a white horse to the Isle of Joy, and Dhoya plunges into the sea (from which his fairy love came) on a stallion. The sexual fantasies connected with the image of horse and rider emerge unmistakably in Yeats's plays, beginning with *Where There Is Nothing*, where the image evolves from riding a horse or unicorn to mating with a unicorn. The dolphin carrying its rider to paradise recalls these previous compound figures either riding to paradise or embodying paradise in their union.

Dolphin and rider do not, however, arrive at the sensual paradise of "News for the Delphic Oracle." Instead, the riders are pitched off their dolphins to be broken against the smithies. In

41 Freud, "A Child Is Being Beaten," *Collected Papers*, vol. 2 (New York: Basic Books, 1959), pp. 194–95.

42 Stallworthy, p. 124.

43 Yeats, *Variorum Poems*, p. 513.

this respect, the ending is similar to the masochistic fantasy of the Real Queen, who dreams of being thrown from the back of a unicorn and trampled underfoot by a mob. Death brings both fulfillment of repressed sexual desire, as symbolized by riding the unicorn, and punishment for the guilty act; but in "Byzantium," as we have seen, masochism is only a part of the picture. Yeats is represented not only by the spirit riders who are broken, but by the marbles that break them.

Yeats's use of a dolphin rather than a horse to carry the dead not only accords with Platonic tradition, but is the culmination of a long line of fish imagery in his own work. The fish in his poems is consistently feminine: writing about Maud Gonne he says in "The Fish," a fish leaped "out of my net,"[44] and the silver fish in the early "Song of Wandering Aengus," who is transformed into a glimmering girl, haunts the poet for the rest of his life. The fish's beauty is equaled only by its slippery coldness, which in the early work is connected both with female sexuality and with emotional coldness and restraint. In another early poem, "All Things Can Tempt Me," he contrasts his "masculine" mood when writing "as though he had a sword upstairs" with a depressed "feminine" mood, in which he wants to be "Colder and dumber and deafer than a fish."[45] The fish, then, tends to be woman in her most disconcerting aspects.

In "Byzantium," the fish loses its most distressing quality, its coldness, and becomes a warm-blooded dolphin, the Platonic "love-beast," who, instead of disgusting or depressing the poet or escaping from his control, helps him by carrying him to purgation. The dolphin's symbolic resemblance to a mother is strengthened by Yeats's depiction of the dead as "wailing" with desire like infants.[46] Moreover, Yeats told T. Sturge Moore, who asked how the dolphin would carry the spirit, that this dolphin could be understood by looking at Raphael's statue of a dolphin carrying one of the Holy Innocents to paradise.[47] There is no such statue, but

[44] *Ibid.*, p. 146.
[45] *Ibid.*, p. 267.
[46] Bradford, p. 7.
[47] Melchiori, *The Whole Mystery of Art*, pp. 212–13.

Yeats's comparison of the dolphin's passenger to a "Holy Innocent," i.e. a child, indicates that he is representing not simply sexual union, but an earlier union of mother and child. The union is interrupted in purgatory, but it may be a spur to purification, a promise of union to come after purgation is complete. Similarly, Yeats describes Dante as risking the purging fire because of his longing for union with the "earthly Beatrice" (*Letters*, p. 731).

Yet the end of the poem presents not death, but life. By the complex movement of his verse, Yeats manages to suggest simultaneous contrary movements: the spirits move inward to be purged and at the same time move outward. They seem to resist purgation, and even as they are being simplified they "yet / Fresh images beget." These images, most probably passionate memories of the past, lead us back to life: "that dolphin-torn, that gong-tormented sea."

Conclusion

I HAVE ARGUED here that the central thread of Yeats's life and work is his tireless, driven effort to "remake" himself, to bring himself as man and artist into a satisfactory relationship both with his impulses and with a threatening reality. In this struggle, he was haunted by certain traumas from his childhood. He grappled with them in his everyday life as in his work, objectifying them in themes and symbols that he repeated obsessively in his writing.

His youthful works, with their themes of death and escape, reflect his early propensity to cope with conflict by fantasy or withdrawal. Again and again in these early works we find an unsuccessful quest for an incestuous love object, a sense of disembodiment or loss of identity, and themes of oral deprivation. Yeats's masochism and identity confusions seemingly derive from his unsatisfactory relationship with his cold and despondent mother. From this relationship came his weak self-image and his difficulties with women, problems clearly mirrored in his work. Fleeing from these problems into fairyland proved no solution. When he saw his insubstantiality objectified in his early work, he deplored it and began a series of psychic maneuvers that led to a strengthening of both style and self.

With uncanny instinct the maturing poet found or created conditions that could help him overcome the self-defeating ways that had hobbled him as a man and as an artist. In one instance Yeats found a friendship with Lady Gregory; in another he created an immaterial relationship to a presence he called *Anima Mundi*. In Lady Gregory he found a surrogate mother who helped him to construct a new identity and to create the heroic figures he needed as models. He became more confident as a man, more vigorous and creative as an artist. He conceptualized his insights with his theory of the mask and a new aesthetic form. The spiritual presence of *Anima Mundi* served him as an emotional refuge, as a source of sustenance when emotional pressures threatened to overwhelm him.

With all these new strengths and sources of support, Yeats could work directly to gain mastery of early trauma, notably obsessive fantasies of the primal scene. Yeats characteristically dealt with such fantasies by turning passive suffering into active mastery. In *The Player Queen* he imagined his hero in control of a previously overwhelming situation; in *A Vision* he acted in his own person, imposing on his readers the confusion he himself had originally felt.

In the last twenty years of his life, Yeats found it increasingly difficult to believe in his mask. Tormented by the bodily humiliations of old age and the fear of impotence, he was visited anew by his youthful fears of fusion and we see him indulging in the regressive fantasies of *The Herne's Egg* or making protestations (through his persona Ribh) that betray fear of impotence. Yet his best late works, like no others, come to terms with his fears of dissolution and death. Whereas in earlier works he had used a talismanic object more or less crudely to ward off castration anxiety, in "A Dialogue of Self and Soul" and the Byzantium poems he uses the same device brilliantly to come to terms with aging and death. In "Sailing to Byzantium" he assimilates to himself the object's permanent and beautiful form and so triumphs over death. But in "A Dialogue of Self and Soul" and "Byzantium," there is a further triumph: with the support of his talisman he is able to swing away from its static perfection and accept imaginatively what previously had terrified him—the amorphous dangers of life itself.

Index